ANGELS FALL

The True Story of a Young Girl
and Her Shattered Heart

Mary Beth Holliday

Order this book online at www.trafford.com
or email orders@trafford.com

Most Trafford titles are also available at major online book retailers.

Printed in the United States of America.

ISBN: 978-1-4269-4135-1 (sc)

*Our mission is to efficiently provide the world's finest, most comprehensive book publishing
service, enabling every author to experience success. To find out how to publish your book,
your way, and have it available worldwide, visit us online at www.trafford.com*

Trafford rev. 09/11/2010

 www.trafford.com

North America & international
toll-free: 1 888 232 4444 (USA & Canada)
phone: 250 383 6864 ♦ fax: 812 355 4082

*This is dedicated to all of my angels and all of my demons.
You know who you are and you know what you did.
And this is also dedicated to Tyler Jolley. This is for
all the stories that I didn't get to tell you.
Thank you*

Chapter 1

Angels Fall

You live and breathe air in life. Babies are born. You have friends that you can rely on that are yours forever.

I lived and breathed air when I was a child, and then I died. Memories are important, but how much is one to remember after they have died and then came back? How many nightmares can one hold and remain so silent? I've begged and pleaded with the girl that I once was and with everyone else in life. I've lived and I've died. I've loved and I've hated. I've laughed and I've cried.

Every school friend that I've had has thought that I've had everything. Every picture of someone famous, every autograph that's been signed, every toy, every book, est., est. I've been envied for what little that really shows. I've envied others for the lives that they've lived. Envy for simply just walking and talking. For having a moment of their own that is not interrupted by others saying that it's simply the wrong thought.

My Mom, my brother and I were at a garage sale. Joe and I were across the street in the car, while Mom was looking at the things that were for sale. I was annoying Joe as we were both in the back of Mom's car. It's something that every little sister does to their brother. Joe wanted me to go see what Mom was looking at, but I started to argue and protest. Finally, I decided to go across the street. I looked both directions three times before I stepped into the street. And then there was nothing.

A thought that has never left my mind for even a second: I was run over by a car at the age of six on September 10th, 1994.

That was the day I died. My self confidence was over, my friends, my family life, everything was taken from me, and it only took a blink of an eye for it all to end. I wore my tennis shoes, a bathing suit, and my favorite little black skirt. I never got my skirt back. Others have laughed at that statement, but I've only cried.

I saw my body take its last three rolls in the street. The torture of that thought alone has given me nightmares! That moment has never left my mind. The torture that that little girl went through-that I went through! I've cried out in public remembering that and I've cried myself to sleep over it too.

Before I went to Heaven, I saw the woman who committed that act. "She wasn't looking where she was going", others have said, or, "I bet she's sorry." No and no. The woman, Rosic, wasn't looking where she was going and no, she isn't sorry. I saw into her soul that day. I learned more than anyone would ever like to know about such a dark spirited soul, for which I have only seen a few souls that were that dark in my life. Rosic wore a black dress-suit; with her blonde hair pulled straight back by her black headband. Her icy blue eyes stared out in rage. There was no sympathy in her at all. She looked as though she expected an apology in the act that she committed.

I was sent to Heaven. I have been asked what I saw by few people, and have been called stupid and crazy by others. My nanny was there, who is my great grandmother. My mom's old dog Troy was there. I was at peace, but I knew that I had to come back to Earth.

I told stories of how Nanny and I played games to help me remember. I came back to Earth for my mom.

My Mom felt Nanny and her grandfather in my ICU room the second day at the hospital. I was with Nanny. Everything was going to be okay.

When my family came to visit me in the hospital, my Brother Mike's girlfriend Shannon passed out at the sight of me. One of my sister Tracey's friends also passed out after seeing me in a coma.

The hospital where I stayed I have very few memories of. I was in a few different rooms. I was in a coma for the first two months that I was in the hospital. When my brothers and sisters had come to visit me while I was in a coma, I kicked my brother Tom. The nurse said it was because I recognized him. Mom would play Barbie's with me; she'd place the Barbie's in my hands and do the voices.

I had a tube that went directly up my nose to provide me with nutrition.

On Halloween night '94, I was taken down to a Halloween party. I had my picture taken with Ben Savage. I started waking up from my coma after that.

The last room that I was in, I can remember the most. Mom stayed in there with me. The roommate that I had was this Asian girl Mary and her mom. Mary had broken her leg, while I had other problems. Mom slept on a chair that turned into a bed in my room. On the weekends I came home, but it is a time that I simply cannot remember. The room was outside of these picnic benches that were inside the hospital.

I wore diapers for a few months.

I did school while I was in the hospital; learning basic things from a time that I remember very little of.

I was released Christmas Eve day. A picture was taken by someone of Mom and me walking out of the hospital. I pushed my wheelchair out of the hospital with my Raggedy Ann in the chair with Mom right there with me. I came home, and there was a big banner saying "Welcome Home Mary Beth!" on it. Pictures were taken, but it is still a time that I cannot remember.

My first words came five months after leaving the hospital. My best friend was a girl from across the street, Meggie. She was always talking and we would always do crazy things. She and I would argue, so my first words were, "Shut up, Meggie!" Her older sister Tarin was a lot of fun!

I was place in West Valley Special Ed. I loathed West Valley Special Ed. for its horrible teachers, and terrible students. I hated my teacher Roberta. The other teacher George was fine. I don't remember having a problem with him. The students were so obnoxious! There were these twins who had Down syndrome, or something else that was horrible. There was the nice twin, and there was the mean twin. They were both in my class, and they rode the same bus as me. One day on the bus, the evil twin who was sitting next to me took my glasses off my face and threw them out the window. I could not say anything at the time. I was shocked. I had absolutely no confidence in myself at all, so I just let it happen. It angers me that I would allow such a thing to occur.

I was in the restroom another time, and I was done. There was another student waiting to use the restroom. When I was done, I came out and was going to wash my hands. The other student, Jose, was next in line to use it. It was just the two of us down the hall in the restroom at the time. As I was done washing my hands, I turned around to get a paper towel to dry my hands. When I turned around to do so, I saw Jose's penis. I looked to see that he was smiling at me. Why would he do that? I thought, but I couldn't do anything. I never told the teachers what happened, or anyone else for that matter.

I was in a wheelchair most of the time I went to West Valley Special Ed. I went to and from school in a bus that had the wheelchair ramp on it. At home, there was a wooden ramp that was built for me to come inside. My wheelchair came with a tray for me. My name was written in big letters on it. I did want to be like everyone else, though; I just couldn't say it at the time.

It took a long time for me to regain the strength to walk and run. I went to the doctors for so long for my legs and feet. I had to have casts in my shoes to help me walk with a heal strike. I was pressured to do it correctly, but I couldn't get it exactly correct.

I wore a helmet as well. I decorated it with all of these stickers and I would spend hours counting them all. A picture of George and me was taken.

My pony tail was placed in one of the wholes that cover the helmet. There were four big wholes, and the rest were little. My head was half shaven from the brain surgery in '94. Mom braided my half shaven head, so it was easy to put half of my hair through the helmet. I had a "punk-rock-chick" look as mom called it.

There was this one girl in my class, Amada. She was Roberta's favorite student. Then there was the student Victor. He could not talk at all. He would only make sounds. I told my mom about him. She and the teacher shared a communication book, where they would write to say what was going on with me and my schooling and/or needs. Mom wrote to Roberta, I guess saying that I was talking about Victor. Roberta had confronted me about that. I was embarrassed about that, but I said nothing as to not get yelled at by Roberta or Mom.

I don't remember any other students from that class.

Joe had gone to West Valley as well. He was in a more functioning class. His teacher liked him for his art work. The principle, Glenn, was a short, bald man. There wasn't a real good partnership between the principle and Mom.

The school had told Mom that I only needed to use half of my body, because I was right handed. I was always reminded to use my left side as well. It always seemed that everyone was acting like I was going to lose my right side completely. But I got my strength and I proved them wrong.

Chapter 2

Hell, Again

My brother Tom was in hockey in the fall of '94. He said he would beat up anyone if they made fun of me. My brother Mike took Tom to his games and practices when I was first in the hospital. But I was home every weekend.

In 1995, I had my first eye surgery, but I had two that year. I walked to the hospital room by myself after giving Mom a kiss goodbye. I was screaming at the top of my lungs while drops were put into my eyes. I was not allowed to scratch or rub my eyes, even though I was in a lot of pain! The doctor just waved at me and smiled while I screamed my head off and cried! It obviously wasn't fair to me.

My best friend Evie came to my house one day. Evie and I had been best friends in pre-school in Mrs. Davis' class. I was recovering from the hospital, so my memories of that time are not clear. A part of me remembers Evie coming over one day. I have a picture of us that Mom took when Evie and her mom came over. It shows us hugging and Evie looking at the camera. She was my first best friend ever.

I always thought I wanted Mom and her boyfriend Billy to be happy. I don't know if I wanted them to fall in love, but Mom's happiness was a plus in my head. Billy and I were great friends. I never considered us best friends, but we were friends.

On February 14th, 1996, I wanted to see them kiss. I didn't really know why, but at the time I was certain. I was very wrong. Billy had asked, "Are you sure you want to see?" I said excitedly "YES!" Then he said okay and pulled Mom in to French kiss her. His arms moved up and down her body, as hers did on him. I was outraged, hurt, broken hearted, and very confused. I stood there for one brief moment, but quickly ran to my room and cried on the bed. That is the only memory I have of that day, but others have told me otherwise.

Billy came to give me a hug after French kissing Mom. I screamed no at him. I never allowed him to touch me again.

Everyone lies, after all...

Mom first told me that she enjoyed the kiss. That outraged me even further. She wanted to pull away. So why didn't she? Everyone tried to hide the truth from me for years, but I saw straight threw it. I almost wish I hadn't. A child's youth should not be filled with knowing lies from truths. No, it should be that of games and love and happiness. I was condemned to walk in silence when I could, being pushed aside by everyone else for the most ridiculous reasons. But at the same time, I was never truly left alone even though I felt lonely.

I was in all sorts of therapies, day in and day out. There was Occupational, Physical, Speech, Eye therapy, reading, psychological therapy, est. I wanted to scream every day when I was in whatever building it was at the time.

I was placed in three different schools all in the 2nd grade.

My physical therapists weren't very different. Carla and Cecilia were in two different places, yes, but their exercises for me were the same. I stood on a trampoline and catch a plastic ball working with Cecilia. This therapist, Red, was this guy that I would sometimes work with when Cecilia wasn't in. Red had a crush on me, for whatever reason. Then there was this other guy that I worked with, Francis. He was cool.

Billy would pick me up early from school to go to therapy.

I always needed to go down stairs and pay and then go up stairs. I was rewarded with hot cheetos and chocolate milk, but those eventually made me throw up, so I gave those up after some time.

My appointments were usually in the afternoons on Wednesdays and Fridays, but they were sometimes held in the mornings.

I would be in my world throughout most days. A world of make believe, but with people that did exist.

On the days that I wasn't with Mom's boyfriend, I would just be at the YMCA. I made friends, but was quiet in my own ways. I would try and draw things like my brother Tom would, but I was never good at it. When Tom would pick me up and make me up, sometimes he let me sit on his skateboard as he pushed me home.

There was a girl who only befriended me because she thought Tom was cute. I was okay with the friendship, but I felt weird that she thought Tom was so dreamy.

In September, 1995 I went to Mayall St. School. My teacher there was Ms. Heimlich. She was okay. There were at least two other women in there as teacher assistants, the two Jessica's. And there was another woman for this boy Jimmy. It seemed that Jimmy had everything wrong with him. He couldn't talk, and he had to have a hearing aid with him. He had tubes of some sort on him.

I had my best friend Joseph in that class. Joseph was hilarious! He would always call me "Coo-Coo". I just loved being around him. He wore glasses, as did I. His hair was dark brown with spikes going up. We would always walk together at school.

There were other students as well. There was this girl, Nubia. She couldn't walk very well, or talk very well either. Part of me felt sorry for her. But she had an attitude towards me, so we weren't best of friends.

Then there was Bobby. I hated him, because he was always mean to me, or making fun of me.

There was this other boy, Avo, who was in a wheel chair. Then there was this Asian boy, Thomas. I thought he was okay. There were a few other kids.

Every week, it seemed like, the class would take a "field trip". We might go to the store and get ingredients or to a restaurant. We went to IHOP with the class one day. We were to know our orders ahead of time. I got the bacon and eggs meal from the kids' menu. Billy had wanted to get something off of the kids menu when he, Mom, and I went together. He made me order it for him, because he wasn't sure if he could order anything off of the kids' menu.

When we would go out of the school, Nubia had to go in a wheel chair. One of the Jessica's had to push her. I was fine walking.

On a certain day in the week, the class would bake something, like cupcakes. Every day we would have snack time at a back-kiddy-table. We would have goldfish and milk, kind of a disgusting combination. I hated goldfish crackers after that.

After a few weeks of being in my regular aphasia class, every day after lunch I would go to a class room behind my room for "story time". I don't remember that teacher's name, but she did have blond hair. I would burp, or yawn, or something to that effect in that class. One time the teacher looked down at me and told me to cover my mouth. I was young, so I can't recall too much of that incident.

The students were nice in that class room.

Chapter 3

My World No more

I would have physical therapy every week. First I had to start at the Northridge Hospital. There I saw three women named Carla, Lorna, and someone else. Lorna was my speech therapist, while Carla and I did Physical Therapy. The other woman was my Occupational therapist.

Lorna had dark brown, curly, short hair. I remember that she always wore dresses. Carla was a blond, and she wore work out clothes. The other Therapist was a sort of a heavy set, black woman. I don't remember being at that hospital for too long.

My eye doctor on both eye surgeries performed in 1995 was Dr. Borchette at children's hospital. I can remember screaming when the drops were in my eyes. I wasn't allowed to scratch them. Dr. Borchette smiled and waved as I screamed out in pain. The first was on both eyes, and the second was on my right, but there was no success for either surgery after they were completed.

My best friend Meggie was a year younger than I was. Her sister called me "Monkey Breath." Her older brother was this boy Ben. He would get into trouble from time to time. Ben and Joe were somewhat of friends some of the time. I remember I liked Meggie's mom, Roberta. She was nice. Meggie's dad was never really home. He drove a yellow car, and every day I would check to see if the car was there. Meggie and I had our spats from time to time, but we were best friends. She moved after I was eight. She was always known as Meggie to me. It was only years after she moved that she wanted to be called Megan. We tried to keep in touch throughout the years.

We would play in her house, and in mine. She shared a room with her sister. Meggie's family was close friends with this boy Casey's family. They lived down the street. Casey's older sister, Megan, was friends with

Tarin, Meggie's older sister. Personally I detested Casey's family, other than Megan. They were all mean to Joe and the rest of my family.

When I had turned seven in '95, I guess that Casey had come to my birthday party. There are pictures to a time I can't recall from memory.

Across the street, next to Meggie's house was this boy AJ's house. AJ had to be Tom's age. And then on the other side of Meggie's house was this other boy David's grandparent's house. It seemed that David was always over there.

My first crush in school was this boy Drew. I was at Tulsa St. Elementary School the second part of second the second grade, as well as the third, and part of the fourth grade. I may have been older than Drew. At Tulsa, I, of course, had my enemies. My biggest enemy there was this girl Stephanie Kummar. She was this little blonde twig that always had to get everything that she wanted. She and I shared the bus together.

My teacher, Mr. Richter, was a nice man.

I liked Drew, but so did Stephanie. When Drew liked me back, he pulled me over one day in class, and he old me that he liked me. Stephanie was being a little bitch and interrupting him all the time. She would make movements behind him and act really stupid. On the ride home, she made fun of me for the way Drew liked me.

Mr. Richter's class was nice, other than that.

When I was finally in the third grade, there were two new students, Leslie and Carlos. I first thought that Leslie was just being mean to me and that she didn't like me. I cried in front of Mr. Richter. Mr. Richter spoke with Leslie and me one day. I was crying, but we talked it out. She and I became best friends after that.

There were other students in there as well. David was another boy that was in that class. He and Stephanie came to my 8th birthday party at the park. We played baseball. When it was time for cake, Stephanie got the first slice. The person whose birthday it is always gets the first slice, so naturally I was very angry and heartbroken. I stomped off and went and locked myself in the car. Eventually I came out and had an okay birthday party. I definitely hated Stephanie.

We hit a piñata for my birthday party. It was this giant bird with a purple hat on its head. Mom took a picture of David, Stephanie, and me with the hat on my head.

There was this other boy Nicky. Nick and I were friends. There is this picture of us in front of the class, and Nick's arm is around my shoulder. Nicky was cool. He had speech problems, but to me he was just Nicky.

Then there was Jonathan. Jonathan had a massive crush on me. I went to a birthday party of his once. When Billy and I were at the mall one time, we saw him on the little kiddy train. I wanted to go on it, but I had changed my mind when I saw him. Billy did "the right" thing, and paid for Jonathan and I to go on it together. I cringed in disgust. I went anyway, but when Jonathan and I were sitting on the little seats together, I moved my legs and blocked the little space there was between us as not to touch him. When the train came around to where the adults were, I tried to pull Billy in.

There was this little Mexican girl, Hanzel. She was nice, I guess. Not too many memories of her. However, we did take summer school together in '96, and she and I were on the same bus. She lived at these little houses at the park, so the bus driver would drop her off first, of course.

There was this other boy, Edward. Edward had a crush on me. It was easy to tell. Then there was this girl Scarlet.

My first assistant was Ms. S. in Mr. Richter's class. She was a blonde, but I really liked working with her. My speech therapy started at school at Tulsa. Ms. S. and I would go to my O.T. therapy once a week.

On a day during summer school in '96, it was my birthday. Ms. S. and I went to my O.T. appointment as usual. I can remember walking back to the class room with her. We opened the door and the entire class was there wishing me a happy birthday! I remember Edgar coming up to me and saying, "Happy birthday, Mary Beth."

During the regular school year, every day after lunch I would go to Ms. Mann's classroom for story time. It turned into me going there for lunch time as well. Her class sat at some tables near her room that were also near trees. When lunch ended, I had friends to play Chinese jump rope with. Johnny was a blonde boy with short hair, and then there was Mrs. G's daughter, this girl Elizabeth, and a few others. My crush in that classroom was a boy named Joey. Joey had dark eyes and black hair that he combed back. He was very into sports. A ball that Joey was playing with came at me one day, and Joey rushed over to block it from me.

I was invited to go to the Children's Museum with Ms. Mann's class. Elizabeth and I were partnered up. We went to the candy shop where you only had to pay for the bag, and then you could get as much candy as you wanted. I stopped after a while, but Elizabeth kept going.

There were these two others girls that I was friends with in that class. Marissa and Taylor lived right next to each other. Marissa had an older sister that went to Tulsa as well, and then her mom worked there too. Taylor was a great friend to me. She seemed like a sporty girl, while Marissa was more girly. They were fun to just hang with. I would play Chinese jump rope with Taylor at lunch time in front of Mrs. Mann's room.

Elizabeth lived at Petit Park, as did Hanzel. Elizabeth lived in the apartments there. Mom and I went to get her one time, and I remember her brother answered the door.

I had therapy every week, Occupational and Physical, so I would be picked up after lunch, or get to school late. It didn't bother me too much, although my mind was just being processed at that point.

After the third grade, I was placed in another classroom outside the gated area I had grown so fond of. I don't remember my teacher's name there, but I didn't last that long there. Ms. S. had gone to work in another class. At that point she was Mrs. Parr.

I went to a back room after lunch in the fourth grade for a math class. It was fun.

In my new class, Edward and Scarlet were there. Stephanie and I had class together, again. I could never escape her. Maybe I should have felt sorry for her. She lived with her Grandmother.

There was a boy named Matthew, but I can't recall too much there. The teacher's aide would walk Matthew and I to these back classrooms after lunch.

My next aide was a lady named Kat. She was cool. But she was only there a week or so, and then I had my next aide, "Mrs. Butter-Butt". I didn't know what her name was. I said that I was tired one day to her, and her response was, "Maybe you should get more sleep." I told Mom, and she was so angry.

The next day, Mom took me to school and we went to the Principles office. Mom said she was really angry, and told me to tell the principle what happened. I turned around in a circle, and then explained what had been said. Mom and I left after a few more spats and I never returned to that school ever again.

I was home schooled for about two weeks after that. I could only handle one hour every day, and then the teacher would leave.

I went to my home school, Haskell, after the first six weeks of the fourth grade had started.

The class had introduced themselves in a circle to me. I remembered some of the people from the YMCA that I went to every day after school. Jacob and LaPorche were there. LaPorche lived right around the corner from me. Jacob and I would hang out with our friend Rachelle at the YMCA every day. Rachelle was really into reading.

Ms. Emery was my 4th grade teacher. She taught Tom when he was in the fourth grade. The seats in the class were moved around so often. I always sat in the front due to my vision problems. Jacob was on the other side of my desk with someone sitting next to him. Ms. Richter was my aide at the time. She was a blonde as well. Her goal was to become a police officer, but she started out as my aide. She sat next to me, and that never changed for that year. I was discussing Tom with Jacob one day. He said I should go and ask Ms. Emery if she remembered Tom. I was too nervous, but I guess she caught me staring too much, so she asked if I needed something. I finally asked if she had a student in the past named Thomas Holliday. She thought about it for a while and said that she did. I explained that was my brother.

Jacob and I were best friends on the weekends. We would always go to play miniature golf. I would get angry when the stupid golf ball wouldn't get to the stupid whole. Mom would take my club away from me. I got over it after a while. Jacob and I would go play in the arcade afterward. When we got out of there we would come back to my house and play house. He was the husband and I was the wife. I had such a crush on Jacob. I was convinced I was in love with him.

Jacob and I wore rings for each other only for a while, though.

When Billy and I were at the mall one day and we were in JC Penny's. Billy and I signed me up for wedding things for Jacob and me, but we did it just for laughs. I think I was 9 years old. For a few years I really did think that Jacob and I would always be best friends forever, but people grow up and change, I guess.

Brianna and I were friends in the fourth and fifth grade. I thought she was cool. She and I played tag on the trees out on the play yard at recess and lunch time. This Indian girl, Sarah was there too. I felt comfortable there. Sarah was originally from India, so she had an aide as well to help her with the school work as well.

I first called Ms. Richter by her first name, Danielle. She asked if I could just call her Ms. Richter as the other students had to anyway. I got used to it, so it didn't bother me at all doing so. She would sketch out copies of hand writing for all the students to practice.

I was really mad at Ms. Richter one day. I forget my reasons why, but I was in tears. Susannah told her what was going on, so Ms. Richter apologized. I forgave her, but it might took a while.

I always did imagine that Jacob and I would get married and live our lives together forever. It was crazy and stupid. We were both young and naïve, I guess. No other explanation.

I would go to the nurse's office just about every day because I would have a stomach all the time. Sometimes I would fake it to get out of class. Sometimes I just needed a break from everyone else, but I never said that to anyone.

I think the girl Homa was Sarah's cousin. I sat next to both of them at one point in the fourth grade.

There was another girl, Yvette. She was sporty, way more than I was. Then there was Stephanie Solis. I wasn't best friends with them, but we hung out at school. There was Giselle and Angela, completely different people, but they were the same height with the same hair style going on.

I had a crush on Vincent Estrada. I loved boys with their hair smoothed straight back. I called him once to see if he wanted to hang out, but he was busy.

Ms. Emery had the class write poetry from the board every morning before class started. That was where my obsession with poetry started.

Mr. Postal was the special Ed. teacher that Jessica Whitlock saw all the time. I never liked him after the 5th grade. I had no problem with him in school, but one summer killed that.

Before summer came after the 4th grade, I hugged Ms. Richter goodbye. She had changed her mind about being a policewoman. I influenced her enough to want to become a kindergarten teacher. *Spending enough time with me really gets to you,* I thought.

During the summer of the 4th grade, I went to summer school, again. Ms. Rozo, who worked in Mr. Postal's, class, was my aide when that happened. I had a good time. There was an assignment that the students had to write. We could write based on fantasy or something that happened to us. I wrote about Stimpy, my cat. The students were to read there stories to the class after the stories were all completed. Then the other students could ask questions to the stories. I raised my hand at the wrong time, actually wanting to read mine next, but I thought of a quick questions to ask instead.

That was my best summer while attending summer school. Until one day when I saw this boy at the YMCA. I thought he was cute. He wore a Mighty Ducks purple and green hat. He wasn't nice at all, though. The YMCA had snack time at around 4 pm. We usually ate pretzels or crackers.

Occasionally we had cookies. There was always juice or another beverage that the kids could have.

Mighty-Ducks-hat-boy was paying attention to me, and my heart flew, until he was mean to me. It was almost time to go back inside, and Mighty-Ducks-hat–boy threw a pretzel on the dirty ground and told me to eat it. I had no will power or common since at the time, so I did as I was instructed.

When Mom came to get me, everything was fine, until we got out to the car. I started crying and I told her what happened. She was outraged! We went back inside the YMCA, with me still crying. She asked who it was and I was going to point to him, when Elena, the camp councilor, came over and asked what was wrong. Mom told her what happened and she told Elena that the boy wore a hat. Elena then asked me if it were a few kids that she knew. I cried that I didn't know his name. I then said that the boy who did that to me was wearing a Mighty Ducks hat. Elena then released who it was. I never saw that boy again.

At home that summer, Joe and I were playing around. He came up from behind me and I old feel something dangling from outside his pants. He had me from behind, so I could never see. I fought to break free. When I finally did, I saw him place something back in his pants. It happened a few times. I would run from him, sometimes in tears, after Joe let me go.

I had tried to stab myself I the heart a few times. Joe tried to stop me. He told me that Mom would miss me. I wouldn't let go of the knife, with tears came down my cheeks. Joe had me so angry that I wanted to die. I didn't care. I just wanted to be anywhere but here. I calmed myself down after screaming and crying.

Sometimes when Joe and I would fight, he would hold a knife to me throat.

"Are you scared?" he'd ask.

"No," I said.

"How about now?" he asked as he moved the knife closer to my throat.

"No," I said again.

Joe moved it closer. "How about now?" he asked.

"No," I said again.

"Now?" Joe asked

"Yes," I said. I broke free. *Joe tried to kill me*, I said to myself. I hated him. The summers were horrible.

Chapter 4

Good Memories Do End

On the first day of class, the class was put back into the same room the first day of the fifth grade. We were called into different classes. Jacob and I were both in different classes and our friendship was at a crossroads. Jessica Yunk, my best friend, wasn't in my new class either.

In the 5th grade, I heard that Ivan, a boy from Ms. Emery's class and a friend of mine, had a crush on me. I was so freaked out at that time! I first noticed him staring at me when we got back to school after summer break. I was over the crush I had on Jacob. I figured Ivan had a crush on me, and I was right. My friend Brianna said that Ivan had a crush on since the fourth grade. I was hanging out with my friends over by the trees one day when Brianna came over and said that Ivan was going to come give me a kiss. I started freaking out! I was a little excited too, but it never happened.

I was placed in the most difficult classroom that year. Mr. Scochenski was a new teacher, but he didn't know how to teach us. He would yell at us half the time because the students wouldn't shut up and listen. I listened, probably because I didn't have anything else to do.

My first aide that year I had met before the end of the fourth grade. She was French and her name was Nicole. I first started calling her Nicole, but switched it to Ms. B. after a few weeks. She only lasted a few weeks, because she didn't know how to do her job correctly while working with me. Before she was replaced, she took me outside and told me. I found out that Sherry, who my massage therapist, was going to be my new aide when we went outside. I was kind of excited. Oh, how wrong I was. Sherry only lasted a few weeks. We were at my O.T. appointment. My new O.T. therapist was a lady named Amy. I hated deeply her. I got mad for one reason or another and I walked off. Sherry tried to stop me. After arguing for a while, I just got too pissed off and I said, "Fuck you," and started to walk away. Sherry got really mad and said I was being disrespectful.

I felt that if people were going to treat me like shit then why shouldn't I treat them like shit? That was when it started, but I didn't know it at the time.

Billy picked me up from the therapy place. I didn't return to school that day. He said to show him around the building, but we ended up just leaving. I had no desire to stay.

Ms. Rozo was my aide for a few weeks. Things went fine with that.

One of my favorite aides was Gina. She was so much fun, and she was really nice. She knew how to do her job. Not too many people knew what to do. That broke my heart most of all. I wasn't that much of a complicated kid, and I guess that was what was so complicated. The fact that I was smarted than most of the adults, and it hurt me to a great pain that no one will understand.

Gina wanted to follow me to middle school, but it wasn't the way that it happened.

Ivan Sandoval and I were in different classes. He had Ms. Shannon next door. I heard that he was dating this girl Crystal from our 4th grade class, and then all of a sudden he liked me. I was kind of grossed out. He would hang out with the guys Jacob, Brian, Enrique, and maybe one other. They were mean to me and made fun of me a lot. I put up with it, but I hated them for that. Jacob and I were close the year before, but he changed.

Ivan never came up to me to kiss me.

I was best friends with Jessica Yunk, but she and I were in different classes the 5th grade. She had new friends, like Tiffany. I loathed her because she was just mean to me. She had a really big attitude towards me, and I never understood why. One day, Jessica and I were hanging out when Tiffany came up. They were gong to the girls' bathroom to get makeovers. Jessica told me to come, but I declined because I just didn't want to. Jessica made some stupid comment that hurt me. After that, I thought "To Hell with her." I was mad for the next day or so, and then she came up to me asking if I was mad at her. *Yeah.*

I forgave her when this little boy who would always chase us around came up to us. I cannot remember his name, but he was in love with the both of us and would annoy us to death.

I became friends with a girl named Dalila that year. She became my best friend towards the middle of that year. She and I lived maybe two blocks away from each other.

I would go to Chucky Cheese's with Billy, and play the pinball game. I liked that best of all because I was good at it.

I was ripped off at Chucky Cheeses one day, and after Billy had complained, I got free things from there. I invited my friend Ashley to come with me to the day of getting free stuff and having a party there. I got a free prize and gave Ashley the 700-800 tickets I had been saving throughout the years. We had free pizza and non stop tokens. It was a blast.

Ashley and I would hang out on the weekends and play make-believe. We pretended to have these boyfriends, and we'd pretend to have jobs with computers, so we just typed mish-mush.

When I told her about Ivan having a crush on me, I told her that I had a crush on him. She ran and told a big group of other kids, even though I begged her not to. The crush didn't last that long.

The class had a police officer come once a week. That was officer V. He had somewhat of a beer gut. We had to write a paper for the end of him being there, and then say it in front of the class. I remember that Mom wrote it the day it was due, because we didn't know when it was due. He was part of the D.A.R.E. program. He told us not to do drugs. I never had any desire to use drugs. I was put on medications too many times, and threw up because of it. The entire 5th grade had learned the song, "I Believe I can Fly" for the assembly our parents saw. The entire 5th grade did it. Officer V. sang an Elvis Presley song. It was hilarious, and I loved it!

Melissa M. and I were close friends. She gave me a Scooby-Doo stuffed animal for my 11th birthday. My friends Dalila, Jacky and her sister Brianna had to bring their annoying little sister to the party as well. Jessica came at the very end when everyone was leaving.

When my best friend Jessica asked me if I knew a Joey from Tulsa St. School, I said yes. He was her boyfriend! She told me that he was moving, but he wanted to see me again. I told her that I had a huge crush on him. She said that he told her that he had a crush on me back then as well. I was jumping up and down! She said he wanted to see me again. He was staying with her. Her brother was best friends with him, so she said. I was so excited to see Joey again. I was talking to Jessica on the phone one night and she asked if I wanted to talk to him. I said yes. He sounded a lot different than I remembered him. I was babbling when I spoke with him, just sitting on the porch out front.

Jessica said she changed him to fit her needs, I guess. I loved the Joey that I knew, and I never would have changed anything about him. I loved the way that I remembered him, though. 5 never would have changed anything about him.

When the night finally came for me to see him again I was so excited! Jessica said she was going to come over with him, so I waited. They never came. Mom said Jessica was probably making it up. I cried my little heart out over it. I was really hurt. The next day I asked Jessica what happened. She said that Joey had changed his mind. My mind went to, "Then why didn't you at least call me?" I was hurt.

One day, Jessica had told me that before Joey was going to move, he wanted to have sex with her. She told me that she said no to him, but Jessica regretted on not going through with it. She told me that she wished she had.

When Mom had gone over to Jessica's house one day, she had asked Jessica's brother if there really was a Joey that stayed with them. Mom said that Jessica's brother had told her no. When I approached Jessica about this, she told me that her brother drank alcohol a lot, and would lie or forget about some things. I didn't know what I should believe at that point. Mom said that Jessica wanted me to be in her little fantasy world, and maybe that was true.

When Officer V. was instructing the class, everyone was chaotic one day. Mr. Scochenski said one more out break and the class was in trouble. This girl Tamara walked into the room singing a song out loud, and everyone except me shouted, "TAMARA!" Then Mr. S. said that we had to do standards. Officer V. left and we copied what was written on the board. I just did as was told. I thought it was unfair, but I did it anyway.

Billy and I made up a blues' song to Scochenski's name, "The Scochi Blues", as we called it. He was just that sort of person, someone to just give you the blues, and make you feel down and out.

On the weekends, Mom would always take Tom to his hockey practices. If they were in the afternoons or late mornings, I would usually go. The hockey practices that were at 4 a.m. I would miss. I usually knew when the days were, so when I woke up I would know where Mom was. That was usually the case, except for one morning. It was a Saturday, and I had woken up. I shared the same bed as Mom because I couldn't climb the latter to get to the top bunk of the bunk-beds Susannah and I shared before the car accident.

I freaked out enough that I called Billy's house and cried. He came over and calmed me down until Mom came home.

I lined up my stuffed animals in order of largest to smallest. My largest bear was given to me by Shannon, Mike's girlfriend after the car accident in '94. The other animals and dolls followed him. There were days that I would count all the animals that covered the side of the bed against the wall that I slept by. I was told that "Crazy Bear" was given to me by Tom.

At the end of the day at school, it was always P.E. for us. I hated it. I was good at sports, just not with so many other kids. Giselle passed the all to me in basketball one and it fell out of my hands. I passed it to someone who wasn't on our team, but I didn't know. Again, I hated P.E.!

Our culmination was coming up in June! I was excited!

I had gotten accepted in Valley Alternative Magnet School for the 6th grade the week before the end of elementary school. I wasn't going to Porter like everyone else that I knew.

The culmination was held at Kennedy High School, Tom's school. The week before, the entire 5th grade went to rehearse the ceremony at Kennedy in the big auditorium. We walked there and it was only four bocks away from Haskell.

The day of 5th grade graduation came. There was a knock on the door. I answered it in my pajamas.

"Does Mary Beth live here," a girl asked.

"I'm Mary Beth," I replied.

It was Meggie! She looked so different! I hugged her right away! Mom took a picture of us, again with me in my pajamas! She was out for Tarin's friend Megan's high school graduation.

I spent the rest of the morning getting ready for the culmination. I wore a purple dress that I picked out. Billy came to the graduation with Mom. The auditorium was filled with everyone friends and family. The 5th grade did three songs that we practiced weeks I advance; I remember that at least two were Mariah Carey songs. I had heard that Ivan loved Mariah Carey songs. I thought that was fruity. The last song we did was my favorite out of the three of them; "At the Beginning with you". We were allowed to do whatever hand jesters we liked to that song. The other songs were choreographed to certain routines.

The names were starting to get called. I was in the back row, because I was one of the tall students. We were to look the teacher in the eye and get a hand shake from the principle, Mrs. Erickson. My name was called after three students. Mr. Scochenski called my name. I took a long walk to the middle of the auditorium to get my diploma. I looked Mr. Scochenski in the eye, and he said, "Congratulations Mary Beth." I was proud of myself of where I finally had gotten to. Mrs. Erickson shook my hand and I went to go back to my seat. I sat down, but realized I had to wait for everyone else in my line to came back to finally sit down. The morning continued.

After the graduation, I found Jacob. We took pictures together to have end. Mom only took two. Then I said goodbye.

When I got home, Meggie was there. We went to Casey's house at the end of the street. Meggie's dad, John, came out with a video tape and recorded us. Mom took pictures of us. Meggie was eating a piece of cake.

Elementary school ended.

It always felt as though I was just having a dream. Little did I know it was really a nightmare?

I was very upset one afternoon. Mom asked what was wrong and I told her that it was about the time that she and Billy kissed. She denied ever saying that.

"If I said it, it was to make you not afraid at the time. I wanted to pull away."

` So why didn't she? I was already angry and nervous each weekend that she and Billy were together over at his place. I stayed up at night, waiting for Mom to come home.

Chapter 5

Tell Me It's Over

In the summer of 1999, I went to Valley Alternative to meet my new aide, Stephanie, as well as the principle Terry. I thought everything was going to be okay. I found out that the teachers were called by their first names, so I thought that was cool. It was a small campus, but maybe a little bigger than Haskell was. There was a farm, but I was told that it was for the elementary classes, so I thought that was fine.

On my first day, Mom and I got there early to find Terry. I was nervous, as usual. Terry found a student to show me where my first class was. We walked there and back. Mom was still around, until we said goodbye. I spoke with Terry a few more minutes, and then I went to class. Terry walked me over. She asked this girl Kelly if it would be alright if I sat next to her. I was so nervous, but she said yes.

Terry left, and this other girl came up and said to Kelly, "I thought you were going to save me a seat." Kelly apologized and said that things changed.

Stephanie joined me later on that period. I was given a schedule of my classes. The rooms were letters instead of numbers. I thought that was weird, but interesting. First period was science with a teacher, Nan. 30 kids were in that class.

Second period was History with a male teacher, Mike, but we had a substitute for the first few weeks, Avo. He was an old man with white hair.

For third period, I was supposed to be in Music, which was also in Mike's class. I was placed in Nan's art class instead. I enjoyed that class. The students were different than the students I had in my other classes.

However, during the second semester, adults said I would take a computer class instead. I was going to have a computer to work on in school, instead of writing my notes like ever other student there. That really mad me angry and heartbroken, but I never showed my anger to the adults. I would tell them that I didn't want to work on a computer. "It will help you out, Mary Beth," they'd say. How?

My fourth class was English with Nan. We didn't always do the subject that the class was being held in all the time. Nan would sometimes have us doing science during the English period or via verse.

Fifth was P.E., but for that I went off campus, next door for adaptive P.E. three days a week. On Tuesdays and Thursdays this adaptive P.E. teacher came to V.A.S. for me and this other student Diana. Diana and I became friends fast. I was always open to being someone's friend back then. Diana was a bigger girl than I was. She was over weight, but that wasn't really an issue for me, unlike other kids there.

My whole schedule was changed after a few months. I was placed in math for first period and English for 6th, so I wouldn't miss anything in Jennele's class.

Stephanie only lasted as my aide for a few months. She would write notes for me in my classes, but her handwriting was so hard to read. Stephanie and I were more of friends, though, which was nice for me. There were only so many people that I could trust in life. Stephanie called me "Summer" for a nickname.

I met Jessica after a week without Stephanie. This other aide from the resource room helped me out for the time that Stephanie wasn't there.

I had started getting into writing my own poetry in December 1999. I found this vintage looking book, and had decided to start writing poetry at the age of 11. I didn't write poetry in the traditional way, though. My poems were paragraphs at first, but then I went on to writing in the traditional way.

The first poem wrote was on December 28th, 1999, and was untitled:

As the surgery goes on through and through, I can only think of one thing and that is you. As they put me to sleep I start to cry, 'cause I don't know if I'll survive. I can just imagine if I fought back. I probably wouldn't win, but I would still try.

Summer

Other poems followed. I wrote about love and lose. Everything that I always wished that would happen to me, I wrote down those wishes on paper.

I didn't date every poem that I wrote, but I continued to write. It was the only way to express the loneliness that I felt at times, and the longings and desires that I had. After watching Romeo and Juliet for the first time I wrote two poems to the tale that was in my mind. My favorite was the second poem that I wrote that didn't have a title until the eighth grade.

Romeo is a dear, says, Juliet, for you belong with me. After death shall we still live together at once with every kiss. I fall into his bed just at night to see what is wrong at the first right. Not at which is flying, but lies out dead. Together at once will be what I said.

Love, Juliet

The poetry continued from there on out. It took me two years to finish the small book that I had filled with poems.

At Mulhulland junior high, my P.E. teacher there was Ms. Hidey. The students there were fine. A little weird, but I didn't complain too much. I used to get really hurt in P.E. class. We did hockey once, and at first I was really excited! I loved hockey. We were put on teams, for the few students there were. I was behind this girl, and she lifted her stick too high and it whacked me in the face. I was told by others that the reason so many things hit me was because of my bad eye sight in my right eye, which was untrue to me. The girl didn't get in trouble for hitting me in the eye, but every time I got hurt, I always wanted to beat the crap out of whoever hurt me first. I never did. Stephanie had to stop me a few times. The girl didn't apologize to me, so Stephanie and I left.

There was this boy in that class who couldn't walk correctly. He had a dent in his leg, but he was nice to me. There was a girl who was in a wheel chair, so the two of them never did the running on the field like the rest of us.

At V.A.S., my P.E. teacher was a lady named Robby. Diana only went the first semester of the 6th grade, but weaseled in sometimes. Diana and I would help out in the kindergarten yard from time to time before or after Robby came.

My 6th period class was math with Jennele. She was fine. She was also my computer teacher. I was placed in that class as the only 6th grader. I was working with eighth graders; standing out, as usual. There was one nice eighth grader, Ana. I thought the eighth grader Dan was cute, but Ana and Dan were dating.

I was set up this boy Matthew to work on a project in computer class. Matt and I had to come up with a make believe product. We chose, "Larry H. Parker, "We'll fight with you!"" It was fun.

We had an activity class twice a week after lunch for 30 minutes. My first activity was art, and Kelly was in it, so it was fun. My first big crush was in that class. His name was Josh. He was a 10th grader. He was such a good artist.

I found Kelly really upset one day in art.

"Hey," I started. "What's wrong?" Kelly was crying.

"Kika said we can't be friends anymore," Kelly told me. "Mohammad doesn't like he fact that I' her best friend."

"Oh, I'm sorry," I said as I bent down next to her. Kika and Kelly were best friends, but Mohammad was a part of the popular crowd and Kelly wasn't. I wasn't apart of any crowd. Stephanie and I tried our best to make Kelly feel better. Eventually, that day, she did.

My first best friend was a girl named Anush. She was Armenian. I didn't think too much of it back then.

Josh dated this girl Jessica who was also in art. They were both great artists. I only wish I was that good. The students were in charge of the activity period. Josh had taught us how to draw things one time.

There was another boy, Michael in that class. The guys thought I was really weird, but it didn't bother me at all, because I was.

I switched activities the second semester to Fashion, a modeling class. Sue was my teacher there. Kelly followed, as well as Essence and Diana. Joanna, another girl from my grade, was in fashion period also.

In the 6th grade I had a big crush on this boy Steve that I had class with. He was part of the popular crowd, where as I was simply nice to everyone. Steve gave me nothing but attitude the first semester, until I stopped liking him. Second semester came along, and he started liking me. I was friends with a boy, Mohammad. He was in Steve's crowd. Then there was Ricardo and Daniel. I despised Daniel. He was mean to me, but I tried not to let it bother me too much. I knew that he dated Gaby, one of the popular girls in my grade. Gaby was in my fashion class, as well as my other classes.

I was feeling sick the second semester. I had headaches that I have never had before. I went to see a new neurosurgeon, Dr. Lazereff at UCLA. I was given no choice but to have brain surgery. When I found out, I returned to school on a Tuesday. I was in Sue's class. I was paired up with this one girl, but too many thoughts were going through my head. I started crying in class. Stephanie wasn't there. My new aide, Jessica, was. But she was at lunch. So as I burst into tears, the girl asked what was wrong. I told the girl, and then I was escorted to Terry's office. Mom was called. She showed up, with me just crying in Terry's office. My headaches weren't getting any easier, that's for sure!

I was scheduled to have surgery the first Friday of March, 2000. It was only to check the pressure of my head, or so I was told. I didn't want to do it! I wasn't given a choice, though. Mom compromised a prize situation for going through with the surgery. It seemed fair. I was the one having the surgery; I was the one who was scared, not other people.

My prize from Mom for that was supposed to be a snow trip two weeks later. Billy got me a golden tiger necklace for being brave. My snow trip never happened, though. The headaches never stopped, so I was scheduled for another brain surgery 13 days later, the weekend the snow trip was supposed to happen.

I had the brain surgery on March 23rd, the day after Mom and Joe's birthday. That surgery was to change the siphon valve in my head to a bigger one.

I didn't get my own room for that surgery. The doctors stuck me with the needle of an IV three times, but they couldn't find vein. They said I would need the sleeping gas, so they gave me the choice to have the regular kind, or grape smelling gas.

Remembering how awful the regular gas smelled, and how much I tried to fight it off at the age of seven, I chose the grape smelling gas. The doctors said that Mom could go in there with me if I chose for that to happen. I was terrified, so I wanted Mom to be there with me.

The doctor said to count backwards from 100. I began to count. Mom said something to me about the backstreet boys. The doctor waved and was talking to a nurse afterwards. I dreamt the whole thing of my memories 3-5 times. Then there were butterflies turning into butterflies, and other design turning into other things. There were lots of colors in that dream.

When I woke up, I was really bothered by everything and everyone, even though no one was really around. Billy was by my bed, but Mom wasn't there. She was out in the hallway making a phone call home. The song, "A Small World After All", was in my head as my eyes opened. It was the worst song to wake up to after having brain surgery.

I was transferred to the second level of recovery after an hour or so.

When I got to the second level, there was a little boy in the bed next to mine. There was a drape, so I couldn't see him. When the night was getting darker, Mom and Billy had to leave. Mom stayed at the hospital, of course, but she had to stay in the parents' room, down the hall. The door to the hallway of the hospital was right in front of me. When a nurse came to check the machine to my IV, I started crying. I was so scared and so upset! The nurse tried to comfort me, and took my hand. I cried for a while longer, until I got too tired, and stopped. I tried my best to fall asleep. I woke up early in the morning to see that Mom had come in, but I quickly fell asleep again. She spent the night sleeping outside the room on the bench.

The rest of the day continued with me in the hospital bed. I could walk to the wheelchair toilet by my bed. It was hard to wall anywhere, with the IV in my arm.

Dr. Lazereff came in a few hours later.

"Dr. Lazereff!" I said, a little through sarcasm, and a little through delight. He checked my vitals, and decided that it was okay for me to go home. When the IV came out, I clung to Mom's arm, afraid that it would hurt. It didn't hurt at all, but that didn't stop the fear inside me. I was very fearful when the doctors stitched my head up!

I saw the little boy in the bed beside me before I left, and I said a silent prayer for him.

I rode in a wheelchair to the parking lot, and waited there with Billy for Mom to get her car. Billy drove us home.

I returned to school the next week. Everything was back to normal, other than I had restrictions on P.E. My stitches were taken out 10 days after the surgery. I needed to hold Mom's hand because I was very much afraid. I had to wear a hat to cover up the bandage on my head. Diana wanted to see it one day at school, so I told her I would show her in the bathroom, something that I didn't really want to do. When I took it off, she looked like she was in pain, but I laughed off my own pain.

Mom had gotten concert tickets to see "Johnny No Name", which was A.J. Mclean from the Backstreet Boys. We had a great time.

Steve had a crush on me the last semester as well. I stopped liking him, because he was always mean to me. When I got my year book, Steve wanted to sign it, so he first put, "Dear Mary Beth, I hope you have a great summer, oh, and Daniel has a crush on you – Steve"

My reaction to that was of disgusted, "EW!" I shouted.

"That's not true," Daniel told me.

Steve signed it again saying, "Dear Mary Beth, I hope you have a great summer and Abel has a crush on you!!! – your friend, Steve." After signing his name, Steve always put, "The Ass", but crossed it out both times. A lot of different kids signed my year book that year, but I never really spoke to any of them in that school year.

The rest of the year passed.

When summer time came, I was going to go to a day camp that Tom worked at. I was kind of excited about it at first. There were age groups for the campers. The instructors had nicknames. Tom's was "Lazy". When I got there, the first person I noticed was Michael P., who was a kid in my class at school. He was in the sports group and I was in my age group that was only girls. There were the snooty girls, the sporty girls, and maybe a few others. Our instructors were changed weekly. There was a cute instructor that was nicknamed "Crash". He was in charge of the sports club during the second week. I only last 2 weeks and I didn't go every day.

The first week I went two days. The kids seemed nice. Oh, how I was wrong. I remember this one girl Amanda. She was cool, and a really good dancer. Each week the campers had to do a show on Thursday. I missed the first week. During the second week, every girl in my group was being mean to me. There was this one black girl who was making fun of me because I was dancing weird in front of a mirror. She took the two snooty girls into a room, saw me, and then closed the door to tell them. They came out laughing. I was crushed how people could be so mean to me!

Then the other sporty looking girl was making fun of me. She had the snooty girls were making fun of me too. I was lucky to go on for as long as I did. I was wearing my swimsuit that day, but as the day turned out, I didn't go swimming.

We were sitting in our group area, just waiting for something to happen. I couldn't handle being there anymore, so I up and left. I didn't make it very far until my group leader said I needed to go back. I thought, "No fucking way!", but of course said something else. I wouldn't go back. Then, after a while the instructor of the day camp, "Chucky" came out to sit with me. He was talking to me, and then grabbed both my hands to comfort me. It made me feel worse! Why was this older guy holding my hands? And why wasn't I taking them back? Tom took me to the office and tried calling Mom, but she wasn't there. I ended up staying in Tom's group the rest of the day.

Everyone else in my group was placed on clean up duty for the rest of the day, except the black chick who weaseled her way out of it. Tom asked of I wanted to be the fish in his group for the show. I said no, and sat with the rest of my group that afternoon. Amanda asked if I was mad at her, but I said no. The other girls said they were sorry and gave me a hug.

After the day was through, Tom, Louie and I waited for Mom to pick us up. Mom got mad at me because I didn't go swimming that day. That was just the icing on the cake to a horrible day. I never returned to camp ever again.

Mom and I went to Oregon a week later. She was going to see her friend after such a long time. I tagged along, because I had nothing else to do. I met Mom's friend and her sons.

In August, Mom, Tom, Joe and I went up to Nevada to see Grandma. One afternoon, Joe and I were playing cards at the breakfast table, Tom was in the guest bedroom watching TV, and Mom and Grandma were in the kitchen. The phone rang. It was Tracey. Mom left the room, still talking to Tracey. She went into one of the guest bedrooms for quite, I guess. She was gone for a while, but I was only paying attention to the game that Joe and I were playing. Mom came back a little later and brought Tom. She was crying. She came to the table that Joe and I were at.

"I have to tell you guys something," she said through tearful eyes. "Your dad died. I'm so sorry."

I was shocked! A swarm of sadness and confusion came over me. I got up from the table, and one second later I was crying. Mom came and gave me a hug right away. Tom had left the room, and Joe said nothing. I didn't know how to feel.

I went outside where Tom and Joe were. We were walking in the desert sand for a while, not getting very far, with no real destination. Mom called us back in for dinner.

I cried myself to sleep that night. I didn't even know the guy, and I wouldn't know anything about my father until a few years later.

Soon the rest of the summer passed.

Chapter 6

Friends, Enemies, and Other Things

The 7th grade came. Everything seemed to be in order for the time being, at least.

Michael P. had told me what he heard happened after that day at camp. I tried to let it go.

My history teacher was Rosy, Nan's daughter. A new teacher, Steve, was the other history teacher. Vivian was my English teacher, Nan was my science teacher, again, and Jennele was my math teacher, again.

During the first semester, Michael P. was saying how Tom was my brother, and how much Michael enjoyed Tom as a counselor at camp. In my opinion, I thought Michael was developing a crush on me.

One day, Daniel was making fun of me for whatever reason. I couldn't handle him. "Not now," I said to myself. I got upset, of course, but had decided to walk away. I made it to the end of that class room building, when I stopped and looked back.

"Moe, can I talk to you for a second," I called to Mohammad. He came over, and I was just stuttering for a moment. He was looking around and smiling, until I broke down crying. Mohammad asked what was wrong. I told him my dad died. I was over it, but there was still a lot of emotion that was there, so I found out at that moment. Mohammad heard me and gave me a hug.

"Dude," he called back to Steve and Ricardo as they made their way over. "Her dad died." Mohammad had asked if I wanted to go to the office, but I didn't say anything, so we just started walking over. Ricardo had said that he liked baseball, just to make me feel better. That was what the argument with Daniel was about when I was first standing over with the guys.

Cassandra, the guidance counselor, found us walking there, with me crying, she asked what was wrong. Mohammad told her. Cassandra asked if I would like to go with her to the office and talk. I told her that I would just go back to class and see Jessica.

The assistant for Jessica was there, Amy. They asked if I was alright. I said yes, feeling a little better. When 5th period came around, I went to Steve's media class. The other students, such as Maria, Gaby, Ella, and a few others asked if I was okay. They heard that I had been crying. I told them I was fine, which I was getting there.

For my media class, Steve was the teacher, and I was really jazzed to learn about media, but I was the only one in the class that was excited about it. Anush was in that class after the first three went already went by, and we were cool, at first. The students were to write scripts based on non-smoking. My script was one that was chosen out of 5 of them. I was very excited! I had asked Anush if she would like to take part in the production. She was cast as Natasha. This new girl, Mary, played Michelle, and Tida played Lindsay. I wrote Lindsay as "the bad girl", the one to do drugs. Natasha and Michelle told Lindsay to stop doing that, but the friends broke up in the end. We only shot in three different locations: the outside lockers, made to look like the girls locker rooms; the teachers lounge, made to look like Michelle's bedroom; and the outside field. No one in my group really did anything. Narine helped out the most by making the fake cigarettes. Some of the other students working as my "crew" wanted to be extras, so I cast a few of them. I was to give everyone a grade, which never really happened, and most of them deserved fails for the assignment. When that assignment was over, I got started on another script, but found out that we weren't going to do another script because no one else in class wanted to do anything. We were lectured on why we didn't want to do anything for the rest of the semester, even though I did.

Anush and I were still best friends at the beginning of the 7th grade. Her cousin Ani was in the 6th grade, but I thought she was really annoying. I tried to put up with her though. Anush was really only hanging out with the Armenians at school. I didn't like them at all. They always seemed to have an attitude towards me, and I never understood why. I would find out soon enough.

My history class with Rosy only lasted for two weeks, until our class was switched to Steve's history class. I liked Steve as a teacher. He was entertaining as hell!

Vivian was a really mean teacher. I had her for English and life styles class. In life styles, the students were to learn what it would be like to grow up and have responsibilities. It was an okay class. Michael A. and I sat next to each other in that class. The students had to take care of an egg for a while. We had to treat it as though it were our baby. There was an earthquake practice drill. The bell rang, and I dropped to the floor. Without realizing it, I accidentally knocked Michael's egg to the floor, and it had a crack in it. Michael was really pissed off at me, but it was an accident. He had to go to the farm area to get a new egg. It happened to a lot of students. Thanksgiving break was coming up, and the students were supposed to keep their babies with them. I was going to Nevada, so Mom told Jessica to tell Vivian that I couldn't take an egg on an eight hour car trip. I used a little stuffed animal instead.

After the assignment was done, the students were to throw their eggs in the garbage at school. I didn't know that we were to first crack the egg, so I just threw mine in the trash.

Another assignment that the class had was to be in a group, and to have a pretend family. I was placed in Michael A's group. He was the father, I was the mother, Gayane was the daughter, Able was the son, and Tracey was the doctor. We were to act out a scene of the "kids" getting dirty and having an infection on their arms. The mother was supposed to find the marks on their bodies and then the doctor was to diagnose the cause. The scene that we rehearsed was changed when we did it in front of the class. No one told me that it was going to change, so I stuck to the script that we had first come up with.

Anush, Gladys, and I were in a group project in math class over winter break. We were to come up with a script for Jennele's math class to show the students how to do fractions. Gladys and I went to Anush's place. Her dad was on the couch, and her little sister was around. We practiced shooting the scene. We wrote a script to show how to do fractions. I was second up. Anush's Mom had come back from her job and was going to order pizza for us for lunch. The pizza came. We were given a slice, but I was still kind of hungry, as was Gladys. Anush's sister said we didn't need to wait and put another slice on our plates. I ate the second slice and waited. Anush put another slice on my plate, but I only took one bite. Gladys asked if she could have the rest of mine, so I gave it to her. The rest of the day continued and we figured out what was going to get said.

When school was back in session, Anush, Gladys and I were going to tape the little skit. Well, everything changed, and I got really upset. Amy was there. We switched the order around. I went form second to third in less time than I could imagine.

Confused and really irritated that I was last, I burst out into tears. This was embarrassing and it was making me more furious than ever! Why is everyone changing everything? I thought. Letting everyone know exactly what I felt, they changed it, again. It broke my heart exploding like that in front of my friends.

Then I was first. That went fine.

The final for that class was insane! I was the first to finish my final, but I failed that part. After I went back up with the second part, Jennele said I should do all of the questions to the second part. I ended up failing that part as well.

Joe had me really upset one day in December. He made me read him a page of my diary to him. I was embarrassed and heart broken on how cruel he was being to me.

I was put in the resource math class after that. Four other students were in that class, so I was comfortable. Well, for a while. It was nice because I only worked out of a text book. If I had a question, I could ask for help without feeling embarrassed. Andrea, a popular girl from my grade, was in there. She seemed even more mentally challenged than I was. Maybe she's jut lazy, I thought.

One day, I had gotten my period and I had put a pad on. It leaked in the back of my favorite pair of pants. I was going to the bus, and the other students, and Jessica, saw it. I got picked up 30 minutes early, so Jessica and I were going to go to the bus. Jessica asked if I had my period and I told her that I did. She gave me a pad to change, and then Stephanie's jacket for my butt. I didn't know it had leaked so much. There were two 8th graders in the restroom. They asked if my name was Mary Beth. I told them yes.

When I got home, Mom confronted me and said that I should change my pants.

I had stayed home form school the next day because I had major cramps. I didn't find out what happened until I got back and Gladys had told me. I was so humiliated!

A week later, in Steve's class, Gladys had wrote me a note asking if I had my period.

"Why?" I wrote back.

"Because I just started mine and I was wondering how long it lasts?" she wrote back.

"Oh," I wrote. "Mine usually lasts a few days."

One day I had written Anush a Note and stuck it in our locker. We shared one with Ani, her obnoxious cousin. She never responded to it. I knew that we were growing apart. She was always with her Armenian friends and cousins. I hated the girl Rosy. She was mean to me. She hated me as well; it just took a little longer for her to say it.

Rosy, Ani and I were in the same activity class; fashion. I hated feeling left out when Anush would talk Armenian to them. I was already an outcast, but that made me feel worse!

I had heard a rumor that Anush was dating Steve, who I used to like. I wrote Anush a note, dropped it where they were sitting, and walked away. Anush said it wasn't true, that her parents wouldn't let her date, and that our friendship was over. I was thinking, "It took you that long to figure that out? Wow!" as I walked away. Narine just shouted, "Fuck you!' back to me, but I didn't care. I was done with them!

At home, things got crazy! One day, my bus didn't come, so Jessica took me home instead. I needed to get special permission for that to happen. When we got to my house, there were police cars. I already knew it was because of Joe. Worse off, it was the bomb squad! Tom socked Joe in the arm after the bomb squad had left. I was just embarrassed.

The next day at school, Jessica only said "Hi" to me, and I just stared crying. I was so upset! She took me outside, and waited for me to cool off.

I was alone for a while at lunch after Anush ended our friendship.

There were these two girls came over and started talking to me one day. They had asked if I wanted to eat lunch with them, so I went over. I was over for a little bit, but left after a while without saying anything. I didn't feel right sitting there in silence with girls that I wasn't really friends with. I went back to the stairs where I was before. Then some boys came over with Michael P. They said hi to me, and I said hi back.

"Is your brother a pro-skater?" one of them asked.

"No," I said.

"Are you sure?"

'Yes, I'm sure my brother's not a pro-skater." I said. "Michael, what are you telling these guys?" I walked off after that.

The boys, Clark, Rene, and Matt became my friends after that. I could tell right away that Clark had a crush on me. It didn't bother me, though. His friends would always tell me, "Clark likes you." Clark would say that we were just friends. I got mad at Matt one time for some reason, and I went off on him. I was having a bad day that day.

I was in a fashion show one day, and tickets were being sold. I was hanging out with the guys when an eighth grader came by to ask if anyone wanted to go. I told the guys that I was in the sports section of the fashion show, and then I shouted out, "Holliday!" I was wearing Tom's hockey jersey in that section. Clark looked at me and said, "Mary Beth Holliday." I just stood there, kind of confused. Clark wanted to buy a ticket, but he couldn't because he was on the non-participation list. He had four U's on his report card and couldn't attend. It didn't bother me much that he wasn't going to be there. One of Clark's friends was at the first show.

There was this other eighth grader that liked me, Dante. He would always ask for my phone number. I finally gave it to him, but he never called.

I began to like Clark at the end of the 7th grade.

During the first three months of the year 2000, Ben Teresa, and Conan lived in the downstairs room at home. The Sylmar house had finally sold, and Ben just wasn't a responsible person. I went through HELL with them living at my home! Mom complained that Teresa just picked up her purse and came over, and that was the way she moved, where as Ben had to pack everything. I hated them from there on out.

The school year passed. I became close friends, again, with Kelly and Essence.

Tom had graduated from high school at Kennedy, so of course I went to that. Tom got some awards, which I was very proud of him!

When the summer after the 7th grade hit, things began to get weirder. One day I wanted Joe to go up to Taco Bell for. He owed me for something. He refused. I begged him, in tears. He still wouldn't do it.

"Fine," I said, and I walked up there myself. On the way up, I told myself, "Don't talk to yourself." I always had that tendency to do that. I crossed the street at Gaynor and was going to be heading down Mission, when this guy starts talking to me.

He looked to be about 16.

"Hey," he said. I didn't want to be rude, so I said "hey" back. Then we started getting into a conversation. He asked me how many guys' hearts I had broken.

Oh my God!" I said. "There are 5 different guys at school!" Then I started going off about that. He asked how old I was, and I told him that I was 13. We walked together until I got to the corner. He then asked how old I thought he was. "16?" I guessed.

He laughed.

"14?" I guessed again.

"I'm 12", he said. Then we said goodbye

I went in to Taco Bell, ordered my food, and then waited. That was when Joe came over and said that he saw me waking, talking to that boy. I was so embarrassed! He said he was going to go home and tell Mom. I continued to wait for my food.

After I had gotten my food, I went to the soda machine outside of Lucky's grocery store. There was this other guy there. He said "Hey", and I said "Hey", back. He asked if I had a boyfriend. I told him no. He asked for my number, because he wanted to call me, but I didn't have a piece of paper. I was about to leave, but he asked for a hug.

"Why?" I asked.

"I just want to feel loved," he said. I just stood there, not wanting to and not knowing what else to do.

You want to feel loved? Hug your mom. I thought.

"You don't have to," he said. I took one step behind me, and then just started running. I made it home, called Mom and explained the story. I thought it was funny. Joe had already told Mom what happened with the first boy. I was embarrassed, of course.

Later that summer, mid-July, Mom found out that her aunt Betsy had died. Grandma was best friends with her. So Mom was organizing a trip for her, Joe and me to out to New York for us to go to the memorial services. That summer, Grandma had fallen and hurt her knee, so she couldn't go to New York with us. It was going to be my first trip to New York, but certainly not my last.

Chapter 7

Beginning of a Nightmare

September came, and school was back in session. I had English for first period, even though I was promised P.E. for first period. Mom, Joe, and I were going to New York the second week of school.

I was confused that I was in Vivian's 1st period English class. I had been told that I would take P.E. first period. That was changed the first few weeks of school.

The second week of September came. Uncle Angelo had picked us up at JFK, and we went to Queens. My Great Aunt Mary lived there. She lived in a big three story house, but she was blind, and could only see out of the side of her eyes. It didn't bother me, though.

We went to the memorial. I had met my great uncle Steve beforehand, and his kids that were Mom's age. Aunt Betsy was Uncle Steve wife, so I'm sure it was very hard on him.

After leaving the graveyard, Joe had said, "Mmm, I could sure go for a funeral pretzel," as there was a pretzel stand there. Everyone laughed. We then went to Mom's cousin Pat's house, and sure enough, there were pretzels.

"Umm, I was just kidding," Joe said. But we all enjoyed a pretzel.

On Monday, September 10th, 2001, Mom, Joe and I were going to go to Manhattan for the day and see everything. We were going to go in the Twin Towers, but I always had my height problem. We just went to China Town, and goofed off for the day. I'll never forget, it was rainy when we were in China town and I was trying to be smooth and go under a steel bar. Well, I fell. Joe was ahead of Mom and me. I had fallen in the puddle that was in front of me. When I got up, Joe was gone. Mom started freaking out! Where was Joe? Mom looked up and down the street, but we didn't really move, because Joe would lose us too. Finally, some short time later, Joe was running back towards us!

I'll never forget that.

The next day, September 11th, I woke up at a quarter to 9 in the morning. That was when I heard Mom.

"Oh, Jesus, Joseph, and Mary!" I heard Mom saying.

I could hear from the third story. Something was wrong, I could tell. I decided to go downstairs and find out what was wrong. Mom had gone to Joe's room first on the second floor. I made my way down to see that on the television, there was a plane that had flown into one of the Twin Towers. The second plane had hit at 9, just a few moments later. I knew that the rest of our vacation was over. We were supposed to go out that day, but things had obviously changed. We spent the rest of the day glued to the T.V. Mom was calling everyone at home, asking if they were alright. I spent part of the day in front of the television, and part of it just writing.

We didn't go anywhere the next day. Mom, Uncle Angelo, and Aunt Mary were glued to the T.V. We were supposed to go to Poughkeepsie that day to see Aunt Mary Lee, but we didn't go anywhere.

We didn't make it out of the house until Thursday, and Uncle Angelo only took us to Brooklyn, which was fine with me. You could still see the smoke for the explosions.

Mom was really worried about how we would get home. The airport didn't look like an option. Not anymore. She said the train would be three days, non stop. I actually liked that idea. Our original plan was to leave on Saturday, the 15th, but instead things got turned backwards. I didn't know what was going to happen, and I had a feeling that Mom didn't know either.

We got a flight out of New Jersey for the 16th. Uncle Angelo took us there, hugged us goodbye, and off we went.

We had a lay over in Las Vegas. Joe had asked Mom for his ticket. We didn't have food on the plane, so Joe had gone to Taco Bell at the airport and had gotten us food. He made it back in time for the departure.

When we got back, it was still early, but we had been traveling all day, so I was exhausted! The next day I asked Mom if I could just stay home and rest because I was so tired. She said that was okay, and called the school to tell them. There wasn't any school on Tuesday, so I had another day to recover.

Getting back to school was insane! I was on my way to Vivian's class for first period, and Maria had said, "AW! Mary Beth, you're back!" I got a lot of responses like that for a week.

In Nan's history class, I was to give an assignment to the class about my trip. Well, with everything that happened on September 11th, there was a lot to say. I spent the week getting everything together for the class. I had posters, books, photos, and a lot to say.

When I first got to school I went to Vivian's class. She saw my posters, and wanted me to show the class, but Jessica explained that it was for another class. Vivian said she would still like to see it.

When 4th period hit, I went up to Nan, and asked her if I could address the class with my report. She said she was just waiting for me, and then she told everyone else to be quite. I showed the class the photo album, which I figured that not everyone could really see. Then I spoke of a relative of mine that became Mayor of New York at a point in that man's life.

This girl Margaret raised her hand, and I asked if she wanted to ask a question, but she told me that she'd wait until I was done.

I took questions at the end. Margaret was first to ask a question. I explained what I could in great detail. Steve was in the front row with all of his friends. H had asked a question.

When the report was done, as well as the questions, the students started chanting my name and I simply blushed while returning to my seat.

I was very angry that I was placed back into Jennele's computer class. I was furious! I was told that I wouldn't have to take the computer class again. The response I was given by the adults, "We thought you'd like it, again. There is a new program that Jennele has."

I hated computers! Why couldn't anyone see that? And I was really excited about taking an acting class, but that opportunity was taken away from me. No one had asked me at the time if I had wanted to take the computer class again; they had just decided that I would like it. I did stick around for the first two weeks of it, but I had gone to the Terry's office one day in tears asking why I had to take it again. I thought when she moved me into another class that I would be in Drama.

I got my schedule switched and went to Jennele to sign it. I was being moved to the elementary yard to help out Lori, a 1st grade teacher. There was another student already helping out as well. When I first started out, I was a little nervous, but I got into it. The kids seemed to except me after a short while.

The 10th grader that was already in there said that I wouldn't make it a week. I knew him from Jennele's computer class two years beforehand.

I helped out in the class room by taking students aside and helping them with reading or spelling.

When lunch time came for them at 11:30 am, I was to open the lunches for the kids. After a few weeks, the kids got comfortable with me, and would ask me to come help them. When lunch was over for them, they would go back to their yard, and I would play jump rope with the girls. They would occasionally say hi to me as I was leaving school on some days.

I only saw Josh a few times that first semester. He had a new girlfriend, of course. She was short and skinny. They were the "Barbie and Ken" of their senior year.

I had formed a crush on Clark over the summer. When I tried to talk to him he pretended that he didn't know me. I had asked Diana to ask Dante why he didn't call me, but he was being rude and had just changed his mind.

Another 9th grader, Rebecca, was talking about her boyfriend and how they broke up.

Shabriel and Rebecca were both in my fashion class, so I saw them regularly.

The Turkey Bowl was in November, of course. On Tuesdays and Thursdays, a Special Ed teacher would come and instruct us in cheer leading. Then on Monday, Wednesdays, and Fridays there was another P.E. teacher from another school that came to instruct the class. He wore glasses, so I never saw his eyes, but from the way he looked, I thought he was attractive.

P.E. was a mixture of eighth and ninth graders combined.

Rebecca was in the cheer leading group with me as well. Diana was also there. When we learned the routine for the Turkey Bowl, I was to stand in the back, but Diana stood behind me in the two rows that there were. I knew the cheer that went with it, so we were good.

When the class had to do square dancing, I was moved into two different groups. The second was Michael P.'s group. The coach had to position me correctly, so he moved my shoulder a certain way. My heart soared when he touched me. Michael wasn't nice to me in that class. Nor was anyone else in that group.

Tom was away in Santa Monica attending college, while he also worked. I would occasionally see him on the weekends.

When winter break came, I was excited that the first semester was ending. I was going to on to Drama class. I was back and forth from helping out with the elementary yard to getting ahead on my school work when I could Tuesdays and Thursdays.

Chapter 8

Illness and Unkept Promises

The second semester came at last! Finally I could take drama as my class!

I got my schedule in first period. Reading it, I discovered that I was not in drama for my third period. I was furious! Tears sprang to my eyes out of rage and betrayal. I was put in study hall instead, because everyone else thought that I needed time to complete my school work. They had *promised* me that I be taking my selected elective.

I went to the principles office in a tearful rage. I spoke to her and she had told me, "Your mom thought it would be a good idea to keep study hall for third period."

"No," I told her. "I want drama." They had promised that after all. Terry said she would it changed, so I felt a little better for the time being. I continued with the rest of my day.

When Tuesday hit, I was pumped to be in Drama. The class began and I was sitting in the front row. The teacher began to take roll. I heard right away that my name wasn't called. Malaika looked at me and said, "I didn't call your name."

'Terry said she changed my schedule so I could be in here," I told her.

"Well, go to the office and get the transfer rescheduled," Malaika told me. So I got my things together, feeling stupid, and went to the office. I went to the main office instead of the counseling office in tears. The office lady, Sue, was there. I tried my best to tell her what was wrong. When I couldn't get the words out without crying, I left the room. I decided that I was just going to wonder around campus, *No one will miss me anyway,* I thought.

Sue had told everyone that was in a meeting with Terry that I had come in very upset, but I had left. Well, after that, a search party was formed to find me. I walked away from everyone, until Jessica said to wait out of the counseling office for her. She was going to talk to Chuck and get my schedule redone, again. *"He just didn't have time before,"* I was told. *Everyone has to make my life hell,* was more like it.

As I was waiting outside, I saw Mom coming up to me with that, "I'm going to yell at you, Mary Beth, because you ruined everything" look on her face. I was going to leave, and not be yelled at, but I promised Jessica that I would stay. I should have left.

"You can't just walk away, Mary Beth. Not when everyone is trying to help you," Mom said, and I've heard the same lie over and over and over again for too many times to count. I just cried. I was promised one thing, and, yet again, was naïve enough to believe it. I blamed everyone that day, including myself for believing such a lie. I didn't ask for that.

I was too upset, in tears, to over back to class. I told everyone that I didn't want to go back because I had been crying and everyone would be asking why. I didn't want to explain. Jessica said that everyone would just think that I would be switching my classes around, but I knew that was a lie. So I hung out with Billy for the rest of that day.

I was beginning to feel sick by the second week of school. It was only February and I was terribly sick. I would get headaches and my whole body would hurt all over! I didn't know what was going on. There were days that I couldn't get out of bed. Finally, by mid February, Mom had scheduled an appointment for me to have brain surgery.

Everything was going wrong that month.

My Aunt Carol was in the hospital. My surgery was scheduled for February 22.

On Wednesday, February 13, I had gone to the hospital for something. Later that day, Billy and I were going to the park to play baseball. When I got home, I found Mom crying in the kitchen. Not knowing what was wrong, I rushed over to her.

"Auntie Carol died," Mom said. I broke down crying, but not very many tears came out. I knew that Auntie Carol was in a better place, but for the sake of Mom, I tried really hard to cry and show emotion. I hugged Mom to comfort her.

When that didn't work, I just stayed back, really upset but not crying. Auntie Sissy came over and cried with Mom. Susannah came rushing in, crying as well. I stood back, waiting.

Mom had asked if I was still going to my math tutor. I said I would, and Billy drove me.

The next day, Valentines Day, Mom and I got up early. We were going to Nevada with Auntie Sissy. I just packed a little.

When we got there eight hours later, Mom and I stayed at Grandma's house. My Auntie Sissy had her own place up there.

We went to the funeral home the next day. Uncle Ronny was there. My heart went out to him. Everyone was going to see Auntie Carol's body. Mom said I could wait out in the front room, so I did.

We waited a while for my cousin Erik to show up. He didn't come, so we waited a while longer, but the funeral house needed to put Auntie Carol's body back in the freezer. I would hear Auntie Sissy talking to Auntie Carol's dead body, as well as my cousin Renee. When things started to die down, Erik finally showed up. I was outside for that part. I saw my uncle sitting down, talking to his grandson. Uncle Ronnie sprang into tears when he heard Auntie Carol's name being said, but he didn't want his grandson to see him cry. Erik kissed his mom goodbye. Auntie Sissy and Renee had both seen lights come around Erik when he was saying goodbye to his mom. Everyone thought that was crazy to hear and see. But sometimes you just need comfort in saying goodbye.

After the service, everyone went out to breakfast.

When we returned to Grandma's house, I heard Grandma say, "Carol", to herself, but I knew that she was just saying it for her own comfort. Auntie Sissy and Renee said that she was talking to Auntie Carol's ghost, and when Mom heard that she just thought it was stupid.

The next day, Mom and I drove home with Renee.

When returning, the pain I had been experiencing never stopped. It had gotten worse. I missed so much school just in the first few weeks.

On Friday, February 22nd, I had gotten up at 5 am to go to the hospital. Mom drove, of course. Billy was there when we got there. We went inside just to find that there wasn't enough room for me. The beds were all taken, so we were told to come back on Sunday. They would have room then.

Billy and I just played baseball for part of the day, and I relaxed as best I could for the rest of that day. I was in too much pain to do much of anything else.

Sunday finally came around, and I was going to have surgery. At 5 AM, Mom and I are out the door going to the hospital. There still wasn't enough room, so we're told to come back in the late afternoon. Mom had asked if I would be allowed to have anything to eat or drink beforehand.

The nurse said yes, so Mom, Billy and I went to Subway, and I had gotten a 6' sub sandwich and an iced tea. We were to wait around for a while longer, just hanging out in Santa Monica, and then we would go back to the hospital. They still didn't have a room or a bed for me, but they decided to put an IV in my hand. It hurt like hell, of course. I waited around for a little longer. The doctors came in a little before 12 AM. The doctors said that I was going to have to be awake for the surgery, but I wouldn't feel a thing. I was terrified enough as it was!

Mom and Billy had left the room. The doctors began shaving my head, and I was crying and screaming as loud as I could! This wasn't fair to me! I cried half way threw the operation, but I began not to care in the middle of it. I thought of different things, both to stay awake and to stay calm. I had opened my eyes twice to see that a thin blue sheet was over my head, I guess for the doctors to not make a mess with all the blood and other things they had. When the procedure was finally done, the doctors took off the blanket and I saw Mom come into the room at 12:30 AM. I fell asleep immediately after.

I woke up at 6 AM, a few hours later. Mom had made it back to the room, but my eyes were only half open. I fell asleep, again, after that. I woke up a little after 8 AM. I spent the entire day lying down in the hospital bed. I made it to the wheelchair toilet a few feet away, but that was it.

The doctor came after 5 PM. He said that everything looked fine and that I was okay to go home. The nurse came back to stitch me back up and to take the IV out of my hand. I cringed in fear, not knowing if either was going to hurt, again. I got dressed and rode down in a wheelchair to the parking lot. Billy drove Mom and me home.

When I got home, there was a letter for me to open. It was a "Get Well Soon" card from some of my classmates at school. I began to read it, and then the phone rang.

"Hello?" I asked, as I picked up the phone.

"Is Mary Beth there?" I heard someone say.

"This is she," I replied.

It was Jessica. She wanted to know if I got home okay and how I was feeling. I told her that I was fine. She wanted to know if I got the card, and I told her that I just opened it. I thanked her and said I would be returning to school soon enough.

I spent a week at home, not really doing anything. I got back to school that Friday. Everyone was really excited to see me. I took things easy going back. The headaches were still all there, as well as the body aches.

I continued through school non-the-less, as best I could. Jessica and I worked at the library so I could have silence as I worked on school assignments. We took big breaks, though. I spent nutrition time in the nurses office for 15-20 minutes until Jessica came back to get me. I would just lie down and try to relax in there. Things seemed to get worse, though, as much as I tried. I missed weeks of school.

I wasn't diagnosed until April, having Fibromyalgia. Mom said that her friend Peggy had it as well.

"Great," I thought out of sarcasm. "Maybe we should join a support group. We're two different people, and she didn't have to deal with this when she was a teenager!" I was very angry with everyone always saying that there were other people out there that had the same thing as I did. No one else had to live the life that I lived! I cried through agony and guilt. It was then that my writing took off.

My Brother Joe's art teacher, Dayo, died of melanoma in early 2002. I didn't know Dayo all that well, I only knew that he was a nice guy and that Joe really liked to have Dayo as an art teacher. Mom and Joe were invited to go to a memorial service at Joe's old school that was held for Dayo. A lot of the students that didn't have fathers to look up to, really considered Dayo a father figure for them.

I could only make it one day to school the first four few weeks of 2002. Then I increased it to two days, and then to three, and then four, and finally, by the end, I made it to five days a week. The principle and my Mom made a deal with me that I was going to graduate from the eighth grade, but it wasn't easy.

I started going back to the Northridge Hospital for water therapy. There were good days and then there were bad days.

I stayed at school until lunch every day for the remaining part of the eighth grade, and then Billy picked me up from school just as lunch started. We would go play baseball, or he would take me to my house where I would rest.

Graduation day was finally approaching, and the students were allowed to have a speaker for them. It was my birthday the day I graduated from eighth grade. I asked for my sister Tracey to speak for me, and she was happy to do so. Tom didn't come to my graduation which disappointed me, but I got over it.

My niece Sabrina was out for her summer break. She also came to my graduation.

My birthday was the same day. I opened one present beforehand. I asked if a tiny envelope was my graduation present and Mom said yes. So we were all ready to go. I thought that Tom would meet us there later that morning.

Diana didn't have enough credits on her report card to graduate with the rest of the class, but she did move on to high school.

Another girl, Sharr, had her sister as her speaker, and she was humiliated from her sister telling embarrassing stories of her. A few of the other students had teachers speak for them.

Maria's brother, Matias, spoke for her and he gave her a hug at the end.

Other students had friends and/or family members speak for them.

Pictures were taken after the graduation. Kelly, Essence and I stood together to have pictures taken.

I opened my graduation present after most of the class left. Mom had gotten tickets to see Pink in concert. Diana wanted to go, but Mom and I were the only two that were going.

When we were home, Sabrina wanted me to open all of my birthday gifts, which only a few were left. I had decided against it, because I had to have something to do later on.

I began taking private boxing lessons that August at The House of Champions. I trained with Everton Davis, and would occasionally see his good friend Peter Cunningham. I would see all the guys in there, but it wasn't intimidating at all to me. Everton would train me really hard just in conditioning, though.

The rest of the summer passed and I got used to waking up in pain and having it last all day. It was hard getting used to. No matter what, no one could get used to that pain! There were days that I had no pain and I treasured those.

Dalila was at her grandmother's in Palmdale most of the time. When she was around, we occasionally had the opportunity to hang out. She was over at my house one day and was flipping through my yearbook.

"He's cute," she said as she was pointing to a picture of Steve. I remember the days when I liked him. "Here, show him this picture," she said, pointing to another girl. Dalila was ugly, though. She just thought that he liked skinny girls, which he did. But Dalila wasn't that over weight. I never judged people by appearance, though.

I had an O.T. person start coming to the house. We worked on simple things, which I hated doing. I was like everyone else, but I felt like I was treated like an idiot.

I hated being compared to other people that had Fibromyalgia. Do they also have a brain injury? Do people treat them the same way as they treat me? Questions to answers no one said.

Chapter 9

A New Beginning

Ninth grade had started. I was excited to be a freshman. And then I learned other wise.

A student that I was friends with, Yoana, was best friends with Steve. I told her what was going on with my "friend" in the yearbook. I pointed to her and asked if she could ask Steve if he liked her. He pointed to another girl that he like.

Dalila would write letters to Steve and ask that I send it to him. Steve asked me who Danielle was, and I told him that she was my friend.

Jessica wasn't my aide anymore, and that really disappointed me, but I thought I would be set up with someone that was similar to Jessica. My new aide was going to be a friend of Vivian's; Suzy. I was very wrong in believing that it was going to be a good year. Suzy couldn't do anything right. She wouldn't write down the assignments for Mom to see and she wouldn't explain what was going on. She only last two weeks, thank God! Jessica even knew something was wrong, because I was almost in tears one morning in front of her! Suzy would say really rude things about Mom in front of me.

My next aide for the time being was Irene. Then I finally had someone smart enough like Jessica. I heard that there was a line of people that wanted to work with me.

My next aide, Amber, started off great! She and I had an awesome friendship too! She was friends with one of the janitors.

I had a new English teacher, Marcy, and I liked her class. It was an easy class. We read "Romeo and Juliet" in English and had different assignments. We watched both versions of the movie. Michael P. wanted me to rewind a scene of the movie, but I didn't. Michael P. was such a jerk to me in school. He was the Nancy-boy, though. He got straight A's, but would act so immature.

I had algebra with Brandon, again. It was hard, but I tried to keep a smile on my face. Brandon took things easy with me, so I kept up just fine.

I had this Asian lady, Benny, as my Biology teacher.

I hated Biology, because it was such a hard class. For a project that I was in, the class was dived into groups. I was told before our presentation that I would be asked a certain question, but instead Benny asked me another question that was much harder. Everyone always changed everything around on me. I got it wrong, of course, but after class she asked me another question that had to deal with one of the formulas we learned about. I got that right so she upped my grade.

Benny was out the first part of school because she was having a baby, so we had a substitute for half of the first semester in Biology.

Nan was again my teacher. She taught Life Skills to us that year. It was fun having Nan again. She and I shared a lot in common, as far as our health went. She also had fibromyalgia too. It was nice, because she didn't try to compare our different types of pain and she didn't say, "Hey we're the same! We should join a club together!" It felt that everyone else who seemed to have it would always try to get me on their side and say that I felt the same kind of pain as they were feeling.

My last class was a study hall class after lunch. Vivian was my teacher, but she taught English to four 6th graders, while I was just across the room doing my homework or school work.

The students were talking about the war in Iraq one day, and I happened to be listening to their conversation. They said something that I disagreed with and I jumped in and stated my opinion on the matter. They listened and then we debated a few things that day.

Kelly's old friend Trevor had come back to V.A.S. He left for middle school, but came back for high school. I didn't really like him at all at first, but I told myself that he was Kelly's friend so I should give him a chance.

I was feeling really horrible one Sunday morning. I had to do my homework, but I couldn't get out of bed because of the pain that I was in. I finally got up and got dressed. I was just going to stay in and do my homework anyways. I had to do Algebra, which I was already horrible at. I had completed a problem and I was really excited that I got the answer right, when the phone rang. I didn't want to get up, but I was closet to the phone, so I answered it.

"Hello?" I said, answering it.

"Hey," I heard Billy's voice respond. "Guess who I'm here with?" He was at the airport going to Georgia that day.

"Mandy Moore," I guessed.

"No," he replied.

"Ben Savage?" I asked again.

"No, it not Ben Savage," Billy said.

"Rider Strong," I asked.

"No," Billy said. "It's Nick Carter."

"Nick Carter?" I asked out of excitement and disbelief.

"Yeah, he's right here. Do you want to talk to him?"

"Yeah!" I said. "I want to talk to Nick Carter."

"How are you," Nick asked. I couldn't speak after that. All of my wildest dreams, and I couldn't say a word.

When we had said goodbye, Nick said, "Bye, babe," to me. Billy had gotten an autograph for me on a piece of paper from the airport that was later framed.

"I got to talk to Nick Carter!" I told Mom, who came to the table as I was on the phone. I was suddenly feeling 100% better. I had to go for a run to calm down a little. When I got back, I called Tracey and Kelly.

The next day, I went to school and found Essence. I told her what happened.

One day in English I asked the class if they would like to on a music video that I was recording. Everyone wanted to hear me sing, and when I refused, Kelly told me that some of the students were making fun of me. That was when I found out that Ricardo liked me.

One day, Carlos, this other boy in my grade and one of Ricardo's friends, told me that Ricardo liked me. I thought he was joking around, so I just said, "Yeah, sure" and ignored that. Ricardo started laughing and his cheeks were blushing a little, but I couldn't really be certain, so I dismissed the whole thing. I had nothing against Ricardo. He was nice to me, unlike some of the other boys in my grade; I just didn't really find him attractive. I was still friendly towards them. They were "the popular crowd", though, and I wasn't. I never fit into any one particular crowd in school, and I was fine with that.

Tom had left for Cal State Berkeley in January, 2003. My heart broke. I had never been that far away from Tom before. He was the only one in the family that I looked up to. Now he was gone. I pretended to be asleep on my side when he came in my room and placed his hand on my side while whispering in my ear, "See ya, kid." I cried all day that day, and it was hard because Billy and I were going to see a movie that day. I started crying in the car after the movie and Billy started asking me what was wrong. I wouldn't say. I told him to pull over; I needed time to cry, but he wouldn't. I had to promise that I wouldn't walk away, so he pulled over. I got mad after a little while and was going to just walk away, but Billy grabbed my hand and I cried some more. He began hitting himself, saying, "I'm hitting myself! I'm hitting myself!" Those statements made me feel bad. He was trying to make me feel bad when I already felt worse!

He brought me home. I cried the rest of the day, but knew that I had to apologize because he and to take me to school the next day because Mom was with Tom in Berkeley. I called and apologized and things were good between us again.

School happened on Monday and everything was fine again.

On January 17th, 2003, I woke to this horrible, nauseating feeling in the pit of my stomach. I couldn't believe that anything like this could happen. It was a week after Christmas Break, so we were back at school. But I didn't like the feeling that I had.

I had a crush on Trevor!

It sickened me. Kelly had asked me a few weeks before if I had a crush on anyone and at the time I hadn't. I was thinking to myself "NOT TREVOR! ANYONE BUT HIM!" I tried to convince myself that it was just a fluke. It wasn't really.

When that didn't work, I decided to tell Kelly. Surely she would see how insane this all was and she would talk me out of it.

It was in Life Skills, when the class didn't have anything to do, that I told Kelly.

"Kelly," I started out, as I approached her. "Do you still want to know who I have a crush on?'

"Yeah!" she said excitedly.

I leaned in and barely opened my mouth, as I whispered Trevor's name.

"What?" she asked.

I told her again.

Oh my God!" she said.

"I know!" I said, blushing and covering my head with me arms.

We laughed until the end of class, and then some. Trevor came up to us and asked what we were laughing about. Kelly just told him, "Nothing", while I just simply laughed. I hid it as long as I could and tried to avoid the whole thing.

At the end of January, Trevor and I were talking as I was leaving campus one day for lunch. He asked where I was going.

"Subway," I told him. "I'm in boxing, so it's the healthiest thing for me."

"Cool," Trevor replied. "I'm in Karate. The food there is expensive!"

"Yeah, but a veggie is only $1.99."

Trevor and I would talk by ourselves for a few weeks. We would just walk around campus, talking. It was nice to have someone to just hang out with.

Valentines Day came around. It was at the Valentine's Day dance that I was talking to Kelly about Trevor, again.

"I think I'm in love with him", I told her. She didn't say anything that day.

The weekend passed and Monday came around. I realized that I wasn't in love with Trevor, which was kind of a save for me. Kelly told me that Trevor had a girlfriend in middle school at Taft. I heard rumors that Trevor had asked Kelly out. I was crushed. I asked her about that, but it was hard asking. Kelly said that Trevor had mentioned something, but she just thought he was making a joke or something.

Kelly, Essence and I started going to the Renaissance Fairs from the 9th grade out. We would grade up in costumes. My mom took us, and we had a good time. I had my fortune told.

Kelly wore a green dress, Essence had to borrow something from me to wear, and I wore my handmaiden outfit that Mom made me for Halloween one year. I was Queen Amidala in her handmaiden outfit. I loved that outfit.

Later that semester of the ninth grade, Kelly came up to me and said that she was switching schools in for the 10th grade. She signed my yearbook 20 times that year!

I had asked Trevor if he wanted to come to a boxing match with me one day. I told him about my friend Jacob and how he did boxing.

First Trevor said that he would like to come with me, but one day when everyone was hanging out on the stairs at school, I had told him I would need his phone number in order to tell him where it was. He quickly changed his mind right then and there. I asked why, and he told me that he would get bored. I tried to convince him to still come, or at the very least to consider still coming, but he wouldn't. I was a little disappointed, but I still wanted to go and see Jacob for myself.

I had changed to training with Peter in 2003. Everton was fun, but he trained me too hard and we would only do conditioning. I would always miss the next day of school because I would be in too much pain to go anywhere. Peter and I would do the conditioning, but we also worked on sparring and shadow boxing. I would impress all the guys in the gym without trying.

In my fashion activity class at school, Malaika was my teacher and she had the 9th graders teach the 6th-8th graders how to do the fashion walking routine correctly. I was stock with a very difficult 6th grader, Mariah. She couldn't do a half turn correctly. I tried very hard to show her the correct way of doing a half turn while walking down "the runway" in class.

One day, when Mom came home from work, she just stated yelling at me for what seemed like no apparent reason. She finally said that Jeb had cancer, and that I didn't have it as bad as Jeb did. I was shocked and heartbroken! First, Jeb and I had been friends for a while. Jed couldn't be sick, but he was. Mom was yelling at me, but I didn't know why. It didn't take much to upset her anymore.

I just went to my room and cried on my pillow in both agony and rage for me, as well as sadness and fear for Jeb. He couldn't be sick. It wasn't supposed to happen to him!

Mom came and knocked on my door a while later, acting like nothing was wrong. She never apologized for yelling at me.

As time went by, I sent Jeb a lot of "Get Well Soon" cards.

By the end of May, I finally got over Trevor. I had the worst time when I liked him. I cried and screamed at myself over him. *This was the worst 5 months of my life,* I had said. *Thank God it's over!*

I had an eye appointment at UCLA. It was with a new doctor. He was going to examine my eyes, which I had no problem with, but then he said he had to put eye drops in my eyes so he could see things better. I refused, but had no chose in the matter. I cried and screamed. Mom and Billy were both there, and they didn't do a thing to stop it. When I had to wait for the doctor to examine my eyes, Mom, Billy, and I were in the waiting room. I was crying my heart out. It wasn't fair to me, and it certainly wouldn't be fair to anyone else in my shoes! Mom got mad at me for crying in front of so many other people. She grabbed my arm and pulled me outside of the waiting room. I cried in pain and frustration! When I finally went back into the doctor's office, he said that the only option would be to operate on my eyes, but that it was my decision. Mom let me make my own decision there. I was so angry that I could have my own decisions on *some* things, but on others.

I went to Valley College that summer to register for a broadcasting class that I was going to take on Tuesdays and Thursdays that fall. I was just given that, with no choice in the matter. Everyone thought that I would have a good time in whatever *they* wanted me to do. It disgusted me to no ends, but I wasn't sure who I was at the time, so I just let it happen.

In boxing, things got heated. I was doing fine with all the guys until this guy in his 30s gave me the creeps! Red was his name. He was friends with Peter, my coach, but I didn't like him! When I would train, he would always look at me in a very uncomfortable manner. It disgusted me! Red called me "beautiful" one day in July. Ignoring it, and him, I boxed with Peter.

I finally told Billy one day that I would never go back unless Red was gone, and I was going to keep my word. However, Billy spoke to Peter. I never saw Red again.

I hated how everyone would always say how I was doing. Was I not allowed to have a mind of my own? I was terrified to let out anger, sadness, hatred, love, or joy. I was ready to die to just be in peace, but it never found me.

Chapter 10

My First Love

Although I was convinced that I was in love with my best friend Jacob in elementary school or my Prince Charming Ben Savage, nothing ever defined love like this.

My sophomore year of high school had started and I was super excited to be going to Valley College! I was growing up, and trying to find out who I really was "in this mess called life."

Amber was going with me, so I wasn't concerned in anyway.

The first day there was exciting for me! My class didn't start until 11:20, so I had sometime to kill. Amber and I waited in the cafeteria. When we went to the building where my class was, butterflies were forming in my stomach!

I sat down at the first sear I could find. This guy with glasses and short blonde hair asked if he could sit down next to me. I told him that no one was sitting there, and that he could sit there if he so pleased. So he sat. Then he asked me what my major was. I turned to Amber, confused by his question, but I responded back to him that I didn't have a major. I didn't say why, though. He said that he would sit in the seat in front of him for whatever reason. Class hadn't started yet, so it was fine with me.

This older woman came and asked if she could sit next to me. I said it was fine. Then the teacher came and class had begun.

It was a fairly big class, but I had no anxiety about it.

The teacher said that our first assignment was to get to know the person who was sitting next to us. We were to write introduce them at the next class. So I turned to the woman sitting next to me. Her name was Olga. She was very nice. I asked about her and she asked about me.

"I'm 15," I told her.

"You're 15? That makes me feel old," Olga said.

We took our notes and then class was dismissed.

When Thursday came about, Olga said not to say her age and I had asked her not to do the same for me. She went first. The class all had there turns. I recognized a guy in there as a student that had gone to VAS before, Alex. Then this guy Jesse was in there as well. Jesse was in my computer class when I was in the 6th grade, so now he was a senior.

Amber and I had made friends with this one girl Crystal in the class. Crystal couldn't walk well at all, so she got by in her wheel chair. During the first few weeks, there was this one guy that Crystal was friends with. He was in the class also. Jordan, whom I had met the first day, was now my friend. The other guy Bill was just there.

It was still early September, I was talking in class one day to my friends, and then I hear my name.

"Mary Beth?", someone called.

I turned around to see that it was Bill who said my name.

"Yeah," I said as I turned.

Looking him in the eye, Bill asked, "Is your name Mary Beth?"

"Yeah," I said back.

"Oh," he replied with a grin on his face.

"Okay", I said to myself, and turned back to the conversation that I was in. As the weeks passed on, I would find myself falling in love, again.

Bill always sat behind me in class after the first day that he said my name. I was developing a crush on him, but it felt like something more, *way* too much more.

It was still late September when one day, I was going to go order my lunch in the cafeteria early. I went to order my sandwich, and was just going to pick out my water and then go pay for everything. I turned around and froze right where I was standing. Bill was there just sipping his coffee, but he looked so beautiful. Butterflies swarmed in my stomach! I couldn't move for what felt like forever! Then he saw me. His mouth spit back into his cup a little and then he waved at me. Not knowing what had come over me, I waved back, and found the strength in my legs to continue forward and get my coffee. I walked passed Bill to the refrigerated section to get my water, and then I went to pay for my things.

Bill was sitting behind me again in class that day.

I was seeing a psychologist and I told her what had happened. She asked if it were the first time I ever had butterflies, and I told that it was. I was crying when I told her, because I was so afraid and so nervous! The doctor had told me that it was because I was falling in love. My first love. It was very intense and very scary or me!

Bill and I became good friends after that. Every Tuesday and Thursday I would be so excited to be in class just to see Bill.

When we took notes one day, I was spelling out a word, and had completed spelling it onto my paper. All of a sudden, Bill's hand came up from behind me and took my paper. Amber had asked silently why he did that, and I shrugged my shoulders. Bill's hand came back, putting the paper back on my desk. I looked at it. There was an "es" added to the word. I turned back to Bill with a smug look on my face, and all I saw was a grin on his with his beautiful eyes looking back at me. Bill had said that he was a perfectionist. I despised perfection, because I was anything but perfect, but together Bill and I made sense to me.

The class was always divided into sections working on assignments. I was with so many different groups.

One day, the teacher called Bill and I into the same group, along with Jordan and another dude. We were to come up with a product to sell. Bill had asked me what I thought of it, and I told him that he could make fun of my last name for a while, if he wanted to, for the assignment.

After I had said Holliday to the guys, Bill had repeated my full name.

"Mary Beth Holliday", he said with his beautiful grin and starry eyes.

We had come up with our product, and were going to record the next class, but Bill wasn't there. My heart was crushed. I was too nervous and stuttering the whole time, so the assignment didn't go too well.

One Tuesday, I had turned around in my seat to ask Bill how his weekend was. He said he was busy with work, but that he had a good weekend. Then he asked me how mine was. I told him about my Friday and boxing and then I said that I went out with some friends on the weekend. I described to him how insane my training was.

I was going to miss a day of school one day due to a doctor's appointment. Amber told Gale, the teacher, but went to the class anyways on the day that I was out. From my understanding, the doctor had said that I was very sick. I was terrified!

On the following day in Broadcasting, I asked Bill how his weekend was. He told me that it was fine. He said that he missed me in class the Thursday before. I was MISSED! I told him that I had an appointment that day, but I didn't say what had happened. He told me that he was sure that everything was going to turn out fine.

Jordan and I were arguing over our weirdness one day. He said that he was the weirdest and that I was normal. I disagreed completely and had

said that I was the weirdest! Then I started naming off my weirdness! I told
Jordan that I was run over by a car when I was six, and I started spilling all
of my other health problems. He looked at me with unbelievable surprise
in his eyes. After class, Jordan and I were in the hall way, and he took my
hands, placing them in his and said that he hoped everything would be
okay with me.

Bill was sitting beside me in class one day, which was a weird turn
around for me, but it was still nice. He was talking about something. My
head was turned, but I looked back to see a flier that Bill had put in my
hands. It was to a comedy group that he was in. It was that Saturday. I
so wanted to go! I asked Mom and she said it would be okay, but then I
realized I wouldn't be alone. I was embarrassed to say the least, and I hid
it horribly. Sunday night came along, and I had done all my homework
that Saturday so I was done. I saw Bill through the window. I walked in,
hoping he wouldn't see me.

"Well, well, well. Look who we have here, "Bill said, while I was
looking at the ground. "Hi, Mary Beth."

"Hey," I said back, casually.

Mom introduced herself and shook hands with Bill. The beautiful grin
on his face was there of course. I went into the back and found a seat right
after Mom paid for the tickets. She joined me a moment later.

She came in and asked if she embarrassed me. I lied and said no.

The comedy was hilarious! I fell more and more in love with Bill!
When it was over, Mom and I were leaving. I saw Bill with that perfect
face looking at me when Mom and I were leaving.

"It was great meeting you," Bill told Mom, that beautiful grin on his
face.

Mom told me that she thought that Bill was very good looking.

The next Tuesday, I returned to Valley College to find Bill there. He
thanked me for coming. I told him that I was confused on one part, but
he said that it was all improvised, so I said nothing more.

I was jealous and heartbroken one day when Bill reached out his hand
and placed it on another girl's shoulder before class had begun. My heart
felt like it had fallen *hard* down on the floor, and then smashed into a
million pieces again. Bill sat behind me that day, non-the-less.

Bill would always talk about us being together in the end. I had hopes,
but maybe they were set too high.

Bill had winked at me one day in class. I was falling harder and harder
for him every second of every day.

Bill was talking about sex and how if you have sex with someone, it doesn't mean that you're in love. I disagreed with that completely!

Bill had said that he was taking journalism the next semester. Jordan always said that he should be a politician. Crystal had said she always wanted to do broadcasting ever since her days of high school.

I was fighting my own battle with myself. I wanted to become bulimic. The thought kept running threw my mind, "You're ugly. You're fat. Bill isn't going to be with you forever." But I ignored those voices that said I wasn't good enough. Bill and I are meant to be, I said over and over. I couldn't let the feeling that I had for him go away; I wouldn't. Bill said forever and forever was what is was going to be.

Our final project was a script we had gotten. There were two groups, and I was in the first act as the "Kid." Everyone laughed when I rehearsed for the role, but I only had 3 pages to read, and then it was someone else doing the character. Bill sat to my left that day. He laughed at my acting.

The second group went up after we did. I didn't have a part for that one. Bill was in it for both.

I think Bill changed his mind about us when he found out how old I really was. He thought I was 19, but I was only 15. I told him about my car accident, and then he called me a miracle. I made him shake my hand and promise that he wouldn't tell a soul about my car accident. When Billy came to get me for boxing that day, he asked if I was okay. I said I was fine. He asked why I was touching my face so much, and I said it was because Bill and I shook hands. He pretended to through up outside the car after that!

After that class had ended, I had emailed Bill, but he stopped emailing me after a while. I cried myself to sleep, always wanting Bill to come back to me. Love hurt more than I ever thought possible!

Billy had heard me singing along to a song in his car. I saw that he kept looking at me out of the corner of my eye. When it was over, he said that I had a lot of the singing notes right on that song. He asked if I wanted to take singing lessons, and I said "Sure." I smiled to myself the rest of the day. He found a singing teacher for me when he and I were driving down the street, and I started going every week.

Boxing was fine, until Peter wasn't there one day. I trained with Bernie instead that day. I sprained my right wrist, so I was out the rest of the week. The next Wednesday, I told Bernie what had happened and he said to train without the wraps on my hands. I out found that it was a worse idea to do that. I had sprained my left wrist and had to go to the doctors that weekend to get it checked out. The doctor told me that I couldn't go back to boxing for 4-6 weeks. I wound up staying out for 8 weeks.

In spring of that year, I was back at Valley College taking an art class that I had not signed up for. Everyone else thought I would love it, but I didn't. The only reason I liked that class was because there was a new guy that I liked in that class, Francisco. He was a really good artist. Irene's oldest daughter was in that class. She asked me how I like it on the third day. I told her that it was hard.

I dropped out before it could affect my grade.

Malaika was my English teacher. One day in class, I felt a hard punch in my stomach. The only other student that was anywhere near me was Steve. Immediately, I thought that Steve had punched me. I didn't say anything until I got home. I cried to Mom about it, and she and I went to Terry's office the next day to talk. Afterwards, Mom had asked if I wanted to stay at school or go home. I said that I wanted to go home, and then I said I was sorry about it. Mom got really pissed off at me, and said, "You can't always run away from your fears!" and then she stomped off. I was outraged! What the Hell did she know about fears? I said, "Fine. I'll stay," and I walked away from her, back onto the campus. I didn't go to English that day, and Steve kept his distance from me for the rest of the year.

John's history class was fine. John didn't really do anything with the students, but we were given assignments. The kid, Brandon, was my partner for an art project. He couldn't draw, but I really wanted to. First he did his mock drawings of two things in history. I copied a picture so well from a book that a classmate, Krystal, said it was better than what she could do. I looked up to see her smiling at me.

In math, I was placed in a geometry class. I was the only student in that class for two weeks. My teacher, Janet, did not know anything about geometry. She taught me very little those first two weeks. Then she said that three other students were going to be coming to the class and we would "have more fun", as she put it. My classmates were students that I knew from my grade and one higher than me. Joanna and I were friends for a while and Clay and I were sort of friends also. Dan had a crush on me for a little while when I was in the 6th grade. He had a girlfriend and I never had any interest in him. Joanna and I were competing in geometry, but neither one of us was the greatest.

In April, 2004, my mom's oldest son had moved in with his son. I do not have it in me anymore to call either one of them family. It began as Hell with them and never got any better. Mom's son had left his wife, because she was cheating on him, and his son didn't like his mother anymore either.

I had a lot to deal with that semester. My brother Mike was a Marine and was going to be shipped over seas to Iraq. There was a going way party for him at home that May.

Mom, Joe, Susannah, and I rode with Mike to the train station and there were photos taken of us. Mike gave everyone a hug goodbye. I was choking up, but wouldn't allow myself to cry. Mike hugged me goodbye, and then whispered in my ear, "Take care of yourself." I had to stop myself from crying, even though there were tears in my eyes.

Amber knew that Mike had gone to Iraq. The next day, Monday, I returned to school. Geometry was my first class. Amber walked in and just said hi to me. I started crying right then and there. She knew what had happened, so she didn't question anything.

Amber's brother had told her that he was planning on joining the army, so she and I were in the same situation. We both missed our brothers.

I had a seizure in English class one day. I was feeling very unusual that day after 2nd period. I tried very hard to ignore the feeling all day. My last class was English, and I was sitting at my desk, when suddenly everything went blank. All I saw was fuzz, and I couldn't hear anything or say anything. I was in silence for what felt like forever. When I came out it, Malaika was asking me very silently for something, so I turned around to get whatever it was out of my backpack. The rest of the day passed and I was silent until I got home. I immediately called Mom and told her what had happened. For a while, she did believe me, but after a while, she began to question it and would have her doubts that I was saying the truth on what had happened to me. I was outraged that she didn't believe me and I hated it.

I became good friends with a boy in my study hall class. Matt and I were the only students in that small room, along with my aide, Amber. When Matt and I didn't have any work to do, we would talk about music, marital arts and boxing, or motorcycles. I would share my lyrics with him and he would share his with me.

Every day I would always think of Bill. And I would always miss him, but throughout time, I began to except that he wasn't coming back. The crying at night subsided after some time.

The last few weeks of school were very intense, and not just because of finals.

Mom and I went up to Nevada to see my grandmother. It was an eight hour drive, which I liked the best. My aunt had been up there, but she had gotten very angry at my grandmother and left the week before Mom and I came. I had a three day weekend, so Mom and I were planning for three days. Three days turned into two weeks.

We had gotten there at 4pm, and had only been there for less than one hour. I was in the guest bedroom, writing in my diary, when I heard Mom and Grandma in the living room. Something was wrong. I went out immediately to find that Grandma had a headache, but grandma had never had headaches before in her life time. Mom was very worried, so she called the paramedics. I was frozen on the chair in the living room, staring at Grandma. Mom was crying on the phone, explaining what was happening to the paramedics on the other line.

We were only there for a short while in silence and then the paramedics had made it over.

"Vita, do you know your name?" a paramedic asked her. My grandmother didn't answer.

I was trembling, sitting there in the armchair, seeing what was going on. Mom had called my uncle and had told him what had happened, and then she called Auntie Sissy and told her.

After the paramedics had taken Grandma away, I just hugged Mom, crying. We made it the hospital in Carson City that evening. Uncle Ronny was there.

Grandma was transferred to another hospital in Reno later that night.

Auntie Sissy had made it out the next day. Mom and I were already at the hospital.

We spent the day at the hospital and then went back to Grandma's house for the night.

I spent my time in the waiting room, while Mom and Auntie Sissy were in the hospital room with Grandma. Mom and I would take breaks by taking short walks. I began to take my wallet so I could go get lunch downstairs.

After a few days that first week in Nevada, Mom said she was going to send me home on a plane so I could get back to school. I begged her not to do that. She didn't want me to miss anymore school, but I needed to be there with her instead. Mom had the school send my work over so I wouldn't fall behind. I did my work at the hospital, and spent time in Grandma's hospital room as well.

A week had gone by. Grandma was doing tests one day. When she had got back to her room, she told Mom that she saw her father. When Mom and I left that day, she cried to me. Grandma hadn't gotten on well at all with her father, so naturally my mom was very concerned.

One Tuesday, June 8th, I had this strange feeling that Grandma wasn't going to make it through the next day. I stayed in the hospital room for Mom's sake. When the day was over, I said a silent goodbye to my grandmother as Mom and I were leaving. That night, the hospital had called and said that Grandma had gotten worse.

Mom and I returned the next day. I decided to wait out in the waiting room that day. I didn't want to deal with a dead body. I wouldn't know how to handle that. Mom said that was fine for me to wait there. I was sitting there for a while, jut reading, and then a girl was there with her family. She and I began talking and then we introduced ourselves. Her name was Danielle.

When the evening was approaching, I was turned a certain position, when I felt that someone had entered the room. I turned back to see Mom. I saw the torture on her face. Grandma was gone. I quickly got up and gave her a hug. We made it out to where the elevators were. I sat in silence for a while as Mom went back and forth to the room that still had Grandma's body in it, and where Auntie Sissy still was. Auntie Sissy made the comment that Grandma was still holding her hand. That was where I saw the guilt in my aunt.

When Mom made it out to the elevators where I was, I placed my head in her shoulder blade and started crying. I told myself that I had to be strong for Mom, but it was hard enough being strong fro myself.

Later that evening, when the sun was still out, we had made it back to Grandma's house. We had eaten dinner, so I thought I would just go out to the front of the house for a while. Mom and Auntie Sissy were doing the dishes in the house, but then I heard yelling. I immediately went back inside to see that Auntie Sissy was yelling at Mom. I was very upset and started saying, "Stop yelling at my mother." Auntie Sissy tried to hug me while I started crying, but I shoved her away. Then Mom and I began to pack our things very fast. When Auntie Sissy was yelling at Mom from the kitchen, I started yelling back at her. She called me a child and said that I couldn't possibly know anything. I exploded through rage and sadness.

"I was run over by a car when I was six; I've had seven surgeries; so I think I know a lot more!"

Auntie Sissy couldn't say anything more to compare in that manner. Mom and I left, and had made it to a shopping center before she called Uncle Ronny and cried to him over the phone. We went over there a while later.

We were in Reno at Uncle Ronny's for an hour, when the phone rang, and it was Auntie Sissy asking what went wrong. She couldn't remember the terror she caused, and she blamed us.

Mom and I spent the next two days in a motel close by. I trembled, thinking that we would be found by Auntie Sissy, and I didn't know what she would do to us when she found us.

We made it back home to California on Saturday.

I returned to school that Monday with my school work that I had completed while I was gone. I passed that grade.

My 16th birthday was a complete mess. Conan had the first slice of *my* birthday cake. I had gotten an acoustic guitar from Billy.

That summer I was going to go back to boxing, but there were things that got in the way of that.

Billy and I went to go golfing. I drove the golf cart, which was the only reason I went. We were at the last whole of the nine that he played, and I was driving the golf cart the way I did. He started yelling at me, saying I wasn't driving correctly. I stopped the cart and told him he could drive, and that I was going to walk back. I ended up getting back in the cart. When we had made it back to the country club, he said "That was fun."

I added, "Yeah, it was," and then added very casually, "Until you started yelling at me."

Billy just went, "Well..." He brought me home.

Mom and I were going back to Nevada in July to pack things up. When we got to Grandma's house, it was already empty. It was like a ghost house. We had certain things to do out there, so I helped as much as I could. We were gone maybe a week.

When we returned, I called Billy, but he didn't pick up so I left a message. Mom came to my room and asked me if I wanted to take a walk. I thought that was fine.

"Well," she started saying. "I lost my only friend."

"Billy?" I asked with concern in my voice.

"Someone like that", she said.

"Is that the person?" I asked, again.

"Yes," she finally said. I was confused, hurt, and resentful towards Billy. I thought they would be friends for a long time, but there were signs that pointed otherwise.

Mom had asked me not to hang out with him anymore, and I had no objections to that. He and I fought a lot lately. He tried to control my life, and even my own thoughts and opinions. That wasn't friendship to me.

Everyday, it seemed like, for a few weeks, Billy always called the house asking for me. I spoke to him, but I wouldn't tell him much. He always asked if I wanted to hang out with him, but I always said I was busy. Mom didn't want me to hang out with him anymore, and frankly neither did I. I finally told him that we shouldn't be friends anymore. There were tears in my eyes as I fought them back when I was saying goodbye. He asked if it was someone else that wanted this, but it was my decision. He asked if he could call three days later and I said that would be fine. Friday came, and he called. I had spent only one full day without his annoying phone calls. When I told Mom what had happened and how uncomfortable it made me, she called him and said to never call me again.

Billy sent my baseball bat that he still had to me along with my money I had earned so many years ago from therapy and I newspaper clipping. It was over.

Mom had thought that I had begun to get depressed after Billy was out of our lives, but I was just getting used to doing my own thing. She asked if I wanted to still be friends with him, but I assured her that I did not want anything to do with him.

I had enough of the fights and being bossed around. I was done with him. Part of me thought that she missed him, but I guess I'll never know.

Chapter 11

New Story to Write

Junior year at last!

Excitement filled the air, but I came crashing down, again.

Amber was around…but she was always late to my 2nd period, Chemistry class, for the first few weeks.

First period was keyboarding, a piano class with Mike. It was a mixture of high school students in there. I had my friend Shayna as my partner at the piano. She would sometimes have an attitude on certain days, but we became closer friends as the year went by. Mike would test us on certain songs that we practiced in class. He would give us retries over and over again when we were tested at the big piano. We learned the basics and how to read and write piano notes and were tested on what we knew.

For the first few weeks, I didn't think too much of Amber being absent for 1st period. After the first fourth weeks, Irene was there with Amber one day, and I had no idea what was going on. After all, no one told me anything about *my* life. Like what to expect when there was a big change. I found out later that morning that Irene was learning what it took to be my aide. I was furious that no one told me what was going on! Amber was going to law school, and that was why she was always late. I already had too much to deal with. Why didn't anyone tell me at the being of the year? Did they think it wouldn't affect me? Amber and I had become friends, or so I thought, and now she was leaving?

I had a new teacher for English and History to deal with also. Carmen had started working tat VAS the year before, and yet she didn't have a clue what to do with students that had special needs. Special Ed. just wasn't what she was taught, and she didn't think that anyone should be treated different. And yet, I was treated like crap from her! She was the hardest on me! I hated her classes! When there was an assignment from her, instead

65

of Irene doing her job and getting the information for me, I had to do everything! It didn't bother me that much at first, though.

When I switched my Chemistry class to another class at second period, I was put in Mike's Music History class. There were seven 12th graders, one sophomore, and then there was me. Travis, a senior, was flirting with me the first few weeks of class. He was a jerk to me some of the time.

I would be so upset with Travis in my head that lyrics would just poor out about him. He was so annoying.

Mike only had one text book on Music History, so the class copied everything down from the board. The class could use their notes for the tests. We were to write practice tests and turn them in every few weeks after finishing each chapter.

I went into another room with Irene and did my tests in silence. It was always really embarrassing to me to be taken out and then come back in when the class had moved on to do something else.

After the first few months of Music History, I had asked Travis about helping me with a song that I wrote. Travis was a drummer, so I thought he would be nice enough to help me, but I was never wrong. First Travis said he would help me out. He said he would talk to the other guys in his band. He said he would tell me what happened. I don't know what hurt me more: the fact that he lied or that I still believed that he was a good guy. I always admired Travis playing the drums, but I simply wasn't worth anything to him.

"It's a once and a lifetime opportunity, Travis," Irene told him. But he wasn't going for it.

Irene had asked Dante, another boy in my class, if he wanted to help me. She asked if Travis had said anything, but he didn't. What a surprise. So Dante and I talked a little at first. I was very excited.

When the second semester had come, Music History had turned into Band. I was the only girl with Dante, Travis, and Adam, the sophomore. I was the singer, Adam did guitar, Travis was the drummer, and Dante did the bass.

I was still waiting on what Travis had said to Felipe or Dante. I don't know what hurt me more: the fact that he lied or that I still believed that he was a good guy. I always admired Travis playing the drums, but I simply wasn't worth anything to him.

I found out that Felipe, the lead singer and guitarist, didn't want to help me. Dante still did. When Dante got a copy of the song "My Story" that I wrote in November 2004, Dante seemed excited to help. One day in class, he pulled me over to work out the chords he had come up with. I wasn't feeling it, though.

My last attempt for help was asking Adam. I admired Adam's guitar playing very much. I asked him one day after class had ended. He said he would, so I gave him my phone number. I had begun to develop a crush on Adam. The only reason that happened was because I liked his blue eyes and I thought he was a nice guy, as well as a really good guitarist.

Adam said he would talk to his dad and see of he would allow him to help me. I waited patiently, while at the same time impatiently.

We worked on songs from the 50s and then one form the 60s in Mike's class. During the first few weeks, I was very nervous, because it was just me and the guys, so naturally I did not sing well. On a Monday, Essence had come to that class and was singing with me as the band did its thing. Essence said she was going to switch into Music History/Band class, and sure enough she did.

I was happy there in that Band class. I was more confident with myself now that Essence had joined, and the band had moved onto other songs too. We worked on Elvis Presley, Ray Charles, and a few other songs from the 50s time era.

English was a different matter. Since Irene didn't know how to be my assistant, I was in tears every day afterwards. Carmen had given an assignment to write a fictional story. I chose "The Notebook", but I changed it around. I had asked Irene if it would be okay to write a story like that, and she said yes. When I got my paper back, Carmen wrote that it sounded like plagiarism. I cried hard from anger and frustration. I had worked really hard, but had been given no instruction on how to write it.

An Armenian boy in my class, Moses, completely plagiarized his paper, not even writing a sentence of his own. He never got in trouble for it either. He was just to redo it. It made me so angry that Irene couldn't do her job correctly, or at all. I did another story, concentrating the heartbreak that I was going through at the time.

For that story, I wanted the female character to have some illness, but I didn't want it to be like "A Walk to Remember", where the character had Leukemia. Mom said something about Joe's art teacher Dayo having melanoma, but I wanted to do something original. However, I was stuck with that anyway. In a lot of ways, the story was similar, but it still showed I made sure to add different things to not make it sound the same.

I cried all the time over the classes that I had with Carmen as my teacher.

In History, I had a lot of trouble with Carmen and Irene. Carmen had asked if the brain injury caused some of my mistakes, but never did a thing to ease the tension that she caused.

Mike's band class was getting ready for Jump for Heart and Peace Day.

I was getting ready for my brother Mike to come home from Iraq. I had cried \ myself to sleep every night that he was away. Sometimes the tears were from him being gone, sometimes from the agony of living with Joe, Susannah, Ben, and Conan.

"That's enough," Mom said.

What do you mean, 'that's enough?' I thought. If it were anyone else, you would defend them. You can't even pretend that you're defending me?

Conan ended up getting McDonald's that day and he was congratulated on hitting me by his father.

On a Saturday morning, Mom and I had got up really early and headed down to Camp Penalton to see the marines come back. We were the first family there at 7:30 AM, but we had gotten lost. After finding the place, we helped out another family, tying balloons and string onto chairs.

The marines came out and did their little saluting thing. Then they were dismissed to see their family and friends. Mom went rushing in the crowd to see Mike first. I was standing back, just waiting for her and Mike. He was her son. She should have the first hug from him.

A moment later, I felt a tapping on my shoulder. I turned around to see Mike grinning at me.

"MIKE!" I said, very excited, and then I gave him a big hug.

I turned around to see that Mom was coming towards us. She later told me that I was very loud. She gave him a hug as well.

Mike had to go take a shower, because he hadn't showered in months.

We waited and found everyone else. After Mike was ready to go, we went out to lunch, and then we brought Mike back home. He was off duty for a few weeks.

In school, Jump for Heart was a surprise to both Essence and me one day. We performed outside in the P.E. field. Carmen's 2nd period English class had heard it and came out to see us perform.

After the performance, Stephanie, the P.E. teacher, had come up to me and said what a great job I did. I was flattered and very proud of myself.

I was so heartbroken over life that I would pray at night to not wake up the next morning, only to be disappointed. I still prayed for a better tomorrow. Something had to come for me. There has to be a light on somewhere in life.

Peace Day was the big assignment in Band class. That was what I was really practicing for. It was the day before Spring Break. I went to my first period class. Mike's class was to warm up and rehearse. Mike had other students in there that were doing other projects while we rehearsed. This younger boy, Felipe, was in there. First he was making fun of me, but after I started singing, I noticed that there was this gaze on his face that I don't think anyone could ignore.

The hour had come at last and the class was going to perform. Essence and I did our vocal warm ups. The guys tuned their guitars. Everyone was ready. My name was going to be called first.

Mom had taken off of work for the rest of the day to hear me and Dr. Gale was there as well. We did "Jail House Rock" first. After I was done with the first half verse, it was Essence who sang the second. We traded verses for most of the songs. However, when I was finished with the first verse of "Jail House Rock", I turned to Essence to see her staring at me in amazement.

We completed everything, and the whole school really liked us.

I was congratulated on what a great job I did by everyone, it seemed like. All of the teachers said, "Good job, Mary Beth," with Essence standing right next to me.

An eighth grader asked for my autograph one day. Essence was right there.

"You're that lady who sang at Peace Day?" the kid asked.

"Yeah," I said, a little insulted that he thought I was so old, but I let it go.

"Can I have your autograph?" he asked.

I didn't know if it was a joke or not, so I blew him off by saying, "Whatever."

"Fine, I'll go ask Marcy for hers," he said. Essence was standing right next to me, and the kid said nothing to her, so that was why I thought it was a big joke to him. No one was ever very nice to me at that school anyway. After the kid said that, I felt a little bad.

During my spring break that year, I was only standing in the living room minding my own business. Mom, Joe, and Mom's oldest son Ben were all there. I suddenly felt something hit me hard on my back. It was Conan, my then nephew. I turned around with tears in my eyes, screaming! "OW!"

"I didn't hit you that hard," Conan said with a big smile on his face. Ben then told him that he wasn't going to take him to McDonalds. That was not a punishment to me. I started smacking Conan with my hands, see how he liked it. He had a blank expression on his face.

"That's enough," Mom said.

What do you mean, 'that's enough?' I thought. If it were anyone else, you would defend them. You can't even pretend that you're defending me?

Mom and I went somewhere, but when we got back, Ben and Conan had come back with McDonalds in their hands. *Ben congratulated him and told Conan he did a good job, punching me in the back*, I thought.

I told Mom, and asked her why she didn't punish Conan. *She would punish him if he hit anyone else*, I thought.

I had a doctor's appointment in May that was going to be of 20 eye doctors in one room at the same time over at UCLA. Mom and I joked that I was going to confuse all of them in less than 10 minutes.

The day of the appointment came and I was nervous. After the appointment, Mom had said I confused them all in less than 10 minutes. I was very proud of myself after that. My eye doctor was now at UCLA, and surgery was going to take place soon enough.

I was still waiting for Adam. Mom knew that I liked him. I called him one night when I k new he was grounded that weekend. Irene said that I should call and ask again, so I did. I told Adam that Essence had a crush on him, but he said he didn't care.

I told Mom at the dinner table, and she slammed her hands on the table.

"Are you disappointed in me?" I asked with a chipper tone in my voice.

"Yes," she said in disgust. Part of me was happy with that, but I sat there in silence as I let it sink in me for a long moment. I then got upset and left the room. I went to my room to cry on my bed.

Mom came in and said a bunch of bull shit to me. I screamed that I wanted to be left alone. She left at last.

She knocked on my door once more.

"Leave me alone!" I shouted. I heard Conan ask Mom if she was okay.

"Mary Beth just wants to be left alone," she said. I could hear the torture in her voice as she said those words. I was left alone to cry, which was a rare occurrence for me to have.

Not much later, Mom came back and knocked on my door, asking if she could come in.

'Go away," I said. Then I heard a loud crash outside my door. I thought Mom got mad and threw something.

Mom heard it to and she thought it was me.

"That's it," she said through anger. "I'm coming in."

I was lying on my bed looking at her, looking back at me.

"What?" I asked through a tortured voice.

"It was the ghost," Mom said after realizing that I hadn't moved. She came in and sat on my bed. We talked about what was bothering me. I told her what had happened. That was a mistake, I later realized.

Mom had told the principle Terry and Terry had told Irene not to talk to me about that stuff anymore. Irene was instructed to just stay out of it. Neither one of us thought that was fair, so we ignored it, and I simply didn't tell Mom about what Irene and I talked about. I never wanted advice about love from Mom, because she didn't now what love really was anyway, in my opinion.

I had only liked Adam for six weeks, until I found out that he was really just another jerk that broke my heart. I had told myself to get over Adam. That he wasn't worth getting more hurt over. It took me two weeks to fully and completely be over Adam.

On Wednesday, May 18, at exactly 10:45 AM, I was officially over Adam. I wrote him a letter that I gave to Essence to give to him. He was to read it. Essence said she was going to just give it to him at nutrition, but I told her to give it to him in the class that they shared during 4th period to make sure that he actually read it she agreed.

The next day, Mom, Tom's friend Tom, and I were going to go to Berkeley for Tom's graduation. It was an eight hour drive, and we were leaving at 8:30 AM.

Tom's friend Tom was short and Asian, so he was just known as little Tom to me.

I was pretty much ready. Mom and little Tom were going to get the rental car and then Tom was coming back. I was passing the hallway when I saw the back of little Tom's head. He wore a plain white shirt. He was just sitting on the porch. I would have let him in, but he didn't knock, so I figured I didn't have to. I was still getting ready when Mom came home.

She introduced Tom to me, but I didn't look at him right away.

Mom was still getting ready, so I took my things out to the car and froze when I saw how beautiful Tom was. I saw him stating back at me in that lovey-dovey way. I turned around immediately. *This isn't fair*, I thought. *It hasn't even been a full 24 hours since I got over Adam, and now I meet Tom?* It wasn't fair!

The car ride up there was unique. I didn't look at Tom the entire time, but his face was glued in my head.

We got up to the bay area and we were at Tom and Susannah's place. Tom was graduating on Saturday. Mom and I were staying at Susannah and Tom's place on Thursday night. Little Tom was going to be staying at his other friend's place.

We hung out with the two Tom's and Susannah on Friday. Susannah made fun of me in front of Tom Friday night. Tom just laughed and smiled at me.

Mom and I went to our motel and slept on Friday night. We got up to head back to Tom's place the next day.

Most of Tom's friends were at the apartment and then at Berkeley.

Tom's party was the loudest at the graduation.

I didn't recognize Jesse at first. It had been such a long time since I saw him. His hair was brown instead of being bleached.

After the graduation, everyone was outside waiting for Tom. Of course Mom had to say something to embarrass me about my fear of heights.

I saw Tom after the graduates all came out. I ran up to him and was the first to give him a hug. Then everyone went out to lunch.

There was a bubbly drink that Mom thought was alcohol, and I wasn't old enough for that yet. I made a joke that I was going to talk about my "friend Fred" on the way home. After I was done with the joke, little Tom's face was four inches away from mine. It was only joking, though. Apparently, little Tom thought I was serious and a look of torture was on his face.

After the lunch, Mom and I left. We were driving home and I kept asking about little Tom. Mom came to the conclusion that I liked him and asked me if that was true. I said yes.

When I got back to school, I had told Irene what had happened and who I met. She said that little Tom was in love with me.

I brought photos of my brother's graduation and showed Irene the picture of little Tom. She could see in her mind that Tom and I would have a child and what the little girl would look like. I was so in love with Tom! She had her daughter make three photos of a picture of little Tom. I kept two in my wallet and one in my diary over time.

I was looking in Mom's phone book one day, a few weeks after Tom's graduation, when I came across "Tom (little)" in her book. I asked who that was.

"That's Tom's friend Tom," she said. I made a stupid joke, while trying to not be obvious that I was going to write down his name and number.

I told Irene. Essence and I had a bet that she would pay me a dollar if I called Tom and told him that I liked him.

When Tom went up to Big Bear after his graduation, all his friends were at little Tom's parents place. They were all playing Chinese checkers one night. Jesse made a move that isn't aloud in Chinese checkers. Little Tom pointed it out.

"Dude, you're not aloud to make that move," little Tom said.

Jesse just looked at him in disgust!

"WHAT DO YOU MEAN "DUDE"?" Jesse asked.

When Tom got back from that trip, he told everyone that and I only laughed, falling in love with Jesse all over again.

I called little Tom a lot over the first few weeks of discovering his number, just to hang up after hearing his voice.

I told myself that on July 1st, I was going to tell him I liked him.

"Hello?" Tom asked after answering his phone.

"May I speak to Tom?" I said.

"This is he," Tom replied.

"Tom, this is Mary Beth, Tom Holliday's sister."

"Hey," he said. I could hear a smile in his voice.

"Don't tell Tom I called," I said rather quickly.

"Okay," he replied.

I waited a few seconds, not knowing if I should say the speech that Irene and I had written. I had the words in front of me, but silence was on the other line as I wondered what to do next.

"Tom, I've liked you for the past six weeks," I finally said, at a fast pace.

"Okay," he said. And I hung up.

I was so excited that I had told Tom that, but also really embarrassed. My troubles were anything but over from there.

Little Tom called my house that afternoon.

"Hello," I answered. No one said anything.

"Hello," I asked again.

"Is Tom there?" I heard little Tom say.

"Yeah," I said. "Tom, it's for you." Tom was just at the computer a few feet away.

On Monday, July 11th, 2005, I had to get up at dawn to go to the hospital for surgery. That was why I chose the 1st to tell Tom that I liked him. I waited around until 10:00 for the doctors to come into the room. Mom was there, of course. The doctors drugged me, so I was blacked out until I was on the operating table. This woman doctor told me to breathe in. I had the oxygen mask on my head that I remember hating from the first two surgeries when I was seven.

I woke up two hours later with both of my eyes closed. They hurt, and it felt like both of my eyes had been beaten to death. I lied there in pain for the rest of the day, what felt like a life time, but was only five hours.

I was very much crushed when Tom wasn't there at the hospital. Part of me expected that he'd come to the hospital to make sure I was okay, but part of me wasn't surprised that he wasn't there. It still hurt, non-the –less.

The nurse came and I had to get dressed with both of my eyes closed. I was then wheeled down to the bottom floor and wheeled into the Doctors office. The elevator ride down was the best part of the day.

When I got to my doctors office, both Mom and the doctor helped me to the examining seat.

"Open your eyes, Mary Beth", the doctor said after removing the bandages from my eyes.

"I can't," I told him.

"Come on, Mary Beth," he said again

I finally did.

"Can you see?" he asked.

"Wow! Yeah I can!" I said. It was the best I had ever seen. He adjusted the strings and cut them. It was hard keeping my eyes open when he did that.

Mom drove home with me in the back seat. The ride home was hell. All the turns really made me nauseous, and I did ask her to slow down, but she wouldn't. I ended up throwing up in a big bowl in the back seat. Mom pulled over after that.

Finally, after making it home, Mom had to help me walk in the house. I was crying out in pain as I saw Conan just sitting on the ground staring up at me. I slept for a good two hours, but woke up and wanted dinner at 8 pm.

The next few days were miserable. I was in a lot of pain and had decided to call Tom and apologize. I had a whole speech ready and everything. I had decided on the 20th to call him. Mom was back at work, so I decided to walk up to Subway. On the way up there, I stopped to make the call to Tom from a payphone.

The phone rang once.

"Hello?" Tom asked as he picked up the phone.

"May I speak to Tom?" I asked, not knowing what to say.\

"Hello?" he asked again, not hearing me the first time.

"Tom, this is Mary Beth," I said and there was a pause.

"Hi," he said, sounding mystified.

"I wanted to apologize…"He caught me off.

"You don't have to apologize," he said.

"I wanted to apologize…" I tried to say again.

"You don't have to apologize," he said again. "I thought it was kind of funny."

"I wanted to apologize," I said, again, knowing I only had three minutes to get this out.

"It's quite alight," Tom said for the third time.

"Alright," I said, tears springing up. "Bye."

I hung up. Why couldn't Tom just be a cruel bastard like everyone else in my life? Why did he have to be so nice? I stood there frozen, feeling as though I was going to die, because my feet were frozen as I cried out in sadness. The minutes seemed like hours as I stood there.

I finally found my legs and was able to go on walking, all the time crying. I made it to McDonald's and got napkins to wipe the tears from my eyes. I made it to Subway and got my sub. I headed home after that.

Not being at home for long, the phone rang and I answered it.

"Hello?" I asked. No one said anything.

"Hello?" I said again.

"May I speak to Tom?" I heard little Tom say. I didn't know where Tom was so I called out to know if anyone knew where he was. He was out back. The cordless phone was in Joe's room. His door was open and he was in there with his girlfriend Shauna. I walked in without announcing it. I found that Joe was sitting looking at Shauna whose shirt was undone. I quickly got the phone and went out to give it to Tom in the backyard.

"Ew, Ew, Ew!" I told myself over and over.

I gave Tom the phone.

"This is my house phone," Tom said over the phone. I figured little Tom thought I was stalking him or something after hearing that, which I was definitely not!

Tom came back in saying that little Tom invited him to go camping, but Tom said he had other things to do.

All summer I was so conflicted. It hurt to get through a day and not call little Tom's cell. I was at the weakest point in my life. *Do I love him? Do I hate him?* A million questions filled my head over Tom at a million miles a minute!

I was finally able to record a demo of a song I had written. My singing had started sounding better than before, but there still wasn't hop to be the next big thing in music.

I waited for school to start, and I waited to finally be over little Tom.

Chapter 12

Senior Year

It was senior year, at last! I was waiting for this experience for many, many years. But I very was wrong, once again.

I had Steve as my government teacher. I really liked having Steve as my teacher. Our assignments were power points that we showed on the projector. I hated that part, because I had to use the laptop from school that everyone wanted me to use in the first place. However, I got it all done. Steve liked order with that. As long as you didn't repeat the same thing that was on the board, word for word when addressing what the assignment was, you were good. Essence and I had that class together.

English the first semester was with Marcy. I liked that class, but Marcy was hardly ever there.

I heard that Irene was going to another job. She was training to work at a restaurant with her brother. It didn't bother me at first during the first two months, until Irene was never there at all. I could deal with the first hour and a half alone for a few weeks, but then Irene got sick. I told her something would happen and that she should just concentrate on one thing at a time, but no one listened to me anyways.

I handled everything with grace at first. When I was told that Irene wouldn't be there to help me, I worked alone. I did all my assignments and would get help from the teachers when I had a problem. But after four weeks of that, I began to get very sick. Everyday when Irene was gone I'd always ask, "Is she coming back? When is she coming back?" I would get the same answer all the time, "Irene will be back soon, Mary Beth." And I believed it. I believed that everything was going to be okay, but I was very wrong.

I had six classes that semester, something that hadn't happened in a long time. Brandon was my science teacher, again. That class consisted of two seniors; a few juniors, a few sophomores, and the rest were all freshmen.

One day, during the first four weeks of school when Irene wasn't there, Susannah had come to get my things because Mom was picking me up. She cashed in on the early retirement at their office, so she took all of September off. I was at my desk just minding my own business. Brandon gave the class free time to do what we wished. This sophomore, Daniel, came over and started putting his hands in my face, so I told him to stop it, but he wouldn't stop. He continues to do it again, and I told him to stop, again, but he wouldn't. I then told him for the third time, and I smacked his hand to let him know how serious I was.

"Ow," Daniel said, robbing the hand I smacked. But then he kept at it.

Brandon said he wouldn't give homework that weekend if someone had answered the question on the board correctly. I had already gone to drop my things off at the front office for Susannah to get and Brandon knew that. He was going to pick a name out of a hat and that person was going to answer the question. Sure enough, he picked mine. When I told him I didn't have my things, the whole class moaned. Then Brandon chose another name, but that girl hadn't found the answer either. We ended up getting five questions to do over the weekend for homework.

When sixth period hit, a student in that class, Chase, said, "Thanks a lot, Mary Beth."

I was so upset at what Daniel had done and kept on doing in science class that I left my sixth period class without the teacher noticing. I just sat in front of the main office, waiting for Mom, crying while I sat there. An office lady saw me and asked if I was okay. I just shook my head no. Then she asked me if I wanted to come wait inside the office. I shook my head no for that one as well.

I just sat there crying until Mom came. Then she asked what was wrong. I continued crying, unable to find my voice to speak. When we were finally in the car, a few yards from the school, I told her through a broken voice.

"It was just stupid, and I'm probably making too much of it," I cried to her, still not sure why anyone would be that mean to me. But Mom said I did the right thing at telling her what happened. That was harassment! She called the school when we got home and told them what had happened. I heard that Daniel was going to be in a different period science class starting Monday.

Well, that didn't happen. The vice principle, Chuck, didn't get to that right away because he had other things to attend to first.

"He has better things to do other than protecting a student in school?" I thought, but didn't say.

I had switched form Jennele's computer class to another class for fourth period when school had started. I hated computers and did not want to work on web design. I was in this teacher Lucrecia's class for school events. We were in charge of the Halloween Carnival and certain other events that took place at the school. Mom volunteered for the Halloween Carnival, and of course I was there with her, helping out. The students were allowed to take a break after half of it was through. Daniel and I were in that same class. His schedule still hadn't been changed yet. He was walking by our booth and Mom saw him. She asked if that was the boy who harassed me and I only had to nod yes. She could just tell by his attitude as he walked by with his arm around a girl's shoulder.

A few weeks later, Daniel wasn't in any of my classes. He and I still shared the bus home. Judy, an office person, would get me at 15 minutes to 3 o'clock to help with the buses. I wrote down the order of the buses and placed the bus numbers on a board for the students to find their buses. My bus driver told me to just sit in the front, after the insistent with Daniel. I didn't have a problem with that, and I was the only kid to get along with the driver.

On a day that I wasn't there, Daniel had brought a gun to school. When I heard about that and how he was expelled, my first thought was, "He was looking for me." I was told that he brought it just to show his friends. The school police had to come and take him away. I thought that after that I'd be done with Daniel forever, but I was wrong, again.

When school had gotten out early on Tuesdays, I went up to a burger place that was three blocks from my house. The Kennedy High School students went there, and right away I noticed Daniel. I tried to hide, hoping he wouldn't see me. Luckily he didn't. I stopped going to that burger place from there on out.

In English, since Marcy was never there, the students would act badly, but I still got my work done. It was an expository writing class, and Marcy was always away at contests for different schools. The students in my class had to enter contests. I never expected to win. We wrote about gun safety. My argument was about guns being shot off in the air during certain events and a helpless victim on the street is killed. I won second place for that. Another student in my class had won third. We had to go to a big event to get our awards. I invited my sister Tracey and my friend Kelly as well as Mom, of course. There were pictures taken, and the mayor had come, but Mom, Kelly, Tracey, and I had left before that happened. Arun, the other student, had gotten his picture taken with the mayor.

I enjoyed writing in Marcy's class.

When the other school events were over and Marcy was finally there, she brought her grown son a few times.

During third period, when Irene had come back for good, she and I would either take off going different places that were a destination for me to get things and to learn how to ride the bus, or I would just stay back and do my homework or school work. It worked out pretty nice.

I was to come up with an assignment for Irene to accomplish in my town. Irene and I had gone to Starbucks with on that day. Irene wouldn't do any of the things that I had written for her to do, which was really messed up to me! We went to IHOP for lunch. We missed the bus at 12:30 that afternoon. I could have walked home.

"I'll get lost," Irene said. Irene made me feel guilty, so I waited for the bus.

We made it back late that day. I was embarrassed to come in class with only 20 minutes left to the day. However, the day passed and I got by.

In Brandon's science class, there were at least two freshmen that liked me, Robert who sat at me table for a few weeks and this kid Hovik. I was staring back at Chance one day and he asked, "Mary Beth, do you find Hovik attractive?" I didn't know who Hovik was so I told Chance that I did not find Hovik attractive. I heard this sound of disappointment from behind me. "No offense," I quickly added, while turning back.

Robert made it perfectly clear that he liked me. This other Daniel was sitting next to me, and the three of us had a project to do one day. We made phones, and Daniel and I were standing on one end while Robert was on the other. Robert and Daniel were talking on the phones, and Robert had asked to talk to me. Daniel wouldn't give me the phone, so he kept asking Robert, "WHAT?" Robert finally yelled over the phone that he wanted to talk to me, but Daniel still wouldn't give me the phone. Class was over a few minutes later.

Daniel and I had a final to do for science class. Robert thought he and I had a final to do together, so he was very excited. Daniel and I did our thing and that was that.

Irene and I went off campus for third period one day. We were going to take the city bus to my neighborhood, but we took another bus that dropped us further away from my neighborhood. I knew where I was, so we went to IHOP. After lunch, I went to the payphone and Irene decided that it was time for her cigarette. I called little Tom.

"Hello?" he asked.

"May I speak to Tom?" I said, not knowing what to say.

"This is he," Tom replied. I told him who it was.

"Hey," he responded. We talked a little.

"Did Tom tell you about my surgery?" I asked.

"No," Tom replied anxiously. "What surgery?"

"Tom didn't tell you?" and I began to fake cry. "I'm just kidding."

"What kind of surgery was it?"

"Just an eye surgery," I told him. "Listen," I began nervously. "You can say no, but I was wondering if you'd like to get coffee sometime?"

"Sure," I heard him respond. My heart flew! "I have a few things to do with my family, but after that I'm good."

"Okay, so I'll call you in two weeks."

"Okay."

I hung up the phone and told Irene what happened. I was on cloud 9 for two weeks.

I waited for those two weeks to be over and then I called Tom from another payphone, but the line didn't go through. I was crushed so badly. I told myself again that I had to get over Tom. He just wasn't right for me.

After winter break and after finals, I had gotten high honors for the first semester, despite the fact that I worked alone for most of it.

I was going all different directions with Essence during the year. I thought we were best friends, but she kept ignoring me and hanging out with a student Andrea. Andréa had slept around, probably with the same dorks that we went to school with. She would make fun of me from time to time. She had everything a girl like that would have: the looks, the attitude, the clothes, and est., est.

I was torn between losing the friend that I had and living in the shadows, and I lived in the shadows for far too long!

I had known girls like Andrea my whole life, and I hated all of them. They all thought that the word owed them something because they found themselves as the most beautiful creatures on the planet. It made me sick!

The seniors had a meeting in Marcy's room one day. Essence was hanging out with me, but when we were dismissed, she called out to Andrea without waiting for me.

"Hey, Andrea. Wait up!" Essence said when the meeting was over. It was lunch, so we went off campus. It hurt when Essence left without me. *Am I just not cool enough to hang out with anymore?* I thought.

Essence and I hardly ever ate together at lunch. I would go to Subway all the time while she went to McDonalds, Jack in the Box, or Deltaco. Essence had told me that she wanted to start eating better, so I thought I would have a friend to go to Subway with, instead of always being the *odd one out.* Essence only went to Subway for a short time.

We were still friends, though. Things had just changed.

Susannah had bought me tickets to go see Green Day, the band, in concert. I was very excited! The seats were on the lawn, so I thought they'd be good. Unfortunately, they were up high, and I had my fear of heights problem. Essence had tickets for the concert the night before. She had asked me to get her T-shirt, so I got one for her as well as one for myself. It was a good concert, but Susannah and I left early because she had work early the next morning. The security was harsh, but we got to leave because Susannah told the security guard something. My guess is that she told him about my brain injury, and that was the reason we got to leave.

When the next day of school had come, Essence was to pay me back. Well, that didn't happen right off the bat. It took a few weeks to get my money back from Essence.

I was feeling rejected that she was always hanging out with Andrea, so I told her one day through tears in my eyes. If our friendship didn't mean anything to her then I wanted everything back. She began to hang out with me more often after that.

I was placed in only five classes for the second semester, but I was going to have job training on Tuesdays and Thursdays at Barnes & Nobles. I heard that I was going to be volunteering there with two other students, both of them juniors, but one of the students, Adam had decided to volunteer somewhere else. Part of me wondered if he was volunteering at the other place just because I liked him the year before for the shortest time. *That is the stupidest reason of all not to work at Barnes & Noble,* I thought.

I had gotten straight A's on my report card, except for Science. Brandon gave Daniel and me a B in Science. It was still good for me. I had only had high honors a few times in high school.

I found my super visor Tray at Barnes & Noble to be very attractive. The other student there with me, Elan, thought so as well. We had finished organizing a bookshelf one day, and she had told me to go tell Tray, because she was too afraid. I liked Tray, so I went up and told him. He said we did a good job, and then he gave us something else to do.

After a few weeks, Elan and I only worked with Suzie, our other super visor. She would actually give us instruction and watch us like a hawk. Elan and I both agreed that we liked working with Tray and our other super visor Bert. On days that Suzie was out, we worked with Tray but he would leave us alone to do our job and then check up on us from time to time.

Elan had to take medication every day, so Irene would come over at a certain time and give it to her while I kept at the job at hand.

A few weeks before February had come I told Bert that I wouldn't be there on the 14th. He said that was okay, and he let the boss, Greg, know. I had my pre-operation for my eye surgery on that day. My eye surgeon had to know what eye muscles he was going to work on, because the last surgery only lasted for so long. When I didn't show up for job site, I thought it would be okay because I had let someone know already.

I returned to job site the following Tuesday, and Elan had told me that Tray had asked where I was. I was flattered and also a little mystified. Why would he care so much as to ask where I was? Elan told Tray that I was at the doctors, but Irene was there too, so...

Tom emailed me and said that he was coming out in March, but not to tell Mom because he wanted to keep it a secret. I didn't say a word, but I thought he would be out at the end of March. Instead he showed up in the middle.

I had gotten home from school, and luckily, no one was home. I hated when Ben and or Conan were at home because I couldn't handle the headaches that they would give me. I noticed there was a new message on the answering machine, so I push it and listened. It was my eye doctor's office calling to confirm that my surgery would be held on Monday, April 4th. As I was listening to this message, the door opened. I figured it was Ben or Conan, so I didn't bother looking from behind the corner into the living room to see. When the message was almost over, I turned to my right shoulder to see that it was Tom!

"TOM!" I shouted in excitement. I ran to give him a hug. We sat at the kitchen table and talked for a little while. The phone rang and Tom said that if it was Mom, he didn't want her to know that he was home. I didn't say anything, but she could tell something was different from my voice. I told her that the doctors had called and had a day for my surgery. I saved it so she could listen to it when she got home.

After Mom had gotten home, she listened to the message and said that date would be fine, and then she changed her clothes. She was making dinner when the front door opened again. I was sitting a t the table and I saw Tom. I had already gone through my excitement, so I was calm. Mom said, "AW!" and threw her hands in the air. She gave Tom a hug, and soon enough Tom's friends were at home to take him away and do stuff.

After Tom had left to go back to New York, I had this weird feeling that something bad was going to happen during the surgery and that I wouldn't survive. It was a horrible, creepy feeling that wouldn't go away. I finally voiced my concern to Tom over an email telling him how unnerving this was for me. He emailed me back and told me that it was perfectly normal to feel anxious before surgeries. He said that everything was going to be alright. *But I've never been this nervous before*, I thought, *not his far in advance.* However, Tom had never lied to me before, at least not any time that I had been aware of. *Why would he lie to me now?*

Still feeling uneasy, I typed up fliers to hand to my friends at school. It told them to have a cup of coffee or the beverage of their choice to celebrate my 9th surgery. I had printed a few. I was giving one to Brandon, one to Irene, my friends Clay, Essence, Shayna, and my super visors Tray and Suzie. However, Suzie wasn't there on a Thursday that I had the fliers. I gave one to Tray anyways. People still asked me if someone they knew could have something else instead of coffee, and so I pointed it out that it also said, "The beverage of your choice" to them.

Clay gave me attitude when I gave him a flier.

In science class, I was sitting next to obnoxious guys, after our seats were changed. They made fun of me and I hated them for that.

My brother, Mike, had left for his second deployment. Mom and I drove him down to Penalton and said our goodbyes there. I wasn't too nervous for him this time. He was coming back again, I knew it. It was rough non-the-less to say goodbye.

The day of the surgery came, and I was very nervous! I told myself, *you've done it three times before, you can do it again.*

Mom and I got to the hospital before seven in the morning. We parked in the parking lot, but there was no one to take the money for the parking payment, so we went up stairs first. There was a younger boy before me. I was the second to have surgery, and then there was someone after me. The little boy had his dad there with him.

Mom and I were waiting upstairs for the bed to come wheel me away. I had cream put on my hands to numb them, as I waited for the surgery to happen. I had to use the restroom before hand. One of the doctors came up when I was still in the restroom. The nice part of the restroom was that I wasn't wearing underwear for the surgery so it wasn't time consuming. Mom told the doctor how many surgeries this would make for me. He looked concerned for me to hear that it was my ninth surgery. I got in to the bed and had him take me down to the recovery place. I saw the boy that was before me and then I saw my doctor. He grinned at me.

Another doctor who was very tall introduced himself to Mom and me. Then this doctor in a bandana put the IV in my right hand. My hands were numb from the moister they had used before and again on my hands.

I kissed Mom goodbye and then I was knocked out.

I was told that the surgery only lasted 30 minutes.

When I woke up, I had difficulty breathing. First, I was surprised that I had woken up at all, but then to also deal with doctors in a hectic way… that was not fun.

"You're not breathing correctly," one female doctor said.

I could hear the tall doctor come my way as well.

"What's going on?" he asked.

They put tubes directly up my nostrils. I asked them to remove them because they were very irritating to me. They removed them, and then said to try breathing normally. I took in a few deep breaths. My breathing was slow, but sure. That still wasn't good enough for them, so they had to put the tubes back, going directly up my nostrils, again. I told them again that it was irritating. Then they took the tubes out and cut them, as to not have the tubes going directly up my nostrils. I was breathing on my own thirty minutes after a little help from that.

I was released a few hours later, going to see the doctor again, in his office, having him cut the stitches and having me read the chart. Again, keeping my eyes open while the doctor cut my stitches out was very difficult.

The elevator ride wasn't as fun this time around.

I had called Essence on her cell phone the next day. She was at school during nutrition. I told her to punch Trevor for me and he said "thank you".

I was home for the rest of the week, and, to my comfort, the week after was Spring Break.

When I returned to school, it was difficult. I wasn't allowed to lift anything that weighed over 15 pounds, which made school work a bitch! Luckily, my teachers weren't that hard on me.

For job site, I wasn't allowed to bend over and do the bottom shelves, so Elan did those. I also was restricted from lifting any heavy books.

One day, Elan and I suddenly had a 10 minute break. I had no idea why, but it was nice until I found out the reason of why it was happening.

It was the next day that Irene had told me that the reason why Elan and I had a break. It was due to the fact that Mom and everyone else at the IEP made that decision for me without my consent. I was so angry! Tears of rage spring to my eyes! *How could they do this to me? I was actually having a good time stocking shelves and being treated like a normal individual for once in my life. This wasn't fair!* I thought over and over to myself.

It was a Monday night at my singing lesson when I started crying a little. I didn't do the best job in the world, and Pam and Mom both pointed that out to me. My mind was else where. I leaned into Pam, and she hugged me back, not knowing why I was suddenly so upset.

Mom and I made it outside.

"This is about the job site, isn't it?" she asked with an attitude in her voice. I told her it was, and then we started to argue.

"If you're not going to listen to what I have to say, then I'm not going to listen to what you have say," Mom said after I told her that I didn't want to hear what she had to say. *It's my life, not yours,* I thought.

I gave in and had her have an attitude towards me while she explained why everyone decided to do that without my consent.

She then told me that my opinion didn't matter and that the subject was closed! I was so angry. *How can the subject be closed?* I thought. It's my life! *I'm the one who has to live it, not you!*

I returned to school the next day and immediately went to the main office to find Terry. Tears were in my eyes and in my voice as I saw her. I assumed Dr. Gale had something to do with this decision.

"I never want to see him again," I told her in rage and heartbreak.

"Dr. Gale was actually the only one that said anything about getting your opinion," Terry told me in a calm voice. "We'll change it back, I promise," she told me. And it was changed back.

At job site, Tray was my favorite reason to go and work there.

In school, Andrea wasn't there anymore! I found that to be a blessing! I didn't go to Essence's birthday because her sister said that Andrea was coming and I didn't want to see her. Andrea dropped out of high school as soon as she turned 18. But that wasn't the last time I saw her, unfortunately.

Prom was coming up. I was the first person to buy my prom ticket, but then I started having doubts and I really didn't want to go. Essence said I had to! She and I would argue.

One day, Essence and I went to the main office to ask Terry if I could get a refund from the prom that I wasn't going to anymore. She told me that I'd have to take that up with Essence. I had also asked her for a refund for the senior trip that I wasn't going on. She told me no for that one as well.

Essence and I had it out right outside the main office. I told her over and over again that I wasn't going to the prom, even if it was to prove to the Madame Class president Monica that prom was going to suck based on the location that was chosen just because she was president!

"Then we're not friends anymore," I told her and walked away.

"It isn't like I'm making you do drugs," I heard her say as I was walking away. I spent the rest of the day being pissed off. I told Shayna and she was conflicted that she'd have to take sides, something that she didn't want to do.

I sent Tom an email that day, explaining what had happened and how upset I was about the conflicting situation that I was in.

The next day, Thursday, I was not looking forward to seeing Essence, but she wasn't at school. I spent the day having an argument with myself, not knowing what I wanted to do. Part of me wanted to be friends with Essence, but the other part hated the idea. I mostly hated myself for being so mean. That wasn't me at all.

I had decided that Friday I would apologize to Essence and see if she would do the same to me.

First period English came. Essence and I always sat next to each other, but she moved to the seat next to that one on that day. I looked her in the eye.

"Essence...sorry," I said silently.

"It's okay," she said.

"I just don't want to go to prom," I told her again.

"You don't have to," she told me.

Everything was set that I would get my money back from Terry. Graduation was coming just around the corner. Everyone was to have someone speak for them. I first wanted Tom to speak for me, but he had moved at the being of the school year. Then I wanted Jesse, but he moved to Long Beach and then to the east coast, so that was out of the question.

I finally found hope! Tom was coming out for one of his friends' weddings the day after graduation. I got up the courage to ask if Tom could speak for me at graduation. He emailed me back asking what he would have to say. I told him to just say that I was the best person that he knew! "Ha-ha! Just kidding," I told him. I said that he could talk about how much I've accomplished or whatever he wanted to say. He said he'd do it.

I told Essence that I didn't want to go to Prom because the girl Samantha didn't like me. She passed on the message, and Samantha said she thought I didn't like her. I actually didn't like her because she was making fun of me during my junior year in Mike's class.

I got my ticket back and just decided to go to prom. I had already paid for my prom dress and I was going to pay Essence for the limo, along with everyone else. I didn't want to feel like the loser that I was in high school and go alone; however I didn't have a choice there. I went to prom without a date.

I had changed my mind the week before prom and Essence almost started crying, until I gave in.

I was sick the week of prom, but I had already paid for everything, so I was going. Essence wouldn't let me out of it anyways, or forgive me, so I had to go.

I had gotten an early birthday present. It was a cell phone, which I had always wanted one!

I had my phone, my wallet, cash and my ticket in my purse, ready for prom.

I had a make over done at Essence's house along with all of the other girls that were riding along in the limo.

I told a kid, Jeffery to take a picture of my hand while we were on the ride over to the hotel, but he said he wasn't going to waste his film.

When we got to prom, there were a lot of people there. I looked completely transformed, so no one recognized me at first.

I walked around for a while in the big room. Then I saw the math teacher, Walter.

"Hey, Walter," I said while I stood next to him.

"Mary Beth, is that you? I didn't recognize you. You look really nice!"

I thanked him and then found that everyone was staring at me a lot.

Jonathon was there with the slut Andrea. I saw them at a table, but I was at another table so I didn't have to talk to them. Jonathan was one of the guys that was staring at me.

I wanted to get my prom picture done. I went to the photographer, but he told me that I was to go buy a card first; I had to choose what the picture sizes were. I went to that table and I saw the kids John and Jesus from my class.

"Hey guys," I told them as I chose my pictures.

I went back to get my picture done. The photographer told me to stand in three different stances as he took the photos. H said I could keep my glasses on, but I decided to remove them for the photos.

The rest of the kids from the limo took a group shot that I wasn't invited to join in, and it was kind of irritating me to me that I wasn't involved with that.

I must have gone to the restroom three times with Essence and Shayna, something I never did with friends before.

I had finally asked Essence if I should call little Tom to see if he was coming to my graduation and Essence said yes. I called him, but he couldn't hear me. Essence, Shayna and I just went back to the room where the prom was going on. Terry was passing through the hallway as we went back.

We got our food. I sat there, eating very little of it.

`John came up to me with his date when there was food on my mouth. I met his date Karen and I was graceful.

After a while, I started to get so upset. I went out to where the restrooms and called Mom. I asked her if she could just come get me. She got really pissed off at me over the phone, so I told her that I would just stay. Then she got more pissed off and said that I wasn't having a good time! I was in tears as she was yelling at me. She said that she'd come and get me, and I caved in and agreed to it. I went to find Essence who was sitting the table talking to someone. I tried everything to get her attention, but she wasn't letting up. Her date finally told her that I was there, but I had started to walk away at that point. All the girls were behind me.

The teacher Steve had seen me while I was leaving the room in tears.

When we made it outside the room, I gave Essence my phone and she spoke to Mom. I just went to cry in the restroom. There were chairs there that faced mirrors. I just sat and cried.

Essence, Shayna, and Samantha found me in there. Samantha asked me what was wrong. I didn't want to talk to her, do I didn't say anything. I just cried.

"Look at me, Mary Beth," Samantha said over and over again. 'What's wrong?"

I couldn't tell her. She wouldn't understand!

Essence asked what was wrong, so I told her.

"I'm Sick! And you made me come!" I told her. "Tom couldn't hear me," I cried over and over again. I was living a nightmare.

"What did he say?" Essence asked.

"He couldn't hear me," I cried. I was so in love with him, but he didn't care!

The girls left the restroom, but every other girl from prom was in there, checking up on me: Gaby, Jeffery's date, Jane, everyone.

Jane and I did become a little closer that day, but we weren't best friends. We were just people who knew each other, in my opinion. She gave me a hug to make me feel better but it didn't help.

Terry would come in and see me from time to time. I just wanted everyone to leave me alone! Why was that so hard to understand?

A woman and her friend, total strangers to me, asked if I wanted to talk, but I shook my head no. This lady and a girl who had severe mental problems asked if I wanted to talk and then said that I would be okay.

"The Lord is with you," she said.

The bathroom lady at the fancy hotel asked if my boyfriend broke up with me, I didn't say anything, but she gave me a hug. I just wasn't left alone!

Cassandra, the English teacher, asked if I wanted to talk when she was in there, but I shook my head.

Terry finally came back into the restroom and told me that there was something going on with security and that it would be best for me to wait for Mom out in the lounge. I so badly wanted to disagree and tell her to shove it, but I did "the right thing" and waited out in the lobby. I was so embarrassed. Terry tried to talk to me. She wanted me to tell her about what was bothering me, but I wouldn't give in. Not to her. Not to anyone!

Mom came and got me, and I was embarrassed, of course, but I tried my best to ignore whoever was watching me. Mom had an attitude for sure that night as we went to the car outside.

I went home, and immediately went to the bathroom and changed into my sweatpants and just went to bed. I was sick for the next few days.

I didn't go to school that Monday. I wasn't feeling up to it physically or mentally.

When I did return, Irene said that Essence had told her that she was wondering what was wrong that night with me. I had told Essence at Prom, so why was she asking?

Life passed by after that.

I only had two real finals, and I had completed them early.

I didn't go to school on my birthday, mostly because I didn't have a final. I went to Barnes & Noble and saw Alex and Tray. Alex wished me a happy birthday when I told him what day it was for me. I thanked him. Of course that night I didn't get the traditional first slice of cake. No. Instead it was given to Conan. I tried not to let that upset me, but it sort of did in a big way.

The next day was graduation and Tom was coming out for that one!

I had put on the dress that I bought for graduation, and I was really excited to see Tom. His plane wasn't landing until 3:30, and one of his friends was getting coffee with him. I didn't want Joe or Ben and Conan to come to my graduation. I hated them all and they were never nice to me. Mom invited them and I told her I didn't want them to come. She said she was being polite. When were they ever polite or even remotely nice to me? This angered me to no end, but I said it was only one day, However, I was very wrong.

Tom got there a little before 5:30. I had been searching up and down the school for him. Essence wanted to meet him. Tom's friend Robert was there as well, but he had to leave early because he had band practice. I thought it was really cool that Robert came in the first place.

Essence met them both, and then she and I went to Brandon's room and got in line.

As the ceremony went on and on, I was talking to Essence in my seat. The students were making a lot of noise, and Terry told us to go out to the field if we wanted to discuss whatever it was we were talking about. No one moved.

After she left the microphone, I continued talking to Essence to finish what I had to say.

It was finally my turn. Essence whispered to me that she wanted to give me a big hug before I went to get my diploma. I gave Tom another big hug for being there. He gave me flowers that he had bought, as well as the single rose that all the students had with their diploma. He had not had a speech planned, but Tom said that I was the best person that he knew. I was touched, but part of me wanted to say, "Tom, you need to go and meet other people."

Shayna had her mom speak for her. She came back to her seat in tears of joy.

Essence had her mom speak for her.

After everyone was done talking and the graduation had ended, I said my goodbyes to all the teachers that I liked. I took my picture with Brandon and said goodbye.

It was eight o'clock when we got out and we went to dinner. Ben and Conan came, which I did not want them to.

Two days later, Tom's friend was getting married, so he went. Tom went back to New York a few days later.

Mom and I were going out to New York in July. We left on a red eye and got there early in the morning on a Saturday. We met Tom's girlfriend Cameron, and then fell asleep in Tom's bed.

After a few hours of sleep, we woke up to meet one of Tom's roommates, Matt. I instantly liked Matt.

Mom and I saw where Tom worked at Bloomberg's in Manhattan that week. We had lunch in Central Park everyday with Tom. He had taken half days at work, so he could spend more time with us.

We went to Queens to see her cousins and to Amityville to see her other cousins. We were in Amityville for Independence Day out on a boat. Tom and Cameron came with us.

I had met most of my cousins from that part of the family.

The last day of New York, Mom and I were supposed to have lunch in the city with one of her cousins, but she got sick. Mom and I decided to go to Times Square to see the Naked Cowboy.

The last night that Mom and I were in New York, I was sitting on the couch with Matt watching TV. Mom, Tom, Cameron and I went out to dinner beforehand. Tom had to use the restroom.

When he came out, Tom suddenly announced to Matt and me that he lost 15 pounds. Without trying to be funny or obnoxious, I said, "Thanks for sharing that Tom."

Two seconds later, Matt started laughing. I had turned to him, but I didn't want to be rude and say, "What the hell are you laughing at?" so I chose my words carefully,

"Why are you laughing?" I finally asked.

"I was thinking the same thing," he said.

"I know!" I pronounced with excitement. "Nobody needed to know that much information!"

Things went silent for another minute. Then my curiosity sprang into action again.

"Matt," I said, staring towards the TV with my eyes on the toy dinosaurs on the television set. I could see out of the corner of my right eye that Matt had turned to look at me. "Whose dinosaurs are those?" I asked pointing towards them.

Matt turned his head towards the TV.

"Oh, their mine," he said. I thought that was so cool!

"I like them," I told him.

"Yeah, I have a few at work," he admitted, setting them down on the table that was sitting in front of us.

Tom and Matt were going out that night to do something. Mom and I gave Tom a hug even though we were going to see him before we left the next morning. We said goodbye to Matt, and then they left. Mom and I stayed inside the rest of the night. Mom took a picture of me and Matt's toy dinosaur.

We got up early the next morning and got ready to leave. Giving Tom one more hug goodbye, tears were in my eyes, but I wouldn't allow myself to cry.

I had other things to get ready for when I got home. Italy was coming up and I was very excited to finally be going to a place I had only dreamed of going to since the age of seven, but I had no idea why. I would soon find out...

Chapter 13

Italy... and other things

September 2006 had finally come! Mom and I were going to Rome, Venice, Florence, Sorrento, and Palermo.

I fell in love with Venice when I was just a little girl, but I really didn't know why.

Mom and I left LAX at night and slept on the 14 hour flight to the Heathrow airport. We stayed there for two hours.

I hated planes, but I wanted to go to Italy. We flew into Rome next. We were staying at a little apartment there with three other families. There were these Australians that stayed in the same apartment as us.

When we first arrived, it was night there, so we walked in the dark with our luggage. We got to the apartment safely. We went to the Spanish Steps, but walked down them, instead of going up.

We took a lot of pictures of all the beautiful statues and art work.

Steve Erwin had died when we were in Rome. The Australians that stayed at the apartment with us had said how crazy Steve Erwin was, so they weren't that sorry that he died.

Next was Venice. I wanted to know why I had such a fascination with the place. We were only going to be there for only three days. We stayed in the old Jewish Ghetto in a really cheap place. We got help from Italians who didn't speak English, but they tried their best to help us out.

When Mom and I went to the Doche Palace, I suddenly knew why I wanted to go to Venice, Italy! I had been here before. I remembered walking through the halls, always trying to keep quite, in fear that I would be punished. I could remember crying out, "PAPA! PAPA!" as I was walking down the corridor.

The big room that Mom and I were in I could remember as the room in which I would dance in that former life time. I had everything, but I would walk in silence without having very much. A lot like the life I lived now. I walk in silence while I can, but always wanted someone to walk with, or at least to be there for me when I was going through hard times. I had everything according to everyone else who saw me day in and day out, but I've always wanted more!

When I told Mom about that, first she seemed to understand but later she only mocked me! I tried to just laugh it off and to not let it get to me, but it really hurt that I was treated that way.

We went to Florence next. There we were at the laundry mat and ran into an American study in Italy at college. She gave us an idea to go to the museum to see the David for free, so Mom and I went on Wednesday. It was beautiful and magnificent in every way. We saw a lot of art, paintings and statues. Mom saw a man trying to approach me, but he saw her next to me. The man, whose face I never saw, turned and walked away.

There was a French couple that I had seen traveling on our train that we ran into again in Sorrento, our next destination. Mom didn't notice them.

Mom and I traveled to Sorrento next, and admired all these different things, the art, the culture, and the food. There was a robbery on the train to Naples. This New York cop had his wallet stolen by gypsies and he had accused an Asian girl of stealing his wallet. Things calmed down after a while, but I was still shacking in fear.

We went to Palermo, Sicily next. We traveled on a cruise ship there. It was an over niter, so we got our tickets two days before so we would have a cabin to ourselves on the top level. It was Hell for me! I was sick the whole time on the ship that night. I couldn't sleep at all! All the rocking back and forth on the ship was very unsettling for my stomach.

When we were going to get off I told mom that I was going to throw up. She persisted on yelling at me and saying that she was trying to find a restroom for me. I told her that I wasn't going to throw up after all, and she persisted on yelling and giving me attitude. After she heard me, she calmed down.

It was our last destination, or so I thought. The first day we were there, Mom and I were by ourselves, wandering around a little.

For the next three, we had a person with us that could show us around. She was nice. She had a driver with her, so he drove.

On the third day, Mom had wanted to find our relatives that lived in Palermo. We went to the courthouse to try to find where they lived. The Mayor of Sicily had to be there once Mom found the correct information. Our guide was there translating everything into English as best she could.

After a while, as I sat in the car waiting, our guide came out to get me to bring to my mom. I was confused, of course, but I could tell that Mom was really excited.

The Mayor had found a third cousin and was contacting him to come and meet his distant relatives. Vito was this little Sicilian man that was a second cousin to my grandmother. He came with his granddaughter in this little car as it raced up to meet us. His granddaughter was around my age.

I was excited and nervous to meet these people that I didn't know; people I was related to.

Vito insisted that Mom and I go to his house to meet our other family members.

When we got there, our guide came with us, of course, to translate everything for us, and us to them. Mary was Mom's third cousin. She was very nice, and they insisted on feeding us. Every meal to a Sicilian is a feast! She called her husband who worked in the fields and he came and brought desert as well. It was an all day event!

The husband brought fresh wine from the fields that he worked in. Mom had a little. I was also offered wine, but I politely declined the offer.

Mary's little boy, Ali, was so adorable! He had stayed home from school that day because he was sick. Little Ali was about five years old. Mary stayed home from her job that day to take care of Ali.

Then there were the sisters, Fiorelle and Tlorie. They were nice. Tlorie seemed quite. Fiorelle came with Vito to pick us up.

Our guide was talking to Fiorelle after the meal was over. They were discussing the career of our guide lady. The women in Sicily didn't have much opportunity to work.

They were all very gracious towards us. Mary asked why we didn't stay with them and Mom's answer was that she was shy. It was a wonderful experience meeting family in Sicily.

When the day ended, we thanked our guide people for their help.

The next day, Mom and I had flown back to Rome where we stayed the night in a fancy hotel. We were going to return the next day back home.

After getting home, nothing had really changed.

Ben and Conan were still around. Conan was always mean to me. And Ben was a horrible father and person to Conan and everyone around.

In October of 2006, Sabrina was out here. Mike was back from over seas that August, so they both stayed with us. I hated the living arrangement that was for Mom. Ben didn't seem to care that he and Conan took Mom's room, I on the other hand hated them for that reason, among many others.

Sabrina and Conan were at the kitchen table acting stupid, while Ben was in Mom's old room playing video games. The children were left unattended by an adult. It was made clear to me time and time again by Conan that I was not an adult. Conan was dripping something that was going to hit the floor. I told him to stop. He accused me of always telling him not to do things. He said that I told him that he always did bad things, which was usually the case.

"Fuck you," I said as I was turning off the computer. "Go to Hell."

"Why don't you?" Conan said back to me.

"Because I already live there," I said, going to my room and getting my shoes on to leave.

As I opened the door and was about to leave, Ben left "his room" and shouted back at me, "FUCK YOU!"

I was gone, determined never to go back. I made it to the park, without having anywhere to go. After two hours sitting there I had decided to go back. My decision on doing so was only for my cat. Someone had to take care of her.

I returned and fed the cat and then I just went to my room. When Mom came home, Ben had told her what I did, but he didn't say what he said back to me. *Shocker.* I was expecting on having to defend myself, but Mom told Ben that I was going to college the next semester and that Conan couldn't act up like that again around me.

On November 10th, 2006, I was walking up to Target to start my Christmas shopping early. I was at San Fernando Mission and Ruffner. I glanced across the street and saw this guy with short blonde hair looking my way. I thought he was really cute, but I wouldn't allow myself to stare. Heartbreak followed me where I went. I turned my head forward, continuing my way to Target.

"Hey," I heard from behind me.

I turned around to see this guy.

"Hey," I said back with enthusiasm.

"I'm selling magazines and trying to earn enough points to go anywhere in the world," the boy said. "I'm in this group to try to get to know people better."

"You should go to Italy," I told him.

"I'm actually going to Sydney, Australia," he told me.

"I've been to Sydney!" I told him.

"Would you like to by some magazines?" he asked me.

Sure," I said, and we had a seat on the hard sidewalk against a wall.

He told me he needed 300 more points. I looked to see that every magazine subscription was 100 points each.

"You can buy one for your boyfriend," he told me.

"Why does everyone assume that I have a boyfriend?" I asked out loud. He didn't answer.

I bought three different magazines: Surfer, Marie Claire, and Jane magazines.

"Can I have a hug?" he asked. Not knowing who he was, I wouldn't have hugged him, but we got to know each other fast enough and I felt safe enough giving him one.

"I usually go to the ATM over there," I said, pointing east.

"How far is that?" he asked.

"About a mile," I said.

I talked about my family, and I told him that my father had died.

"I'm sorry," he said.

"It's okay," I told him. "I never knew him."

He told me that his twin brother had died in Iraq. He showed me pictures of his sister and one of him and his twin when they were just kids.

"I'm so sorry," I told him.

"It's okay. Your father died."

"Yeah, but I didn't know him," I said.

He said that he would only date girls who wanted to have triplets and so far he hadn't found a woman who wanted that.

"I think having triplets would be fun," I told him.

We walked to the closet ATM. He had a seat adding up the magazine prices. He first said it was only $100 dollars. It seemed like it would have been more to me, but I took out $100 and went back to the table he was at.

"Did you miss me?" I asked.

"Yes," he said.

I was flattered and touched. "You missed me," said, pulling my hand towards my chest and smiling.

"It's actually $110. Do you have a ten?"

"No," I told him.

He asked if I wanted to hang out afterwards and I told him yes! He said he could pay the $10 for me. Then he handed me my receipts. He shook my hand, while I was expecting another hug. He ran across the street. I was confused. "Should I stay or should I go?" I thought. I ended up walking to Target and getting some of the presents. I walked home, smiling to myself.

When I got there, I was sitting at the kitchen table looking at the name on my receipts. Jeremy Triplett. The phone rang and Ben answered it, but then hung up. No one was there. Again, the phone rang with Ben answering it, but no on was there.

I cried myself to sleep for months afterwards, always wanting Jeremy back in my life. We had spoken of a future together. He would have kept me safe, I thought to myself.

I told Mom about the magazines and she only seemed concerned. I told her over and over that I was fine and that nothing bad had happened. She never believed me. She never believed that I could take care of myself. She thought I was stupid and feared that I was going to make the same mistakes that she made at my age. I swore to myself that I didn't want to be like that. I swore to never get married at such a young age.

College was coming up, so I registered for three classes: English, Vocal and a class to help me out with my school work.

Chapter 14

Trying to Start Over

When I first started college, I thought I was going to be a blast! I was naturally very excited to be going to school! It was something that I always dreamed of doing.

Mondays and Wednesdays I would have singing in the morning. I went to my first class in the music building. I had gotten there early, but I wasn't extremely early for the first day.

I had taken a seat in the front as my vision was horrible sitting in the back.

The class started out with the teacher calling out roll call. I simply raised my hand when my name was called. H looked up and saw me.

We were put into groups to start singing. I sat next to two older women that seemed nice. One lady was a jazz singer, but not a great opera singer in my opinion. The other woman was a massage therapist. I tried to start a conversation with them; my first! I told myself that I was going to break my shy spell! It seemed to work for the time being.

On Tuesdays and Thursdays I was going to have English after a class that I was going to take to become more organized.

First day of that hit, and my first class was changed to another building. I called Mom and broke down crying. I was too over whelmed with anxiety for this! She told me to calm down and take a break. I was going to have my English class at 11:20 AM that morning, so I just tried to be cool until then. Well, that didn't last long.

I had gone to the English building, which I knew very well from back when I had broadcasting there. My teacher was a male. The first person I recognized was Jesus from High school. He sat behind me. I was a little confused because I thought that everyone had gone to Pierce College. I was looking forward to just starting over with my life and not have any of my old enemies anymore to deal with.

I had purchased my English book a few weeks early from the book store located on the campus. I thought I had the right book. The teacher informed the class that it would be working on how to properly write a sentence. I checked with the teacher after class and found that I had the wrong book. He told me to just trade it in.

I had said hi to Jesus when class had ended. He told me that most of our graduating class had gone to Pierce, but had changed to Valley College instead. I was a little disappointed in that.

I had made it out to the bus station to go home. I had to take two buses to get home, and then I would walk the distance from there.

Later that first Tuesday night, I started to cry at the dinner table. I was so overwhelmed with everything; the English book that I didn't have, seeing an old classmate again, the class that I couldn't find and having to do it all alone. Mom and I talked it out and I had decided to only take one class, but it also broke my heart. I felt as though I were letting people down. I didn't want to be that person to let people down. Look at where I had come from. I hated letting Tom, Mom, and Tracey down. I hated myself for that. And most importantly, I didn't want to let myself down. But I also knew that if I continued down this path that I wouldn't come out the other side.

I had decided to drop my Tuesday classes online that night. I returned to school the following week to get my money back. I had to go through everything in the information office. I made it through okay though.

In Vocal, it was tough! First we were in groups of five, then down to four, then three. When the teacher had placed us in groups of two, I was pretty nervous. I didn't sing out loud with this one girl. However, I did accomplish it in my own way.

I had noticed a tall guy in my class, Aaron. He was beautiful and he could really sing! He was always up with this one girl Monique. They were both unbelievably great singers! It made one wonder why they were in that class to begin with. Aaron had his posture to work on while singing. He and I were in the same group only twice. I wanted to be in his group forever! Aaron and Monique were always in the back row of the class, while I was in the front. I would always stare at Aaron and I would find him looking back at me with intensity in his gaze.

During the first few weeks of Vocal class, I was learning to breathe from the bottom part of my stomach. I had learned that I would have better pitch that way, but I was still very quite. The teacher had to walk to the top of the stairs in the class and have me sing louder so he could hear me. I was challenged very hard, but in a good way.

During the fifth week of classes, I had gotten to school early, of course. I found a student that I knew was in my Vocal class sitting on the bench outside the room where I usually sat. He and I were discussing something, when suddenly we were told that our teacher was not going to be there. I was a little let down, but I had just signed my name on the paper to indicate that I was there, as well as the other guy. He introduced himself as Jose and we had become friends instantly. Jose had asked if I wanted to take a walk with him and I agreed to it. We talked about everything under the sun.

When the hour had gone by, he thanked me for talking to him at the end of the hours that we walked together. Then I had to walk to the bus stop to catch my first bus.

The next week, after class, I had asked Jose if he wanted to talk, saying that I can be very annoying in case he didn't want to. I wasn't going to allow myself to get hurt. I promised myself that much. Luckily, he said yes, and we hung out every Tuesday and Thursday that semester after that.

I had an appointment at my dermatologist one Saturday in March. I told her that I wanted a mole from my neck removed. It seemed to me that it had grown out some. The doctor was more concerned with a mole on my leg.

I went to Barnes & Noble to get books on different cancers. The mole on my leg could be cancer, I thought.

I had lunch with Kelly and Essence and I explained what was happening. We were apart for months, so I thought our friendship was in trouble. Luckily, I was wrong.

The day of the appointment came, and the doctor was going to take the ole from my leg first. I screamed! Nothing had ever hurt this much in my entire life! When the doctor was done removing the mole from my leg, I was done with it all together. I wasn't going to be put through that much pain to numb my neck!

I was left with a big scar on my leg for months. It became blue, then green, and then purple. I went back to the dermatologist for cream. I had to apply it on my leg twice a day for a few months.

One day at school, I had told Jose what happened to me and I showed him the disgusting looking scar on my leg.

Little by little, it hurt less.

Little by little, I began to like Jose as more than just a friend, but I wasn't going to let myself get caught up in the moment over that. I had told him that I was trying to work on my music and I pointed to the fliers that I posted in the hallway. He said he was interested and that he'd help me out. Jose was a good guitarist, so I gave it a shot. My voice was lost, so I never sang directly to him and we never had the opportunity to record.

Jose and I became closer and closer. He was a true friend of mine. I had told him of my brain injury and car accident. We would talk about politics, religion, and everything else under the sun.

When our mid-term came, each student was to perform the same Italian song that we had learned. I was so nervous! Our professor had called everyone alphabetically, because no one raised their hand to go first. Jose always looked so weird when he went up. I just tried my best at singing.

Every week on Tuesdays and Thursdays I was working with a woman who helped me prepare to get a job. Betty was alright to work with, but after a while it got to be too much. I walked a mile and a half to the park. We'd meet in the library and go over everything that was on her list of things to do. When I told her that I wanted to work with music or act, everyone always said that was out of reach and that I needed to be realistic. That really made me angry, furious, and heartbroken!

Spring Break came at last, and nothing really changed. Betty had me excited and then scared about my job hunting. I had filled out an application for the library, but I never got call back. I never really wanted to work with books, anyway. Everyone else thought that it would be slow and easy going for me to do, but it wasn't my dream.

I had gone to Barnes & Noble one day. Tray was there and he mentioned that there were job openings. I asked if I could have an application.

"You want to work her?!" he asked, excitedly. Then he sprinted off and got me an application. I said that I would return with it in a week.

I had filled out the application for Barnes & Noble, but my schedule wasn't good for working there either.

I had looked around my town for other job opportunities. Two and a half miles away from home was a Hallmark store that was hiring, so I asked for an application there.

That was the last place I had sent an application to work at, but I never got a call back. One day, Betty just said that it was time and that I didn't have a way out of it. I cried to Mom over the phone, walking home, and explained everything that I was feeling. It was all too much for me and I didn't want to cry about it over be overwhelmed from it anymore. Betty didn't last much longer.

It was so irritating and frustrating to keep being put on the spot of "What job do you want, Mary Beth?" and, "You need to think realistically."

When Spring Break was over, I went back to my class and I loved it. For five hours, no one was bothering me. I had the teacher saying that I sang to quite and I needed to be louder, but he didn't treat me different because of my medical condition. The professor had no idea that I had it either. That was the nice part.

I loved being with Jose. We had such a good time. He told me that he was going to transfer to Valley College as a full time student there instead of CSUN where he had other classes. He majored in three things before, but changed his mind so many times for different reasons. I told him that was fine. He said that he was going to change his major to Music, and I said that it was a great idea. Go for your dreams.

Jose was in a band outside of class. He told me that his band was going to perform at a club. I told him that I wanted to go, and he said he could sell me a ticket. When I told Mom and Susannah that I was going to see Jose's band they said that it was probably Mexican music and that I wouldn't like it. I was made fun of for a few days. Ben said that it was most likely Mexican music. I never asked anyone's opinion and yet they were so harsh on me. I felt like crying when they made fun of me and Jose.

Susannah looked up the name of the band online and told me what it was. I said that she wasn't invited anymore. I had already bought my ticket from Jose. He forgot to bring the tickets to school but his friend was around, so he got a few from him. Jose asked how many I wanted. I told him just one.

The week before the show, I was at school just hanging out with Jose before class, and he gave me a t-shirt with his band's name on it. It was awesome!

Mom came with me to the show, which was always a little embarrassing. She bought her ticket there and then we went inside. I saw Jose and went over to wish him good luck. The first band was horrible. The lead singer could not sing. He played the acoustic guitar well and the other band mates did a good job with their instruments, but the lead singer *could not sing*. It was really sad that they actually had fans.

Jose's band was the second band. They did a good job. It was way better then the first band. The drummer was a girl and she did some singing. She did a fairly good job. Jose sang a few songs and the other guitarist sang as well. After their act, the band was selling the t-shirts that I had already had. I wanted to say hi to Jose at the end, but he walked away to get something in another room. Mom and I left when the third band was playing. They were the best, but it was much too loud to stay.

The next day was a Monday and I wore the t-shirt that I had gotten form Jose. He told me that the first band had done an extra song, so Jose's band wasn't able to do their last song. I told him how bad I thought the first band was. Jose's band had tried to record, but they had no success in that.

Aaron was always there staring at me in class as I stared back at him. It was always nice.

As a class, we practiced Santa Lucia in Italian. It was very difficult for me, so I practiced with the CD that I had in the class book. We were all going to sing Santa Lucia individually for the final. We had to choose a song to perform individually for the class as well. I was looking through the book one day, just flipping through the pages, when I found "Somewhere Out There." "An American Tale," I thought. I decided to do that song. We each had to practice our song in class during the last eight weeks of class. The professor sang with me on one occasion, because I was so quite.

The teacher was out one day, and I didn't hear that he wasn't going to be there. Jose saw me in the hall as usual. He made fun of me for a little bit.

Jose said that we should sing "Somewhere Out There" together, but I thought he was just kidding around because he already had his song picked out for the final.

I watched "An American Tale" to get the song correctly. We spent weeks getting the songs done correctly. Aaron was always there, but he was working with Monique on there song. They would practice at Monique's place, I over heard one day. A little spark of jealousy came over me. But when Aaron would see me in class as he got there, he would smile at me when he entered the room.

A few weeks before the semester had ended; Jose and I were walking out to get our rides. He told me that I inspired him to write a poem. I was so touched. He gave it to me and I began reading it as we were walking outside. Not seeing where I was walking, I almost walked into a tree because I was concentrating on the poem, but I looked up in time to see where I was. We got to the circle entry of the parking lot, and Jose ran to his bus. I waited for my ride, which Jose knew all about. When I got home, I went up to Subway to get my lunch. On the way there, my phone rang. It was Jose.

"Did you read the poem?" he asked.

"Yeah," I said. "I really liked it."

"What are you doing right now?" he asked.

"I'm on my way to Subway," I told him.

There was silence.

"So I guess I'll just see you in class," he said, and then we said goodbye.

When I told Mom about the poem that Jose wrote and dedicated to me she said, "You know what it means when a guy writes you a poem, right?"

"That he has nothing better to do?" I guessed half serious half sarcastically.

"It means that he likes you," she told me, but I found that ridiculous!

The next day of class, Jose was kind of being a jerk towards me, which I did not like at all. I didn't know if he was just having one of those days or not. With time, he got better.

The professor had us sing on tape, which I could not do. Jose was absent that day, but had called and told me to tell the teacher that he wouldn't be there.

I sang, but I was too quite and too nervous!

I had made up my mind that I was not going to class the next day and Mom was really angry at me in the car. I didn't want to explain myself, so I just let her yell at me. Jose told me that he couldn't really hear me and that the professor was probably going to sit down with me and go over it again. Luckily, that never happened.

The last day of my favorite show Gilmore Girls was coming. Mom and I watched it every Tuesday. It was half way through and I was already pretty upset that it was over.

Ben was walking down the hall to the bathroom to change for his night shift at Vons. Mom said something to him, and then Ben started talking. I was watching the last Gilmore episode so I said, "Shh..." Ben kept talking, but then he added a "Shh..." himself. I was so upset! Angry and broken hearted. Mom didn't say anything, so I figured she didn't acknowledge it or just didn't care. After the show ended I started crying. Mom asked if it was because of what Ben had said or if it was because it was the last show. I told her a little of both. She said that she would have made Ben apologize, but she didn't want to ruin the show for me. Too late, I thought. She knew what he did. She knew that it upset me. And still, she did nothing.

The next day, Ben came home at around 6:30 in the morning.

"Morning," he told me.

"Go to Hell," I said silently.

I was going to brush my teeth, so I was naturally walking down the hall where there was a picture of Ben, Conan, and Vicky taped to Mom's door. I tore it off and ripped it up when I was in the bathroom. Ben came over.

"Is there a reason you ripped up the picture?' he asked.

"Is there a reason you yelled at me last night?" I asked him.

He said something stupid, and then I yelled, "YOU CAN GO TO HELL!!!" around the corner of the bathroom door. Mom over heard. I just continued with brushing my teeth.

"*What's going on?*" I heard her ask.

"Mary Beth ripped up a picture," I heard Ben say.

I went outside after that and waited for Mom to drive me to school.

When she was outside, driving me to college, I told her that I wanted to move out if she was going to choose Ben and Conan over me. They made my life Hell and I could not take it anymore. I was yelled at about everything. Mom yelled at me for wanting to move out.

"Ben's looking for a place," she would always say.

On May 29th, I was sitting watching TV, and Conan comes in. Out of playfulness, I tapped him with my pillow.

"Why did you smack me?" he asked.

"Why did you always hit me?" I shot back.

"I was only a kid," he said, acting innocent. And I wasn't? I left, after Susannah yelled at me, determined to never return home. I eventually calmed down from my walk and went home. I only went back because of the animals. The people who lived there, I could care less about!

The day of our final had finally come. The teacher had us do our vocal warm ups and then we had a 20 minute break.

When everyone was back in the class, the professor had asked if anyone had wanted to go first. I immediately raised my hand to go first and get it done and out of the way.

"Mary Beth?" And I went up. I forgot the second sentence to the song, which was embarrassing, but over all I did a good job. I got a "B" in that class, so I was happy overall.

We were given a writing final as well. When I was done, I went and gave the professor my written test. He handed me my final.

I went back to my seat and got my stuff. I told Jose I would be outside. On my way out the door, Aaron was holding it open for me. He had finished both of his finals as well. We got to talking in the hall. He did a fantastic job! Aaron said that the CD had a lower key than the piano, but that he and Monique still did a great job.

If he would have asked for my phone number, I would have given it to him. I got one more smile from Aaron and then we said goodbye.

I wasn't waiting long at all for my ride. But I didn't get to say goodbye to Jose.

When the van was a few blocks away I got a call from Jose.

"Hello?" I asked.

"Hey, I'm running after you right now." I turned around.

"No, you're not," and the phone went dead.

My phone rang again.

"Hello?" I asked after seeing Jose's name.

"Hey. Sorry about that. I guess it's another ride" And we discussed stuff a little more.

The phone went dead again.

It rang one last time.

"Hello?" I asked.

"Hey," he said.

"Stop hanging up on me!" I told Jose.

"Yeah, sorry about that," and then of course there was silence.

"So, I'll just talk to you in a few weeks," I told him. And then we said our goodbyes.

The summer had approached and Mom and I were going to New York.

I was always excited to see Matt. And now Jared lived with Matt and Tom. The new bachelors pad was nice. Same place, but more things. They had a new TV. Matt had a girlfriend and so did Jared, but to my understanding, Jared's girlfriend lived in France.

Mom and I were going to be there for my birthday. I had decided a few months earlier that I wanted to see "Phantom of the Opera" on Broadway for my birthday. Mom got the tickets and Cameron wanted to come as well. My birthday was on a Wednesday.

The week before, Mom and I traveled through Connecticut, Rode Island, and Massachusetts. We went to Harvard and Yale, the two big universities that I wanted to see. I, of course, got souvenirs form both universities.

At Harvard, Mom and I were sitting outside and I saw this really cute guy staring back at me. I blushed and turned away.

Mom and I saw a dorm room at Yale. It was very small, but there was a big enough common room.

Rhode Island was great! Mom and I went to see the TAPS building from the Ghost Hunters TV show. This guy who knew them came over and started talking to us. He gave us a tour of the outside of the building.

Massachusetts was our last stop to return a car that we had rented. Mom got so lost, so I said that we should ask for directions. Mom was so upset that she was crying. There were police officers around, so I thought she would ask them. Instead she asked a drunken man and a blind man. We got more and more lost. Finally, she parked and ran inside a hotel. A nice man gave us directions to a parking structure and he drove us to our destination to get a bus back to New York.

On the day of my birthday, Tom had taken the day off from work because he had some appointment, but Mom and I caught up with him later on that afternoon. We went to a museum and walked around Central Park and then we went back to Tom's place and got changed in to nice clothes. Our first destination was Big Nick's Pizza Joint in our nice clothes. Cameron got to Tom's in plenty of time to come with us. I got a "Happy Birthday" from her and then we left. Tom had gotten me a Starbucks gift card for my birthday.

We got our pizzas and the next event was "The Phantom"! Our seats were on the second level, which I had my heights problem, but I was okay after the show started. It was unbelievably fabulous! It was then and there that I decided that I wanted to be Christine from Phantom of the Opera. I had decided that I was going to take acting that fall at college.

That night, when we got back to Tom's apartment, Tom and Cameron had cupcakes ready for my birthday. My wish was to get a happy ending at last.

Matt was supposed to be back at the apartment from his job the next day. Thursday came, but Matt was not back. Matt had told me the week before that he was going to make me watch a TV show.

"No, you're not!" I told him.

Matt laughed.

Mom and I went about town by ourselves that day.

On Friday we were supposed to meet Mom's cousin in the city and have lunch, something that I didn't really want to do. However, Mom's cousin was sick that day, so instead we went around Times Square. We found the Naked Cowboy. I had been talking about getting my picture taken with him all week. Here was the opportunity, but I was too nervous to take a picture with him. I went up anyways. The Naked Cowboy was really nice to me. He had asked where I was from and I told him. He gave me a hug and then Mom paid him three dollars for the photos she took.

Later that day, Tom had gotten off from work and was with Cameron. We were all going to have dinner that last night. Mom told Tom that I had my picture taken with the Naked Cowboy.

Tom response to that was, "He's not naked." Then he saw the pictures.

Tom's next response was, "Mary Beth, I don't want you taking your picture with anymore naked guys."

The first response in my head was "Why not?"

Instead I said, "Hey, Tom, you said so yourself: he's not naked!"

We had our dinner and then went back to Tom's. Cameron was staying over that night on the couch with Tom.

The next morning, Mom and I got up and got ready. Our flight wasn't until sometime after 10 AM. We took a taxi cab this time to JFK airport. We said our goodbyes and left. I came back to the miserable family life I had back in California.

I registered for an acting class in August and I was waiting until September for it to start, not knowing what to expect. I knew Jose was still going to be in the Music building, so I at least had someone to talk to at college that I knew.

The guy who called and threatened me in February called again in the summer. I received the message when I was at the park one afternoon. I was terrified, again, and I told Mom. We called and got a new number for my cell phone. "The police would never have done anything to protect me anyways," I thought.

I was still dealing with Hell from Ben and Conan. Conan always called me stupid and fat and he would always say, "You got run over by a car," and he wouldn't stop until I was crying. I hated him from there on out. Everyone thought I was mean to him, but no one ever said anything to him about being mean to me. What a shock!

Joe was making fun of me one day and I completely lost it. I picked up a chair and was going to bash it into his skull.

"Make fun of me one more time," I said with the chair raised over my head. I was making my soup and Joe persisted on making fun of me. He thought the soup was disgusting. I dropped the chair and I ran out of there before the microwave went off and before anyone did any real damage. The damage done to me was already complete.

I went up to the park in the middle of the afternoon and just sat down to cry. Not too long after I was just sitting there crying, this guy comes over. He asked if he could have a seat. I was trying too hard to be calm. I told him he could sit.

"Do you have a smoke?" the guy asked me.

"I don't smoke," I told him. "Smoking is stupid and my uncle died from it."

I began to touch the ring I was wearing for Jeremy that was on my middle finger.

"Who gave you that?" the guy asked.

"My boyfriend," I lied. And tears came back to my eyes, very hard.

"Can you not cry?" the guy asked. "It makes me uncomfortable."

"I was here first," I said back to him. "If you don't like it, you can leave."

"Well…" the guy said and then there was silence.

"What if your brother did something horrible so long ago and got away with it," I started to say, referring to Joe saying "Yes" after I was run over. I had never been over hearing that. Why did he get away with thinking such a horrible thing and I was doomed in Hell?

I don't know," the guy said. "Can you please tell me what you're talking about?"

"It's too painful," I cried out to him. He wouldn't understand.

"Can I read you something?" he asked.

"Sure," I said through the harsh tears that I was fighting back. And he said what sounded like a passage from the bible.

"That was nice," I told him when he was finished.

I started to cry once again.

"Just think of the good times you have with your boyfriend," the guy told me.

"Just please stop talking," I told him.

He asked to walk past me a while later, so I moved my legs down from the fence they were on. He walked out to the outside of the batting cage. It was silent for a while.

He then came back in the same way. Then he got something out of his pocket. I thought I saw a cigarette.

"Is that a cigarette?" I asked.

"Yeah," he told me. I got up to leave. "I won't smoke it, if you stay," he said again.

"No. I have someplace I have to be," I told him. I walked home. I found that the microwave was never opened and that it was still beeping. I opened it and dumped the soup in the sink. I didn't have lunch that day.

Mom was home a little later and I told her what happened. Nothing ever happened with the situation at hand. I should have guessed that nothing would, I thought.

Chapter 15

Different Types of Hell

On the first day of school, I was out on the field in the back. I called Jose. I thought her would be there.

"Hello?" he asked.

"Hey, I'm here. Where are you?" I asked.

"Who is this?" he asked again.

"Mary Beth," I said.

"Who?" he asked, again.

"Mary Beth," I said.

"Oh, hey," he began again. "Did you get a new phone? Your number's different."

"No, I had to change my number," and I gave him very few details while still being honest about my phone threats.

"Are you here?" I asked again.

"No, I got into the music school at CSUN," Jose told me.

I was a little disappointed. Jose was living up to his dream, but I thought I'd have a friendly face to remember. I told him that I had a present for him. We spoke a little longer and then said our goodbyes.

Beginning my acting class was a little nerve racking, not to mention all the stress from home. I liked not being at home during the morning hours and part of the afternoon. The first day of my class, we all had to write three things about ourselves, two that were factual and one that was not. We were to stand in the front of the class and tell what it was on the cards. The other students that asked the questions were to guess what was right and what was wrong.

I as sitting next to a girl named Mary on the first day and then she was sitting next to another Mary. My teacher, Cathy said it was the first time she ever had three Mary's in the same class. I made it loud and clear that my name was Mary Beth, not Mary.

During the next few weeks, there was this one girl that I found to be interesting. I was walking out to the front of the college, passing this vending machine when I saw this girl from my class, trying to decide what she wanted from the machine.

"Are you choosing something to eat?" I asked.

"No, I don't have any money," she said.

We got to talking a little.

"I'm really bad with names," she said. "You are?"

"Mary Beth," I answered. "I'm also awful with names. What was yours again?"

"Alyssa," she told me. We parted ways until the next class.

This other girl liked my name when we were sitting in class with our papers ready.

"Oh, I like your name," she said. I found it to be ridiculous that everyone liked my name, but after a while I got used to hearing that comment. There were these twin guys that were in my class, Albert and Gregory. They always seemed to it next to me after the first month.

I found that the girl's name was Jennifer. She loved acting almost as much as I did. She came from a Mexican family. Her older brothers still lived at home with her. She had to share a bedroom with one of her brothers. She would get into fights with her mother and father, always thinking she was mistreated. She didn't know the half of being mistreated by family members. I explained my story to her about Ben and Conan. She said I could file for restraining order based on emotional abuse. I was thinking of that more and more as the first few weeks of college disappeared.

One weekend of September, Mom told me that she really missed her room. I was so furious with Ben and Conan already. They treated everyone so horrible. I hated Ben because he thought that everyone owed him something

There was a boy in my neighborhood that I grew up with, knowing that he was there, but we never spoke to each other. He must have been three years younger than I was. I saw him staring at me during the first few weeks of September, and I stared back. He had grown up and was very good looking. However, I knew that I was much too old for him. He worked at Albertsons and I would see him there as he came over to bag Mom's groceries. He would look at me and I would look back always thinking, "When is he going to make his move!?" He never did.

One day, I was in the bathroom and I saw Ben walking into it. I was coming out, but I whispered, "Go to Hell," to him. I was too loud and he over heard me. He started laughing at me. Then I screamed "STOP LAUGHING AT ME!", but he never stopped. I slammed the door on him. He continued laughing. I screamed at him to stop laughing, and then I don't know what came over me. I couldn't see anything but the hatred that I had. I had finally said that I was going to get my bat, and went to my room. I could not see what I was doing; I was in too much angry and rage. I can remember seeing the bat, but I can't remember going back out to the kitchen. Ben was still laughing at me.

"I want a restraining order," I told him through the raging tears that streamed down my cheeks. Ben was still laughing at me.

"I'll dial for you. You're holding the bat," he said with a laugh.

It was then that I realized what was going on. I did have the bat in my hand. The rage and pure hatred that I had against Ben had finally come to this. I hated myself, but I wouldn't put the bat down.

"You take one swing, it will be your last," Ben said. I could see that there was nothing but coldness in his eyes. No concern for anyone but himself. He wouldn't help me or anyone else. Ben would just take everything that wasn't his and he never had any regrets about the whole thing.

Not knowing what to do or where to go, I ran outside with nothing but the bat. No shoes on and no socks on. I ran down the street, not knowing where I was going, or what to expect when I got there.

I began walking when I reached the end of the block. I was going to head to Tom's friend Ara's house. Maybe he would let me stay for the night. It was over a mile away. I never wanted to go home, because I knew that Mom was never gong to get rid of Ben and Conan and it was my entire fault. I was blamed enough as it was for the fact that everyone else made mistakes. I was the victim of everyone else's grievances. No matter what I was feeling, and even if Ben had killed me, she would never kick him out.

Not knowing where I was exactly on Hayvenhurst, I turned down a random street, thinking that Ara lived down there. Mom had showed me where Ara lived before, but I had forgotten. I saw a lady walking down the street, so I screamed out to her. "EXCUSE ME?!...EXCUSE ME?!..." I kept saying, but she never turned around. "Help," I whispered mainly to myself.

"EXCUSE ME?!" I yelled again. The woman stopped and turned around to see me. I went up to her crying, the bat in my hand.

"Do you know an Ara and/or Jesse live?" I asked, tear in my eyes.

"No," the woman said. "Why do you have a bat?"

"For protection," I said, just remembering that I had it. Tom was robbed at gun point and I was threatened from someone in that neighborhood, and I wasn't taking any chances. I told the woman that I ran away and I couldn't go back home. She told me that she didn't know where I could find who I was looking for. She told me to sit down and calm myself before I started to search for them again. She told me to not take my bat to the doorsteps of the houses, because other people would get the wrong impression. I took her advice, and she said, "May God be with you." I thanked her anyways. I made it to the end of a corner, and laid my bat behind me on the grass. I sat at the curb, crying. I tried my best to keep as calm as I could be, in spite of everything.

When I started crying again, I saw this blonde woman and her dog walking across the street. She saw me there crying.

"Are you okay?' she asked and came over.

I shook my head and explained what happened, without saying how I had my bat. I asked if she knew where Jesse and Ara lived. I told her that I ran away and I was not going back. It was a nightmare and I didn't want to go back to see what else was there for me to have to live with. I told her that I was going to find the house, so I got up to leave, taking the bat with me.

"What do you have that for?" she asked me.

"For protection," I screamed, again.

I went off to the house on the corner, remembering what the first woman told me. I left the bat out, titled against the garage. I went up to the door and rang the doorbell. I didn't hear anything, but I thought that the owner would hear me. I saw that the house had pigeons in a cage on the front porch. No one answered the door. I saw a man walk past the door inside. I rang the bell again when I heard him talk to someone in what I can only assume was the kitchen.

"I'll get it," he said.

He opened the door and saw me there. I didn't say anything. I could only stare in shock and fear at the man that was standing before me.

"Can I help you?" he asked after a moment.

'Does Jesse and Ara live here?" I asked through a cracked voice, trying to keep the tears down.

"No," the man said.

I looked partly behind me. "Do you know where I can find them?" I asked out of desperation.

"No," the man said again.

"I ran away and I can't go home," I told him, the tears starting to come to my eyes.

"Do you have social security?" he asked. "You could go find some place at a home," he started to say.

"I can't go home," I told him. I began to turn around. "I'm sorry to have bothered you," I told him through tears in my eyes and cracked voice. I turned back towards the driveway. I made it to where my bat was, took it, and then went down the driveway. I was going to head down to the next corner and beg them for help, only hoping to find Jesse or Ara. I had quickly changed my mind after getting across the street. I started heading back after I knew I would never find them. I made it to the previous house that I was at. I saw that the man was standing outside watching me, his wife there with him. I could feel the terror on my face as I saw them staring back at me. I checked my feet to find that they were pitch black from the ground I was walking on.

"Do you want to sit here?" the man asked, as his wife quickly walked away. "We have different pets."

I cried, looking down at the ground. "No, thank you," I said through a torn voice and the tears that fell from my cheeks.

I began walking away and I had turned south at the corner. I started heading down Hayvenhurst again, not knowing where I was going to go or where I was going to end up. "Anywhere but here," I told myself over and over. I walked in tears that were so fierce, as they ran down my face; I could barely see what was in front of me.

When I made it to the corner of Hayvenhurst and Devonshire, I stopped to see the red light in front of me. I pushed the button to have it change green again. I turned my head back to see the man running out in the street, looking both ways. I thought that he was just trying to see if I was okay. I continued waiting for the light to change. When I started to cross at the green light, it was the first time that I saw the other cars on the road through the corner of my right eye.

I continued heading down Devonshire, telling myself that I'd go to the fire station. Hopefully they would have room for me to stay the night. Where I was going the next night, I didn't know and I didn't care. I began to hear police sirens coming from behind me, but I didn't stop to see what was wrong. I figured it was a car speeding out of control or something to that effect.

I finally made it to Balboa and Devonshire to stop and wait for the light to change. I had push the button when three police cars pulled up.

"Drop the bat," a police woman said kindly, but firmly to me. It fell out of my hand and hit the ground. I leaned down to pick it up and place it to the side of the poll. It fell again and I tried again.

"Just leave it," the woman said again. I did as told. "Turn around and spread your legs apart," she told me. I did as I was instructed. I placed my hands together as well. The first woman came over to face me.

"I have a brain injury," I told her, hoping she wouldn't be too hard on me.

"I'm sorry," she said. I began crying again.

The other police woman took my hands and was going to put them in cuffs.

"Lock your fingers together," she told me to do. I tried, but couldn't get my fingers all the way together. She hurt my hands when she put the cuffs on me.

'I ran away from home, and I can't go back," I told the first officer. How many times was I going to have to tell people this? I wasn't harming anyone. I was just trying to find a place to stay for the night and then I would be out the next day. I would never come back and no one would ever have to pretend to worry about me ever again.

As I explained my story to her, I saw that the second woman was writing it all down in a notebook.

"Search her," the first officer said. So the second police woman searched every part of me, including my groan area.

"She's clear," the second officer said. I turned my head to see the man whose help I pleaded for. He was three cars down, standing with his arm folded in front of his chest. He turned me in, but why? I didn't do anything to him and I said nothing to get myself in trouble with the police.

The police woman said she would take me to the car. I asked if I could have the cuffs off. "Not yet," she said. "Watch your head," she told me as I was placed in the police car. I began to cry hard once again.

I explained my story over and over to them. The first police woman was in the front seat as the second officer spoke to me in a calm voice. She asked very specific questions and I told the story the same way to both officers.

The first police woman was typing in her computer when she asked the second officer to ask me something that I over heard at the time. I explained everything in my own words. The door closed on me twice and then the officer locked the door. I was in handcuffs, so I couldn't go anywhere even if I wanted to. They had guns, I didn't.

Eventually, after I was crying for what seemed like forever and as I was trying to get as comfortable as I possibly could be in the back of a police car, the first police officer came back and said to the second that the guy wasn't pressing any charges against me. "I didn't *do* anything to him!" I said to myself. "All I did was ask for help."

"Do you have anywhere to stay?" the first officer said. "is there anyone you can stay with?"

"What do you think I was trying to do?" I thought to myself. "No." I said to the officer.

"Could you give your home number?"

"Please don't!" I cried through fear and sadness.

The police women walked back and forth.

"Watch her," they said to each other as a new one came and went. I explained my story, again, to the male officer. I kept it a little shorter, but still saying what happened. I was so tired of being in this situation. The male officer is just a change of face, I thought.

The first officer came back and asked if I had other family I could stay with. I told her I didn't. She asked once again what my home number was. I gave in and told her. "You're not going to get out of this," I told myself. I told her Mom's full name.

The second officer told me her story of why she decided to become a police officer. Her father would beat her mother and she had tried running away many times, but was picked up twice by the cops because she had weapons in her hands. She wasn't picked up when she had a bat, though. "So why am I?" I thought.

I heard the first officer call home and ask for Mom. "I don't want to go home," I kept thinking over and over again.

"A pretty girl like you shouldn't carry a bat when she walks alone at night," the first officer told me.

"I am not pretty," I thought to myself. "So why does it matter?"

I saw Mom talking to officers outside of the police car that, a few feet away. An officer opened the door and I placed my feet on the ground.

"Not yet," she said. "You have to put them back in." So I did as was told. I waited only another minute before I could go out. I stood in front of Mom crying when the police woman unhand cuffed me. I cried to Mom. When both of my hands were free, I hugged her and told her how sorry I was through the tears that were streaming down my cheeks.

"It's okay," she told me over and over.

We were almost done, but the second officer gave Mom her card and said that if there were any problems to call her. I realized I didn't have my bat. I saw that the police were getting it out of the first car. Mom took it. I tried to carry it, but she hissed at me, "I got it." We thanked the officers, to this day I don't know why. Then Mom and I left.

"Do you want to go for a ride?" she asked me when we reached the car.

"Yes," I said through tears.

We headed down Balboa and were in the hills when I said to myself, "I don't want to go home." I was so quiet, I don't know how Mom heard me, but she did.

"*That's it*," she said, and she pulled into a parking lot. "I could have told them of how you almost attacked Ben or about a few weeks ago with you and Joe," she yelled at me. I couldn't fight anymore, so I just cried more and more. I figured she knew what Ben had said. How he threatened to kill me. "She just doesn't care," I told myself. I cried some more.

"Do you just want me to drop you off at Lenore's? Or Billy's? He would be so excited to see you," she said out of disgust.

"No," I told her. I wanted Ben and Conan gone forever. I never wanted to see them again, and I told her that over and over.

"You can stay in the hospital night," she said to me out of rage.

"No," I told her. Why couldn't she act like a caring parent towards me? All of her caring ness went to Joe after he did something wrong, Susannah after she did something wrong, or Ben and Conan after they did something much more wrong than I could ever imagine!

"What am I supposed to do?" she asked me through hatred towards me.

"Throw them out," I said.

"No," she told me in hatred.

We sat there for a little longer. Mom wanted to know if I was hungry. She was thirsty and wanted something to drink.

We ended up at home.

"You can stay in the car or come inside," she said through hatred towards me. I wanted to run, but I got up and went inside. I could see Ben sitting in front of the TV, not giving a damn at what he had put me through. How surprising.

I went straight to my room and closed the door with force.

I tried to sleep, or do what I could at rest. I was too fed up with everyone. I hated the family I had from there on out, but I knew I'd have to come out of my room eventually.

Mom entered my room at one point, but I pulled the covers over my head. I was not going to see her or talk to her. She would make me feel worse, I knew it.

After a few hours of silence in my room, I told myself to go out and apologize to Mom. I found her and Susannah standing in the living room staring back at me. I could tell they were talking about me before I came in. I came over to Mom and hugged her. I sat in front of the TV and Mom brought me a tub of water for my feet.

The night did pass, but the memories lived on.

Returning to school that week was much better than having anything to do with home. I was free to think for myself. Everyone thought that everything was my entire fault, so getting out was better for my mind, body and soul.

Jennifer was there and so were Albert and Gregory. After class on that Tuesday, Jennifer and I got talking about our weekends.

"I had the worst weekend ever," Jennifer started to say.

"Nothing can compare to how horrible mine was," I told her, choking up inside. "But you can go first."

Jennifer started describing how her brothers were and how her parent treated her. That was nothing compared to my weekend! I started to tell her what happened to me after she was done.

"And the police put me in handcuffs," I said. I left out the fight with Ben., "just because I was carrying a bat."
"I live in Van Nuys. Don't carry a bat," she told me.

"I just want to move." There was no other way to live through a family from hell.

Tracey had called and wanted to see me. We were going to have lunch. I didn't know why, but I soon figured it out.

On our way to get lunch, she told me that she heard what happened. She didn't judge me, though.

She made a pretty crude joke when she dropped me off. I had already told her that I asked Mom to get rid of my bat. Mom said she took it somewhere that I would never find it.

By October 11th, Albert and I were in an improv together. We had to do a fighting scene. We only had so much time to practice for the next 1 and a half.

"We should be a couple," Albert started to say.

"Why do we have to be a couple?" I asked. "Why can't we just be strangers beating each other up?"

"We should be a couple and one of us cheats on the other," Albert said.

"Fine," I agreed. "We're married. My character cheats on yours." And we started to practice beating each other up. We had everything worked out and we went over it a few times. We took our seats after eight minutes of rehearsal, and we waited for our turn. While we sat there waiting, Albert looked at me and said, "I'm going to take your hand at the end." I agreed, having no objection to it, and thought he was only going to take it.

Our scene finally came up and the fighting began. We slapped each other, I kicked him, and he pulled my hair. Then he takes my hand.

"Okay, let's go have make up sex," Albert said, taking my hand with him. I laughed and so did the rest of the class. We had not rehearsed that.

I was getting better at pretending that Sunday didn't happen. Or at least I was better at trying to move forward.

I had tried to search for the right monologue to do. I wanted to do a scene for "10 Things I Hate About You," but Cathy aid it was best to not do movies.

By October 16th, the mid term had come. I found a monologue to do. My character was writing a letter to her father who was in jail. When I first found it and read over it, I laughed. It started out so incident. Then she asks how jail was treating him.

Another guy in my class, Oliver, was going over it with me. I helped him with his monologue and he did the same with me. We weren't supposed to do a scene from a movie, but he did. Oliver was a cute boy with blonde hair, but I didn't act any differently towards him.

I had gone to a support group that Mom had taken me to twice. That night was my second time. We were there a little late, but only by ten minutes. When we walked in, there was this girl that was bitching about her father taking up all her time because he was in a coma. I hated her right then and there. When she was talking a little bit, I started to get upset, so I told Mom that I was going to go to the bathroom. I didn't say why. When I got back, she was still bitching on why she didn't have any time of her own due to the fact that her father was in a coma and was taking up all her time. When she wouldn't stop complaining, I started to cry again. I was in a support group that I didn't want to be in and I was in it with a woman that hated her father, because he was in a coma and was taking up all her time.

After the woman was done, Mom started talking and saying how it had nothing to do with her. It was her father that was suffering, not her.

No one there really knew what it was like to have a brain injury. There was another woman who would smile at me and her husband who had a brain injury. I was finally crying my eyes out and decided to leave. I just went out to the elevator and waited for it to get to that floor. The elevator got there and I went down stairs to wait. I was fighting with myself and with everyone else. I waited for over an hour and I went back up stairs to get Mom. Everything was done. Mom said that the rest of the people in the group really liked me, but I did not care! "What the hell do they know about having a brain injury, always be introduced that way, being a teenager, and being a girl all at once?" The only other people in there that had brain injuries were men, so I stood out, again.

I told Mom I never wanted to go back again! For once, she didn't make me, but I had other things that she was making me do.

Susannah wanted to get a dresser, so I had to move my air hockey table outside. The weather destroyed it. But Susannah got what she wanted.

I was battling with everyone and everything in so many different ways. I was battling with myself. Maybe life isn't that hard, I thought. Maybe you're just making it seem harder than what it really is. Then why do I want to die? I argued with myself. No one else has to deal with everything this way.

The mid term came and went on a Tuesday. My teacher, Cathy, wanted me to do it again, but I explained that I wasn't going to be there the next week, because I was going to be out of state.

By Thursday, Albert thought I wasn't going to be there.

"Do you want me to leave?" I asked out of sarcasm.

"No," he said quickly. "I just thought you said you'd be gone today." That's cute, I thought, you were listening.

That weekend Mom and I went to Nevada to get her stuff from storage in Nevada.

Life seemed to pass by with me being in hell and going deeper and deeper into it. I thought there was something to look forward to in the end.

I had become friends with a girl, Julisa, in class. So Jennifer, Julisa and I would just hang out after class.

On Tuesday, October 30th, I was standing outside of the Theatre Arts building. I check my phone to see what time it was. I found that I had a text message from Jose. Checking it, he asked how I was.

I answered to him that I was fine, and then I asked if he wanted to hang out that Friday at the bookstore, something we had always talked about. First he said yes, but a little later he said he had to work. He texted me back and asked if I wanted to go to see an opera instead. I started jumping up and down! "Is this a date?" I thought.

Julisa came over and I told her what happened and asked what she thought. She told me that it was a date. Jennifer said it was a date. Mom said it was a date. I emailed Tom and he said it was a date. I emailed Kelly and asked her, and sure enough she said it was a date. I still wasn't sure.

I waited until November 2nd and I went to CSUN. Mom came with me to find the building. We got really lost. She made me feel stupid. I didn't need my mommy there to hold my hand.

I found Jose sitting outside the music building. We had an awkward moment beforehand. I didn't know whether I should hug him after we hadn't seen each other for months or not. We went inside and found our seats. The opera was incredible. Then there an intermission break and we went out to the front. Jose's friend came over. He was talking to Jose. Jose pretended to forget my name, so I introduced myself to the other guy. Then Jose and I went back to our seats to see the rest of the show.

The end came and I applauded. Then Jose and I went back out to the lobby area. His friend came back over and the guys were talking a little longer. Then Jose and I were going to go outside and wait for our rides.

"It was nice meeting you," I told Jose's friend.

When Jose and I were outside, we talked about everything that was going on in our lives, just like the last semester.

'So this was fun," I told him.

"Yeah," Jose started. "I've seen this three times."

"Why the hell would you say that to a girl that you're going out with?" I thought in that one brief second.

"And the first time I saw it, I thought of you."

"I was thought of!?" I said, pulling my hands to my chest. I thought that was so touching that he thought of me first.

We talked for a while longer, and then his ride showed up. He spoke to someone and waited with me for my ride. Mom finally came and I said goodbye to Jose.

I still missed Jeremy like crazy! I cried every night, always praying for him.

By November 19th, I had made friends with a guy on a dating site online. We traded email address and Ryan and I became friends. We emailed each other for a while, but then he stopped. I was hurt. What did I say wrong? What did I do?

Julisa and I became partners for the final. We did a dialogue called, "Juliet revisited." We both wanted to cynical character, but I got it because I found the dialogue.

I really enjoyed doing an improv with Gregory during the last few weeks. We were placed in the same group to do a fairytale. We had "Jack and the Bean Stock." Everyone had their parts except me. It was decided that the giant had a wife, so I was her. I just needed to be annoying, something that I was natural at.

"Fee fie foe fum. I smell the blood of an English man," Greg said. I come out.

'We were supposed to go shopping. I can't believe you forgot we were going shopping. We were supposed to get curtains, and I was going to get a hat and a purse…" Someone else came out. "And what about this…" I went on.

"Shot up!" Greg shouted, covering his ears. The audience laughed. After the class, Gregory said I did a good job.

Julisa and I continued to practice for weeks and the final finally came. We had gone first in class.

We had our laughs from the class. It was hard for me to keep a straight face.

Mom was going through a lot with her heart doctor appointments. She told Ben that she needed her room back. He said he was going to move out by the end of the year and I was excited to get rid of him for once and for all. That never happened.

I was angry with hatred and furry in my blood. It was then that I told myself that I was never related to him. It at least made me feel better for the time being, even though I still felt like dying.

I emailed Ryan over and over, but he wasn't responding. I decided to move on. But I also swore I'd get my revenge on him.

Jonathan was ignoring me now, so I had nothing to lose in the love department.

Christmas was coming. Susannah had asked me if I wanted to pick a name from a hat.

"No," I said. "I'm going to get the people who deserve presents." I said this with Ben sitting at the table. And he knew why.

Tom had come out for Christmas. He got me a purple sweatshirt that I loved. It became my favorite sweatshirt from him and Cameron. Mom was doing well with her heart, but that only meant that Ben was never going to move out.

Mom's friend Mary Beth died on Christmas morning. I somewhat remembered her. I went to the memorial with Mom. People that I hadn't seen in years were there, and no one really remembered me. Mom said I was named after her, but I knew that wasn't true. That wasn't the story she originally gave me. Chuck had named me. I only received so many good things from him.

Chapter 16

New Revenge

I had gotten back in contact with Ryan for revenge. I swore that I was going to break his heart the same way he broke mine. I'd show him what it felt like. I changed my email address while still keeping my old email address. He picked up right away and we became friends instantly. I swore to myself that I wasn't going to be the one to get hurt this time. No, it was going to be Ryan. I still liked him, but my revenge was more important to me.

He wounded my heart.

Every night felt like my last. It was a weird feeling, like I knew something was coming for me and I could stop it. I said my all my goodbyes and prayed every night, but it felt horrible and terrible that this could be the end of me. I'm sure everyone else would have been happier without me here on earth. That was the reaction that I got from everyone. I was unappreciated and it hurt. But there was nothing I could do about it.

"If you didn't want me, then why id you bring me back from the dead?"It seemed that everyone was always acting with me and said that they loved me and wanted me there. Why? So they cold tease me about carrying a bat? Or they could make fun of me, because I tried to kill someone? Or maybe they just wanted to kill me themselves?

I spent my nights crying. I cried, not just for Ryan, who half the time was ignoring me\, but for the end that I knew was coming. I hadn't done much in life. I was never really given a chance to do anything that I wanted. Everyone wanted me to do what they wanted or what they thought was right. And if I got something wrong or wasn't successful enough, it was my fault.

Mom had forced me into Psychological therapy without my consent.

"You're going, and you're not getting a choice here," she told me. I wanted to protest, but I could never find my voice. It made me angry that I was the one who was blamed for everything. I wasn't the one who let Ben and Conan move in or the one who made them stay. She took all of anger out on me because I was the weakest and the easiest victim. She could say whatever she wanted to me and I would just take it. I wouldn't be given a chance either way. So I went.

I had gone back to college, again, even though I didn't really want to. I just wanted everyone off my case, so I chose the safest way to do that which was agreeing with them. I learned very soon after the first day that that wasn't the way to go. Everyone had their opinion of how my life should go, but it was *my* life. Not theirs. They just didn't get that.

The singing class that I was in for a day was interesting. The teacher had us doing a poem by Emily Dickenson. I was in the group of people that did the high notes because I didn't know where my vocal range was. I was in the group with this nice girl that I met. She thought she had seen be before in another class at night, but I assured her that it wasn't me. She was nice to talk to. That was my first and last day at that school in that class. It broke my heart to quit, but no one ever had to deal with the anxiety that I had to deal with. And I hated being compared to everyone else. Did they know what it felt like to come back from the dead? Did I miss something?

I was in contact with Jose through text messaging, again. He told me that he was in an opera. I told him that I wanted to go, so he got me a ticket to see it. The opera was over at CSUN. He said he was playing a cat, which I thought nothing of at first. Then the opera started. This guy comes out, playing a little boy being mean to everyone and everything. Then the objects around him come to life. Jose was the cat. Then there were the stuffed animals and other toys coming to life all around the little boy.

I laughed all threw the opera, but I tried very hard not to. Jose's only line was "Meow." I was thinking, "You must have really had to practice very hard for that one!"

After the opera was done, I wanted to see Jose, so I waited downstairs. I took a picture of him and these other girls. Then Jose and I were going to hang out for a while, or so I thought. I opened my arms for a hug, and I had warm butterflies when Jose gave me a hug. We hadn't seen each other since last October. But it felt like it was a good thing. Was this where I was supposed to be?

The cast was going to get something to eat, but Jose was going to stay with me until my mom came back for me. I met the guy who played the child. He was nice and had an incredible voice! The guys hung out with me for a shot amount of time.

I assured them that I was fine standing there on my own. It was a university. Nothing was going to happen.

"Are you sure?" Jose asked, and I could hear a little anxiety in his voice.

"Yeah," I told him. "Don't worry about it."

"Okay," Jose said and then he gave me another hug for goodbye.

I said goodbye to the other guy as well and then I watched them both walk away. I stood there with nothing but the street light on. A skateboarder came by, and then I saw Mom in the distance. I began walking over to her.

I told her of the opera and how Jose played a cat. She and I both thought that was hilarious!

I had asked Jose, a few weeks later; if he wanted to just hang out at the book store with me, something that we had always planned on doing. He asked what time and I asked if 12 o'clock was okay with him. First he said yes, but then he asked if 10 AM would be okay. I told him that would be fine. It didn't go that way, though.

I had gotten to the bookstore a little before 10 AM. Mike worked security in that parking lot, so he was there. I had texted Jose that I was there. Twenty minutes went by, I texted asking where he was. Forty minutes, "I'm so angry at him," I thought, but I tried texting him again. No response. An hour went by, "I'm never talking to Jose again," I thought. "He'll be here soon," that little voice inside me said.

Mike came by a few times and asked if I was okay. He knew that I was meeting one of my friends, but he wasn't there yet.

So I waited…and waited.

I went to get coffee at Starbucks while I waited.

An hour and thirty minutes had passed. I got a text message on my phone, "I'm so sorry that I'm late," Jose wrote.

"Where are you?" I asked. No response. So I continued to wait, tears springing to my eyes.

I went inside the bookstore alone and then came out again. I waited twenty more minutes, and then I went inside. I rushed to the restroom with tears in my eyes.

"This is just like high school," I thought. 'Am I just that unlikable?" I stayed in the restroom with the stall door closed, just crying there, until someone came in. I wiped my tears away. Then my phone started to buzz. I got a message from Jose.

"I'm here," it read.

Coming out from the stall, I wiped my eyes and straighten up in front of the mirror.

I pretended to look at a book while I saw Jose came around the corner.

"Hey," he said cheerfully. I wouldn't look him in the eye. "Are you mad at me?" he asked.

"No," I lied through a cracked voice, still looking at the book in front of me. I got over the mood I was in pretty fast. Jose's friend had dropped him off, so we hung out for two hours. We laughed and joked around. He bought CDs and books.

Mom had gotten there. She and Mike were standing together to the side.

I didn't give Jose a hug goodbye, because I felt that he didn't deserve anything.

"Adios," I said as I turned away.

"Bye," I heard him.

Now that I wasn't going to college, I felt that I had let Tom down, and it broke my heart. I didn't really care what anyone else's opinion of me was, but to let Tom down was the most difficult thing to deal with. The thing was that no one really understood why I couldn't go back to college. It didn't mean that I didn't want to go back. More than anything, I wanted to go back and be as normal as anyone else.

Mom had me get help finding a job. It wasn't the job I wanted. The only thing about it that I liked somewhat was that I was with other people. The part that was horrible was that Leslie, who "helped" me, said that I needed to be realistic about my goals. I said I wanted to work in music. I wanted to do something out of the realm that everyone always had me in: a grocery store bagger, or a receptionist. I was neither and no one saw that. I wasn't seen as anything more than a freak of nature to people and it hurt. I fought back with everything that I had, even though a big part of me had given up.

"No one wants you to live your life, fine," I told myself. "But they will be sorry," another part of me said. "I will not do what others want me to do."

I tried very hard to be pleasant and to work things out with Leslie, John, Mom, Tom, and Tracey. They all wanted me to go back to school and to get a job.

"Take anxiety medication, Mary Beth," they'd all tell me. I was still trying to work things out from just going to psychological therapy once a week. I was hating the person that I had become. I told myself that I'd never give up on my dreams and I wouldn't give up on my life, but so many people were pushing me in too many different directions. It hurt to keep going down this path, but it hurt worse giving up.

"When I decided to come back to earth, I didn't mean for it to end this way," I always told myself. I was fighting the biggest battle ever. It was a war field between me and everyone else. I wouldn't let them win.

I had started not feeling so good by the end of February, but now in March, I began feeling worse. I had dizzy spells that lasted quite a while, but they would go away eventually throughout the day. I thought I was dying. "I'm going to die without having my first kiss," I'd say to myself. "Great."

To get me through the night each night, I'd pretend that Ryan was there with me. But it had been a few weeks since Ryan last contacted me. I was broken. Why had I fallen in love with Ryan? He said he'd fallen for me, but I knew that he was better off without me. I couldn't handle the pressure of being in my own shoes, and I didn't expect that he could do that either. He lost his first love, and I lost all the guys that I loved.

I wanted so badly to go out to New Jersey to see him. Things at home were getting more and more difficult to deal with and my health problems weren't helping any. I had made up my mind that I was going to go to New Jersey, but then I quickly changed my mind because I had to save my money for New York. I told Ryan my plans. He said that we could meet in Central Park. He had fallen for me and I was falling for him, again.

After only a few weeks of texting and emails, I had said to myself that it was enough. I had to end things with Ryan, because I didn't want to hurt him. I didn't want him to hurt me after finding out the truth about my brain injury. It seemed to be harder on me than I had originally thought, but time healed everything.

By early April, Mom told me that we were going to go to Oregon to visit her friend Peggy. I wasn't too thrilled about that. Peggy drank alcohol and that completely made me sick. The only reason I'm going, I told myself, is so that I can see Jeb.

I had told Mom one day at the grocery store that I was too dizzy to walk to where she was at, only a few feet away.

The job hunting experience was getting more and more difficult to put up with. I hated Leslie for saying, "You need a job that is realistic," and I hated John for saying, "We'll get there eventually, but first we should start with something a little more easier. You could bag groceries." I told them that I wanted to work with music, but my dreams were stupid to them and my opinion about *my own* future didn't matter to anyone.

By May, the New York trip came. I was worried about the cat. Who was going to take care of her? I had begun hating Ben more than ever! I hated how he was always at home, how mean and selfish he was towards everyone, and how he got away with it. I was treated worse than shit, but he was treated like a king. Just writing his name would even disgust me. I hated that!

Mom got upset at me one night because I had left the dinner table at dinner time. Ben had used my hot sauce without asking whose it was.

"Do you want me to cancel the trip?" she said through hated towards me.

I turned back. "Please don't," I said. I could see the rage in her eyes towards me. I went to my room and tried to block out Ben's voice. He had a volume to his voice that no one else had. I listened to my CD player and wrote a new poem, but I couldn't escape the pain I was in. I got up after the poem was finished and had put my shoes on. I wasn't going to stay at home anymore and put up with this shit. I had yelled at Mom enough and had been yelled at way too much for things that I couldn't control. Some were little mistakes that I made, but I was yelled at for all the things that went wrong. I was the easiest target.

I was only gone for one hour and ten minutes, making it down to these apartments. I asked a man what time it was and decided to go back home. Who was I kidding anyway? I came back and apologized, but I knew that nothing was going to change.

Joe was yelling and screaming in his room one day. He was throwing everything out into the hall way and he kept marching in and out of the house. He yelled and screamed at no one. It scared me, so I emailed Tom right away and told him what was going on, and then I got my shoes on and decided to go to Starbucks, two and a half miles away. I made it out the door okay. Then I called Mom and told her.

When I got back about an hour later with my coffee, Joe's car wasn't home. I found that there was a whole in Joe's door, about the size of his shoe.

By May 23rd, I told myself that I wasn't going to fall in love for a very long time. "Not anymore," I told myself. "You get hurt to much."

I wasn't over Jeremy, Tom, Ryan, or Matt, But I swore that I was going to be.

Mike's girlfriend Ashley, who was only two years older than I was, was pregnant. While we were in New York, Mom got upset at me for being afraid of heights. We saw her cousins.

A few mornings, we went out for breakfast at The Flying Saucer, a small coffee shop in Brooklyn. It was so good. It was where Tom and Cameron always went. They had great bagel sandwiches and really good coffee there. We would sit outside and have our breakfast.

On our last night in New York, Cameron, Tom, Mom, and I went out to eat. After that, Tom and Cameron wanted to go to the bar close to their house. I was only 19, but they said I could get in, because no one checked IDs at the door. It was one of the oldest bars in Brooklyn. I had no objections. We went to the back room where there was a pool table. Cameron was going to get the drinks.

"Mary Beth, do you want a soda?" she asked.

"No, water's fine," I told her. Mom, Tom, and I sat back there and waited. Eventually Cameron came back with the drinks. I could officially say that I was drinking in a bar in Brooklyn.

Tom said that his friend Robert was interested in seeing some of my writing. I was very excited that I could have a new friend to show my writing to. Robert had a band, but Tom told me that he was going to talk to Robert about helping me out with my stuff.

I had decided to leave all of my old loves in New York. They weren't bringing pleasure to me at all anymore. So on May 31st, and I said goodbye to all the loves I had. I was going to be a free woman and not think or cry about any other guy again!

Tracey had come to Susannah's birthday party in June. She made me feel really bad about giving up on the job hunting experiences that I had. No one knew what it took for me to go through that shit. I never liked throwing in the towel, but I was throwing in the towel on everyone else's hopes and expectations for my future. They didn't see me doing much, I could see that.

I had found out that one of my friends smoked. He was ruining his health, so I did research again on smoking and all of the horrible things that could happen when you smoke. I passed the information along to Pam.

On Saturday, June 14th, Mom and I went to an improv in Sherman Oaks. We usually went to improv shows together from time to time. I was to write down some quirky saying that I used in every day conversation. I was going to write, "Use your diaphragm," but Mom was laughing at me and told me no. I was still going to use it, but she kept saying no. I finally said, "To hell with it," to myself, and I told her I wouldn't write anything. She had to control my life, fine. I stayed silent.

"Oh, I'm sorry," she said. I wasn't hearing any of it, because I knew that she couldn't be that sorry. "Here, write, "What do you mean 'dude'?"" she said. I wasn't having it though. She had to twist everything around all the time on me.

Then it turned out that my slip of paper wasn't chosen in the big pile during the improv. Imagine that.

The actors were hilarious! I fell in love that night, after swearing to myself that I wouldn't fall in love for a very long time. His name was Tyler.

I kept looking over at him and he chose to do some of the options that I yelled out. I got a smile from him, even though I'm sure he never saw my face that night. I had butterflies the size of wasps in my stomach.

When the next day rolled around, Sunday, I was doing research to find out who this beautiful man was. He had everything that I wanted. I found his myspace page and I said to myself, "What the hell?" I sent him a message, expecting nothing in return. "Hoping for the best, but expecting the worst", was my motto.

I checked my email the next day to find that I had a new one. It was from him! Tyler wrote back and thanked me for the compliment that I gave him. He said that I should go see him in his show that was on Fridays. My birthday was on a Friday! I was super excited!

For my birthday, Mom and I were going to go to the beach, but it was turning more into baby sitting at the beach. Conan and Sabrina had to come. I put my foot down and said no, but Mom said I didn't have a chose in the matter. It was my birthday and I wasn't allowed to say how I could spend it.

Ben said that he was going to take Conan to the mall later, so Conan wasn't coming. But I was still left with suffering with Sabrina. My birthday never seemed to be about me. I tried to put up with it. "After all, you and

Mom are going to see Tyler tonight," I told myself. The good part was that Mom didn't know about Tyler. I wanted to keep her out of my love life as much as possible. She just made me feel bad about everything that had to do with that kind of stuff.

I got a wicked sun burn at the beach. I had put on sun screen all over my body, but it wasn't enough. I put up with Sabrina being the little brat that she was. She said, "I have a boyfriend," like she was rubbing it in my face. She found out that Ashley had gotten pregnant, and she seemed really excited about that. I did have a good time with Sabrina that day, but I was gearing up for that night.

Mom found the improv. We were, again, to write down things to say. I didn't know why. Tyler was there and that was all that mattered to me. Tyler smiled at me when he needed a name for one of the groups on stage. The Jolly Roger won!

Another actor, Zeke, asked me a lot of questions for part of the improv.

I was falling madly in love with Tyler. Part of me said that it was true love. It had to be! I battled that issue with myself, maybe a little too much.

Tom had come out on June 22nd. Mom and I had gone to the store and had gotten ice for the BBQ that was going to happen in the back yard.

Tom and his girlfriend Cameron had gotten to the house early.

Mom and I had just gotten back from the store, when we saw Jesse and Ara getting over to the house. I gave Jesse a hug and then Ara. I carried in a bag of ice, and Jesse helped out, carrying in the other one. I waited what felt like forever to get a hug from Jesse. I still had a crush on him.

Susannah was talking about little Tom, and for the first time ever, I didn't have any emotion towards that. It surprised me, because normally I would explode into tears or rage, but for once, I felt nothing.

It was the first day that I was ever comfortable in a large group of people. I wasn't making friends right away, but it was amazing to me that I was in a group of people.

I had asked Essence to come, but she was seeing a concert that day instead.

I socialized for over two hours, which was a major improvement for me to do. I was very pleased with myself, but I ended up in my room. Socializing for me was overwhelming and exhausting.

I heard Ben talking about Ashley, "She doesn't look pregnant," he said. "I bet she's faking it." This upset Ashley a lot, and surprisingly it upset me also.

Mom was mad at me for God knows what reason. I didn't spend enough time outside. I was just getting comfortable with the big transition that I was making with my own life. She should be happy, right?

The next week, I got up the courage to ask Tyler out to coffee. In modern times a woman can ask a man out. It was only coffee, I told myself, and if he said no, the world would not end. I asked him the week before that last weekend of June.

Sure," Tyler wrote back. "I can't go this weekend because my sister is getting married." I was sitting down at my computer in my bedroom when I received the email.

I looked over both my shoulders and had three different reactions to that.

"I didn't need to know that much information… I don't know how to respond to that; and *I didn't mean right now!* My head turned back to my laptop. "Ooh, are you going to catch the bouquet? Oh my God," I thought.

I wrote back that it was fine. I didn't expect anything anyways.

I wrote down a date and Tyler had agreed. Tyler and I were supposed to meet on a Tuesday, but I wanted to look really good. I asked if the 7th was good for him and he said yes.

I was out with Essence one night and I told her about Tyler. She said that I should email him back with the question, "Did you catch the bouquet?" She thought it was funny. So I did.

Tyler's response to that was, "No, I did not catch the bouquets."

"Well, I'm sure you'll be invited to another wedding," I wrote. "Don't lose hope!"

Sabrina was the only other person that I told besides Essence about my coffee date with Tyler. She was very excited for me. The kid had a boyfriend already!

Tyler told me to where a nametag, so I searched high and low for one. I told him I would be wearing my Harvard hat instead.

On Saturday, July 5th, I wasn't feeling too good. The tube inside my neck was hurting me a lot. I was also very dizzy. It was coming and going a lot lately. "No," I told myself. "You're going to meet Tyler and it will be wonderful!" I didn't want to cancel again, so I got up the courage and stuck it out. "You're doing this because you like him and if he likes you back, great. If not, it's not the end of the world," even though it felt very much like it.

I had butterflies in my stomach for two days straight before the day happened. "It's going to be the time of your life. You'll see." I tried to brush it off. Essence and I were supposed to go shopping so I cold get a cute outfit, but I ended up shopping with Mom. I found a pair of cute jeans and a cute blouse. I am not going to make a big deal out of this, I told myself over and over. "It's just coffee. It's just coffee." The butterflies were swarming more and more in my stomach.

I had drawn two pictures of hearts. One had a dagger threw it, while the other did not. Sabrina really liked them, so I told her when I was done I'd make her a copy of it. Mom really liked them as well.

I told myself not to tell Mom about the coffee experience. "She will just make you feel bad and she won't want you to go," I told myself. "This is your day. No one else's! And there is still a chance that he won't be there."

"It's not the end of the world, though," I told myself over and over. "If he doesn't show, you'll be okay."

Tyler emailed me on Sunday and had asked where this Starbucks was. "I can just see it now," he wrote. "We'll be I two different Sawbucks' at the same time. Just like the movies!" I laughed and then I looked up the address. I gave him specific details about the location; other stores that were there as well, just in case. "I hope to see you there," I wrote at the end.

I set my alarm for 6 AM the next morning.

Chapter 17

Love at First Sight

Monday morning had come at last. The alarm went off.

"Why did the alarm go off?" I thought at first. "OH, MY GOD! TYLER!" How could I have forgotten? I got up and ate breakfast, trying hard to pretend that everything was normal, even though on the inside I was howling at the top of my lungs! I didn't tell Mom that much information. I said that I was going up to get coffee that morning at Starbucks.

I didn't want to feel bad or stupid about the choice I was making on my own.

I finished my breakfast and was taking a shower when Mom left. I wanted to look good.

I left at eight o'clock. I wanted to have time to write a letter to Tom. I was going to be sending him a picture and I wanted to explain why I did the picture. I knew that he and Cameron were going to be out of the country soon on a trip, soon enough.

I was heading down Mission Blvd. towards Hayvenhurst. I knew the way to Starbucks. I figured I'd be there an hour early so I could write the letter to Tom. That wasn't what happened.

I crossed San Fernando Mission on Hayvenhurst just fine, but I forgot to turn left.

"Where am I going?" I asked myself when I was passing some apartments. I turned around and started heading down Hayvenhurst.

I finally got to Starbucks. I checked the clock that hung on the wall. 9:30. "I still have time to write," I told myself. I ordered myself a large coffee and sat down at an empty table. There was someone behind me at another table. I just began writing.

Every time I heard someone come in, I looked up to find that nothing was really going on. Tyler wasn't there yet. "It's not 10 yet," I told myself, trying to remain calm. "What do I talk about? What do I say?" I was overwhelmed by this feeling. "No," I told myself. "Stay calm. Stay cool and collected. It's going to be okay. You'll be fine." I tried to motivate myself as much as possible. I looked up from my sketch for the last time.

I froze in my seat. Here he was. The most beautiful man I had ever seen. I stared in wonder, knowing that I looked like an idiot. "Look away! Look away! Look away!" I told myself over and over again. But I couldn't. My eyes were glued to him. "He came! How do I act? What do I say? How do I look?" My eyes were frozen on him.

He got his coffee that he was waiting for.

He turned to me with his head tilted back a little and his eyes on me. "Harvard," he said.

I was overwhelmed with a million different emotions. I looked down at my papers, a little embarrassed. My heart was pounding. Butterflies the size of moths filled my stomach.

"Have you been waiting here long?" Tyler asked me.

"No, not long," I told him. "I've been here since 9:30. I left my house at 8, but didn't get here until 9:30, because I got lost walking over here." I looked up to see him smiling.

I went on talking a mile a minute, not knowing what to say.

"My mom's a paralegal." Stupid, I thought. Why would you tell him that?

"What does your dad do?" Tyler asked.

"He's dead," I told him.

"Oh," Tyler said.

I told him that I hated the color red just because some guy in boxing was named Red. Why would you tell him that? I thought. You're an idiot!

"Well what if his name was…" Tyler gave me three things to think about, and I told him that it didn't matter to me. "What if his name was Harvard?" he finally asked.

"You're over thinking this," I told him, looking back at the table. It was the safest place to be looking when you didn't have a clue what you were doing.

"I'm going to make you like the color red," he told me with a smile on his face as he was looking down on his half of the table.

"No you're not," I said with a smile on my face. *How stupid could you get?* I thought to myself. I looked down to my shoes to find that Tyler's feet were stretched out to my side of the table. *Did he mean for that to happen?* I thought. *Was it an accident? Do I just make him feel that relaxed and comfortable?* I let it slide without asking.

Then I went back to talking a mile a minute about everything and nothing in particular.

"I need napkins," Tyler said. He left and went up to the counter.

Don't say anything stupid anymore, I told myself. Ask about him.

I was half surprised when Tyler came back.

"Do you have any brothers or sisters?" I asked. That seemed like a safe subject.

"Yes," he said calmly. I have one older brother and two younger sisters. They are all teachers. Growing up, my sisters were the ones to get all the attention from my parents. My brother and I were saying, "Well, what about us?"'"

"Yeah," I said. "I heard that the middle child is the rebel." He was an actor, they weren't. That was my philosophy on the whole thing.

"I always thought that it was the youngest?" Tyler said as I was looking at the table.

"So what does this mean about your sister?" I thought.

"I always thought it was the middle child," I said.

Then I looked into his beautiful eyes again to find that he was looking at me.

"Do you have any brothers and sisters?" Tyler asked in a calm voice.

"Yes, I have five brothers," I told him, but a short while later I would forget. "I never met my oldest brother, Griffin, though. I think he lives east. My brother Tom lives in New York. He went to college at Berkeley. He is studying at Pratt University to become an architect. And Joe is into production. He did a short film and got an award from," I started rolling my right hand, "that guy that played the dad in Selena."

"Edward James Almos?'

"There you go," I said with my right hand moved out towards him. "It's just Joe and his stupid friends running around in tunnels wearing gas masks. How is that considered good?" I looked back to see that Tyler had that same playful look on his face.

"Well, maybe it just depends on the person," Tyler said.

"I still don't understand," I told him, shaking my head.

Then I went on talking a mile a minute about others things. Making a complete ass of myself, and Tyler just sat there and took it all in. The expression on his face almost reminded me of, "Oh my god! How much longer am I going to have to sit here?" But he sat and listened. I tried to make a joke, and I could tell that he was laughing out of kindness.

We spoke of other things. He told me about his friend Zeke.

I finally had a story that I remembered that had some laughs to it before.

"I was in New York this last May. My mom, my brother Tom, his girlfriend and I went out to dinner the last night there. After dinner, Tom and Cameron wanted to go get a drink in a bar. I'm only 20," I pointed out, pulling my hands to my chest. "But they don't check IDs at that bar, so I could get in. So I can say *for a fact*," I closed my eyes and tilted my head back, "that I was drinking in a bar in Brooklyn." I quickly opened my eyes to find that I was staring at Tyler's grey shirt. "It was water," I assured him, moving my hands erratically. "But non-the-less," I looked up to my right side, and then went back to tilting my head back and closing my eyes, "I was drinking in a bar in Brooklyn."

I opened my eyes, acting normal again, to find that Tyler had the biggest grin on his face. He looked beautiful.

"You can use that as an improv," he told me. "So are you coming back?"

I was shocked and flattered.

"Eventually," I said looking to the right.

I then told him the other part of the story. He just looked at me as if he thought I was adorable. Then I went on jabbering away, talking a mile a minute about nothing particular. He had that same gorgeous look on his face, like he was concentrating on every word I was saying. I was howling at the top of my lungs on the inside.

"HE WANTS ME TO COME BACK!"

Silence came for a second.

"I like the pictures," I said, turning my head towards the wall. I turned back to him.

"I always wanted to steal the pictures from IHOP," he said.

"You could take a picture of food that you make and hang it up at your place," I recommended.

"Yeah," Tyler said. "I could cook a dish of pasta and put the picture up a t my place."

He liked pasta. I began falling harder and harder in love. We joked around for a few seconds more.

I spilled my coffee on myself on accident. Tyler was nice enough to hand me one of his napkins.

"Thank you," I said, taking the napkin and cleaning my shirt off.

"Do they have a restroom here," Tyler asked me.

I pointed behind myself. "I think there's one over there."

"Okay," and he left. I couldn't help but turn my head.

He is probably going to leave me here like an idiot, I thought. I turned my head back to the table. "No, his sunglasses are still here. But that doesn't necessarily mean anything," a small voice inside me said. I sat there in silence and waited for whatever was going to happened next.

Tyler came back.

"There are no pictures in there," he told me.

"Aw! I want to see!" was my first thought.

Instead the words out of my mouth were, "I don't even know how to respond to that." There was a brief moment of silence, and then Tyler began talking again. There was another moment of silence. Tyler had that adorable look on his face as he looked behind me.

"I'm trying to come up with a joke," he said.

A question popped into my mind.

"How do you guys come up with the stuff that you do?" I asked.

A questionable look came across Tyler's face.

"What do you mean?" he asked.

I looked to my right again.

"I mean do you come up with stuff beforehand or just say whatever's on your mind?"

I turned back to see that Tyler had bent his head down to the side again and he had that adorable smile on his face, again.

"No, we come up with jokes beforehand. It can be really scary, because sometimes you tell a joke and then no one in the audience laughs, and we just say, "No one's laughing….Maybe we should just do Phyneox now. It can be really scary."

I understood. Another crazy story came to my mind.

"I have another story to tell. This one is of my brother Tom's friend Jesse. Jesse's the funny guy in the world," I said, but then quickly added, "besides you guys." I looked to see the small playful grim on Tyler's face as he looked back at me. "It was after Tom's graduation. The guys were all over at Tom's friend Tom's place at Big Bear. When Tom and Tom went to Berkeley together, I always wanted to call up Tom and say, "Hey, Tom! Is Tom there?" but he'd probably get mad at me after the second or third phone call and say, "STOP CALLING ME MARY BETH!" and then just hang up, so I never did." I looked back at Tyler and told myself to not look away this time. I saw that Tyler was making a fake phone with his hand and then hanging up. He smiled as he did this. "Anyways," I went on, "so they're hanging over at little Tom's place up at Big Bear playing Chinese checkers one night. Woo-hoo, Chinese checkers, party hard. And brother Tom," I out my hand over my head to indicate the height comparison between the two Toms, "friend Jesse makes this move that your *not* allowed to make in Chinese checkers." I looked at the table. "And little Tom says, "Dude, you're not allowed to make that move," or, "Dude, what are you doing?" or something with the word "dude" in it. I don't know I wasn't there." I looked down at the table and said, "I can't say this with a straight face, but Jesse goes, "WHAT DO YOU MEAN "DUDE?"" I looked up to find that huge smile back on Tyler's face, again.

"I've never known anyone who wasn't called "dude" before," Tyler said with a big grin.

"Not everyone is called "dude"", I said. I couldn't help but defend Jesse. Apparently I was a little too loud and the Starbucks guy told me to keep it down. Tyler and I both turned back to listen.

"I think he's talking to you," Tyler said with that serious look on his face, again.

"I'm usually quiet," I told Tyler, looking behind his shoulder. We continued talking.

"What?" Tyler said leaning his ear into my direction. I told him whatever it was again.

We sat there in silence for a little while. I stared at Tyler's blue eyes and the grin he had on his face.

"So this was fun," he said with his face turned down again. "We should do it again."

I was so excited in that brief moment. Eight different reactions came to my head.

"Oh my God! Is he talking to me? Wait a minute, is he talking to me? Hold on. Slow down. Take a deep breath. It's going to be okay! It's going to be okay! It's going to be okay!" I then turned my head all the way to my right, trying to check behind my shoulder. "Wait is there a bear or a clown making funny faces or doing funny tricks behind me? Are there cheer leaders doing cheers or people doing the wave?" I turned my head back after that one brief second. "No, nothing's there. We're just sitting here in silence."

"Sit here in silence?" I asked aloud. And as the words left my mouth, I was thinking to myself, *'You idiot'*

Tyler turned his head back to me.

"Yes," he said through laughter with his eyes closed.

"Sounds like a game plan," I said. "I like it!"

"I'm going to Oregon this weekend," I told Tyler.

"Okay, so you'll have more stories to tell next time."

We both got up. Tyler threw his cup away first and then I did the same with mine. He had the cutest bounce to his walk. He opened the door for me.

"Thank you," I said. I froze where I was, but he went a few more feet in front. Tyler's head was looking toward the ground. I didn't know what to do. I felt so stupid standing there like an idiot, so I walked to where Tyler stood. Still not sure what to do, I stood there in silence for a few more seconds. Then I turned and stuck out my hand for a hand shake. Tyler shook my hand, but my eyes couldn't move away from our hands. "You are such an idiot!" I thought to myself.

"So are you going to wander back home?" he asked me.

"Yes." I told him. I went on my way. Crossing the parking lot, I didn't look back at Tyler, but maybe I should have...

I smiled to myself the entire time I walked home. "Did I just do this?" It was the greatest day of my life!

I reached home at about 12 PM. Mom called, of course. I didn't tell her what happened or where I was. I wanted to independent and lead my own way in life.

I told Kelly and Essence over emails and the phone. The day still pasted as usual.

. Butterflies filled my stomach with joy instead of heartache for once. It was nice. Sabrina, Mike, and Ashley came over that afternoon. I looked at Sabrina and smiled.

"Oh my God!" she said, remembering what I told her about. She knew what happened.

"He said he wants to see me again!" I told her, and I was jumping up and down.

"Mike and I share the same age difference as you do with this guy," Ashley said. If she could have Mike, then I felt that I had every reason to have Tyler in my life.

When I reached my singing teachers house that night, I told her what happened and explained why I couldn't tell my own mother about it. I should have listened to that voice inside me.

"So who is he?" Mom asked after we got home.

"What are you talking about?" I asked.

"Who is the guy that you saw?" she asked.

"I don't want to say," I told her with a smile on my face.

"Is he from the improv?" Mom asked.

"Yes," I said. "But I don't want to say."

"Is he Tyler?" she asked.

"Yeah," I said, but that voice inside me said that I would regret that statement.

"Isn't he in his late 20s?" she asked, sounding concerned and over protective.

Yes," I lied, thinking he was most likely in his early 30s. But age didn't matter to her in either of her marriages, so why should it matter to me? I was in love again and I was the happiest I've been in a very long time.

Chapter 18

A Whole New Thing

Mom wouldn't stop talking to me about her concerns on the matter of Tyler. First she thought he was in his late 20s, and then she thought he was in his 30s. It was my decision. No one else mattered in my opinion. It was me against the world.

I was getting ready for the trip that Mom and I were going on. Oregon. I was going to see Jeb again. We hadn't seen each other since we were kids. Mom and I were leaving Thursday afternoon.

Wednesday morning hit. I woke up at 4 AM and went to the bathroom, thinking I was going to through up! Sure enough I did. I told Mom that afternoon, but I was feeling better by then, so I thought it had passed. I had waited until that afternoon to email Tyler. I was so nervous, but also very excited. I told him that I was still laughing from Monday morning. I asked if he would like to hang out again on the Monday, July 21st. I was sure that I would have more stories to tell him. I had decided that I was also going to tell him about my car accident. There are two things that can happen, I told myself. Either he'll care or he'll leave. I'd been down both roads before.

Thursday morning came. I woke up at 5 AM, went to the bathroom and threw up. Later that morning I told Mom what happened and she asked if I wanted to cancel going to Oregon, but I assured her that I was fine.

Our flight was in the early afternoon. I knew I would be okay. I hadn't seen Jeb in a really long time and he and I had real changes in our lives that happened over the years. Jeb had recovered from cancer and I had fibromyalgia.

Mom and I got to Oregon after 7 PM. We ate something at the airport. Mom called Peggy and told her we were on our way.

We got a ride from a woman taxi driver. She and Mom were talking the whole time. The driver said that she had grown up in the circus. Mom was laughing at that, but I found that a little strange. The woman said she slept with the baby tigers in the circus and hung out with trapeze artists. She would walk the tight rope and have clowns around her all the time. She was a very interesting person. We finally got to the place where we were going to meet Peggy. Mom paid the driver and we thanked her for her stories.

Peggy got there and she and Mom gave each other a big hug. I gave Peggy a hug as well. Peggy said that Jeb was looking for a girlfriend, but I found that a weird conversation.

We finally got up to The Dalles where Peggy lived. I saw Jeb. He and I gave each other a hug. Peggy offered Mom and I Jeb's room, but we decided to stay in the trailer below. It was more comfortable then staying in the main house. Mom and I unpacked our things. Jeb had asked if I wanted to for a ride with him in his truck, and I agreed. It was a time for us to catch up.

Jeb got my door. He drove down to a building to get his pay check. Jeb did handyman things.

On the way down there, we talked about what we had been up to: school, his work, family, books, and music. Jeb had asked what my favorite music was. His favorite music was country, but he liked everything.

When we got to our destination, he went inside as I waited out in the truck just listening to the music. It was country, I could tell.

Jeb came out a little later.

"Sorry it took so long," Jeb said.

"That's okay," I assured him. "I was just listening to the music. Who is this?"

"Kenny Chesney," he said.

"A friend of mine turned me onto Garth Brooks," I told Jeb. We spoke of a lot of other things as we made our way back to the house.

Friday morning came, and I woke up rushing to the small bathroom to throw up. It was a little before 7 AM. I was extremely dizzy after that. Mom said that she set up an appointment for me to see Dr. Lazereff, my neurosurgeon, when we got back home. I agreed. Whatever I had wasn't normal and it wasn't going away. I felt better, again, after throwing up. Only mucus came out all three days that I was vomiting.

Mom, Peggy, Kalib, and I were going to go on a train ride. Kalib loved the train. He wore his conductor hat. It was nice. The scenery was incredible! I only took so many pictures, though. There was only so much I could see and not be sick of.

Peggy picked up pizza to cook from the store and we had that for dinner. When we left the main house it was pitch black at 9:30 that evening. The sun stayed out all day until 9PM.

Saturday came along. Mom, Peggy, and I were going to go more into the city to see Peggy's mom. Peggy's Mom Jacky was nice, but I was so bored up there. The only conversation that was going on was how old everyone was. I had a really uncomfortable feeling being there that I never wanted to experience again. Jacky was nice though. She gave me a Valentine looking present. It was a nice day. However, instead of throwing up, I had really bad diarrhea when we got back to the cabin. We were gone for five hours when we were with Jacky. The drive there and back was my favorite part of the day.

I had been thinking of Tyler the whole time. I told myself that it was love, but at the same time I didn't want to get hurt, so I convinced myself that it was only infatuation. Either way, I was on cloud 9!

Mom, Peggy, Rick and I were supposed to go to the lake on Sunday. I didn't really want to go, but I forced myself to keep a bright smile on my face. "Just think of Tyler," I told myself. He seemed to be the only thing that would make me smile.

Sunday came around and I was feeling my worst! Nothing was coming out of me, but I did not feel good!

I stayed the entire day at the cabin just sleeping. I must have been asleep for a few hours, because when Jeb came down to check on me it was around four o'clock. I was just lying on the bed when I heard him calling. He entered the room and asked if I wanted to go back to the house.

"Okay," I said. Jeb told me that he would wait outside. I only needed my shoes and socks. I went out and we walked up to the house. We sat on the couch and watched TV. An action movie was on.

"Do you want something to eat?" Jeb asked.

"No. I'm alright," I told him. A few minutes later he asked me again, and I said yes.

First Jeb fed his brothers. Mieshak was first. He made it over to the dining table. Jeb fed him. Jeb put Mieshak back in the back room. Kalib was next. Jeb fed him as well. Then Jeb went into the kitchen and started cooking something. I sat in front of the television watching a food critic on the Travel Channel.

Jeb made us omelets. Mine was good.

When Jeb and I were done with our food as we watched TV, we watched this other food critic. He went to India and tried these different foods. It grossed me out with what the guy was eating.

"Ew," I said at last.

"What?" Jeb asked as he turned to me.

"I would never eat that!" I told him.

"Really?", Jeb asked. I want to try everything at least once.

"Good for you, Jeb." I told him.

Jeb and I had some good laughs throughout the day, as I began feeling better.

Mom, Peggy, and Rick came back from the lake after 5. They had got some fish to cook and eat. Mom showed me her pictures of the lake. It was beautiful.

You could still see the snow on the mountains of Washington that were out across the way of Peggy's place.

I had told Mom once again how bad I was feeling. She told me to start keeping a log of everything that I was feeling.

Monday was my first day out to the city portion of Oregon. Mom, Peggy and I went to dress shops and I found a really cheap jacket that I fell in love with and bought. I was still not feeling well at all.

Mom had told me a few nights before that she had a crazy dream that I was so sick. I was dying in her dream.

When Mom and I left on Tuesday afternoon, I managed to give Jeb half a hug.When we got home, we were lucky that the house was still standing. Ben, Joe, and Conan did a horrible job at keeping everything under control. Stimpy started meowing a lot when Mom and got home. We didn't know what to think of it, so we just kept her as comfortable as possible.

I checked my email when we got home to find that Tyler emailed me back on Thursday, July10th. He said that he had gotten sick, but he said that he should be better by the 21st so I could tell him more stories.

"Okay," I told myself. "This is it. You have to tell him about your car accident, and no matter what happens you'll be okay. Even if he leaves and never wants to see or hear from you again, you'll be fine. But this is the last time you will *ever* fall in love. I won't let you keep hurting yourself, kid. It wasn't fun the first billions of times and it won't be fun again."

I wrote back to Tyler and told him that I had a lot of crazy stories to tell him on Monday. There were a lot of different things happened that I wanted to tell him about. He asked what time we would meet and I wrote, "The same time as last time."

I hadn't received a response that week, but I told myself not to freak out. I was still going to go up to Starbucks. I was arguing with Mom about it. She said he was too old for me, but I didn't care. I was in love.

What did age matter, anyway?

Mom kept on being over protective. She made it clear that he was wrong for me. It wasn't as if Tyler and I were going to go get married after the second cup of coffee that we would have together. I had no idea what he really thought of me anyways.

I brought up the subject of Mike and Ashley. That seemed to keep her quite for a minute.

Chapter 19

When Happy Endings Don't Come

On Monday, July 21, 2008, I got up at 6 AM. I was going to see Tyler again! Mom knew what was going on. She wasn't over protective that much today. I didn't care either way. I was doing this for me. Sink or swim, I could say I did it on my own.

I had breakfast and Mom left at 7:30, as usual. I finished getting ready.

I was done and out the door by 9 this time. I told myself that if Tyler wasn't there that it wouldn't break my heart. I'd be okay. It certainly wouldn't be the first time it happened, but a part of me said that it would definitely be the last. Still there was a part of me that was too excited to see Tyler! I had what I considered good stories written down and I knew how to act them out.

I got to Starbucks at 9:30, knowing that I was early; I sat down and wrote my pros and cons list for having my eye surgery. I had made up my mind that it would help. What else could go wrong? 10 o'clock came, but Tyler wasn't there.

"Just a little longer," I told myself. "Maybe he got up late or there could be traffic." 10:05 passed. 10:15 passed.

Heartbroken, I left by 10:20. It seemed that everyone was staring at me. I wasn't crying, so why were they staring?

Was my mascara running? Was my lip gloss messed up? I didn't know and I didn't care. All I wanted to do was get out of there! I forced myself to keep everything in until I reached the park. The journey was only two blocks away, but it felt much longer.

Making it to the park, I found an empty batting cage and fell down crying on the bench. A big part of me wasn't surprised.

"How stupid can you be?" I shouted at myself in my head. "Of course he doesn't like you! Why would he? What the hell do you think you have to offer him?"

I cried through the violent tears that came streaming down my face. All these different questions came to my head at once.

"Mom won," was the first thought in my head. "She didn't want me to see Tyler. Fine. She got her wish." So many other emotions flooded my mind. "But why would a mother not want her own daughter to be unhappy?"

"Was I too nice? Was I not nice enough? Was I not funny enough? Was I too funny? Was I too loud? Was I too quite? Was I just not pretty enough? Am I just not worth remembering? Am I not skinny enough?"

Of course, I didn't have an answer to any of these questions, so I sat there for three hours and cried. I blamed myself; there was no one else responsible.

"You knew what you were getting yourself into, kid. You knew that you never had a chance."

"But why?" another part of me was questioning the other. "He said he wanted to see you again. Why would he be so cruel and lie?"

"Because he's a good actor," both sides answered.

After crying and arguing with myself for three hours, I gave up and went home. "There's no point in staying and getting hurt any longer. Besides, you already expected this. It's no surprise."

I made it home by 1 PM. I went to my computer and deleted his email address. The phone rang.

"Hello?" I asked threw a cracked voice. It was Mom.

"Hi," she said. "What's wrong?"

I told her that Tyler didn't show up.

"Oh, I'm sorry," she told me. I knew she was lying. 'She's probably jumping for joy,' a voice inside me thought. "I was being over protective. I'll back off," Mom said. A small part of me believed her, or at least that part of me wanted to believe her. I was too crushed to tell the difference anymore.

I emailed Kelly, Essence and Tom and told them how heartbroken I was. I was never going to love again, that was for sure! I tried to do whatever I could for the rest of the day, knowing that this pain wasn't going anywhere anytime soon. It found me and it's staying, I told myself.

I checked my email at 2:30, an hour and a half later, to see if I got any replies back from anyone.

"There's a new message," I read. "Maybe it's Kelly or Essence."

It was Tyler.

"21st," he titled it. Having no awareness of what I was doing, I clicked the message.

"Sorry," it said. No you're not, I thought. I read more. He said that he had just moved into a new place and that he mainly forgot. You've heard this all before. The old, "The dog ate my homework," routine. Enough's enough.

Tyler had asked if I wanted to get coffee another time. "I want to hear your stories about your trip to Oregon."

Fighting with myself, I decided that he most likely was sorry.

"It happens all the time. Enough is enough, though. What? Are you going to forgive every person no matter how much they break your heart? You said it yourself, kid, 'This is the last time.'" The argument continued inside me. Finally, a minute later, I decided to write back.

"Sure," I typed. "I can't do it today," it was 2:30 and I had singing at 6, "but maybe another time."

Having too much going on already, I didn't know where to place myself. The dizziness was there. The nausea was coming and going a lot. My body hurt like never before!

I went to see Dr. Lazereff the next day, Tuesday. Maybe he has an answer, I thought. Mom came with me, of course. I explained all my symptoms to him. A student was there with him. She was nice.

Dr. Lazereff said that the only option he could think of would be for me to under go surgery to change my entire shunt. I described how the tube in my neck was causing me severe pain. Both Mom and the doctor said that it was impossible for that to happen. Tubes don't have nerve endings. They are simply tubes. I was to have an MRI to see if anything was wrong with my shunt. Mom said she could tell if there were something truly wrong, but I wasn't showing symptoms for that now.

"But it hurts!" I would cry and yell.

Dr. Lazereff said that the surgery that I would undergo would be dangerous. And there was no real guarantee that it would solve the problem.

I was considering it, though. This could solve a lot.

Tom called on Wednesday. He and Mom spoke for a while. Then Tom asked to talk to me.

Tom and I spoke for a while. He told me of the monkeys that he and Cameron saw in Asia. I guessed to myself that the only reason Tom wanted to talk with me was to make sure that I was alright. I was at least good with faking being okay.

Tyler started starring in my dreams.

I was getting all negative things from everyone around me. I started to lose sight of who I really was. I was letting everyone around me treat me like crap and I couldn't take it anymore! Just because their lives were fucked up, didn't mean that I wanted, in anyway shape or form, to be like them!

I started starving myself. Tyler thought that you were fat and that's why he didn't come back, a voice inside me said. "Shut up! Shut up! Shut up!" I told myself. "Fine, I won't eat, but I will *not* be controlled by anyone either!"

I was feeling more and more depressed. Tyler wasn't coming back.

Why did you let this happen to yourself? I thought. He isn't the only man out there in the world. And even if he was, you'd be fine on your own.

My broken heart didn't matter to anyone at home. It was always about Joe, Ben, or Conan. I wasn't so surprised, though. It hurt like hell.

I was living in hell, but I wasn't surprised.

I started the application for social security and it broke my heart. I never wanted to give up on life. Not like this. I was meant to do extraordinary things. Not have everyone else have their way and I would be thrown to the ground all the time. It wasn't me, but yet this is who I've become.

My friends weren't there for me during my time of suffering through my stupid broken heart. I was there for them through everything, but I was suddenly left to deal with this heartache alone? It wasn't right.

I would get yelled at from Mom for being upset and crying at the dinner table. I cried even harder when the yelling would start! I wanted to break everything in my room and the whole house, but I knew that it wouldn't get me anywhere. I was going no where fast and it hurt worse than hell.

The heartbreak never stopped. I was battling a war inside and out that could never end and there was no way to get out of it. I was up against myself, the world, Mom, Tom, Mike, Joe, and every other person in it. I wrote more and more over the broken heart, but it didn't help me feel better. I was in this battle alone and no one knew how bad it hurt. To lose the love of one's life because it made others feel nervous? Since when was one love that a person felt for someone else, anyone else's business?

To change my mood, I tried ignoring the pain, but that never worked. I cried myself to sleep for weeks; turned into months.

Pam, Chad, Mom, and I were going to an improv at LA Connection one Saturday night. I prayed that Tyler wasn't going to be there. Luckily he wasn't.

The comedians did a skit and they needed someone from the audience. Mom, Chad, and Pam all pointed to me. I went up. I was on a "dating show" with the other comedians. My job was to ask whatever question I had. I did fine and I got some laughs. I chose the homeless guy in the end, because he had the most personality to him.

In life, I wanted to give up! Nothing was coming for me and love didn't exist for me. *That* was clear enough!

I felt so broken after only four weeks after the only "date" that I would ever have had with Tyler. I hated the way that it made me feel. When did love have to control anyone like this? Grabbing them and never letting go. It wasn't supposed to hurt this way! That was for sure! I faked being okay, but I knew that everyone could tell that I was never going to be okay again. Love broke me.

I felt like tearing up my entire room and not stopping. I wanted to break everything and tear everything else up into little pieces! I wanted nothing but dust to exist. I screamed at the top of my lungs, but only to myself.

I had told myself to ask Tyler again if he wanted to get coffee, after I calmed down a little. I had made up my mind that I was going to tell Tyler about my car accident. "If he leaves and never wants to talk to you again, you'll be okay, kid," I told myself, again. "It certainly wouldn't be the first time that anyone walked out on me, and it probably won't be the last."

I left the house by 9 AM, getting to Starbucks by 9:30. I was early, but I waited for 20 minutes after 10. Tyler wasn't there.

"You're okay, kid," I told myself. "You already knew that he wasn't going to show. It does hurts, non-the-less, though."

I went to the park and cried for a little while, and then I went home to delete Tyler from my email and myspace. I logged on and found that I found a new message. It was from Tyler.

"Sorry," it read. He explained that the reason he couldn't be there was because he had to work. I had given him my number over an email and he reciprocated by giving me his number as well.

I texted him and said that it was okay. I asked if Thursday was a good day for him. He replied that Thursday was bad. He told me that he could give me a ticket to the improv show.

Tuesday night came. "Just tell him," I told myself. "He won't reply, but you'll be fine."

I texted Tyler.

"Friday should be good," I said. "Listen, I have to tell you something, when I was six years old, I was run over by a car." Just to ease the tension that was forming in my throat, as I typed it out I put, "There are some funny things to that as well." Tears were pouring down my cheeks as I pressed "Send" on my phone.

"He's never going to talk to you again," I told myself. "But at least he knows the truth. You'll be fine, kid. You're better off without him anyways!" I turned over my phone as I put it on "Silent" and went to bed. I cried myself to sleep, not able to fall asleep until 2 AM.

I dreamt that night that Tyler did reply to the text message that I sent him that night.

Wednesday morning I woke up to turn over my phone. I found that I had a new message. It was from Tyler.

"You texted me about an hour ago. Are you still up? Can we talk?"

Confused by this, I wrote back, not knowing what to say.

"I'm fine," I wrote.

Mom had her heart appointment. I was freaking out about that. I prayed that she was going to be okay. Sure enough, Mom was healthy.

I had enough to freak out about with my own doctor appointment with Dr. Lazereff. He said that I could have a surgery, but that it would be dangerous. However, it would be my decision. Mom had to have her say, though.

"NO!" she screamed at me. I was in such severe pain that I wished I would die and instead I was yelled at for it.

I was starting to think that I was making it all up.

I was at my computer one afternoon trying to find out if I was insane and just making up this pain. I couldn't be, I thought. What kind of sane person would make this up? Even if I were insane, why would I *want* make up the kind of pain I'm in?

I had ended up sending Tyler an email, apologizing about telling him about my car accident. I knew my chances weren't good anyway. Did I regret telling Tyler about my car accident? No. He had to know eventually, anyway. Everyone had to know if they were to really know me. So for the people who stay in my life or leave, at least they would know what happened to me.

I received a message back.

"Why would that freak me out?" Tyler asked.

I only had to think of it a second, but then I wrote, "Because you don't hear it every day," and I hit "Send."

I waited expecting something else, but nothing came.

I had started getting nightmares of Ben. I would yell at him in them. He deserved *much worse* I thought when I woke up from the dream. I did the stupid thing and told Mom. I was yelled at for having nightmares of someone that I used to consider family. He was too mean and selfish to even be considered anything close to being anywhere near family, I told myself.

"Just suck it up, kid. You've had worse," I kept telling myself. No matter how much I screamed and whatever I would throw, everything would be my fault. "Everyone blames you for everything," I knew this too well. "You could die and everything would *still* be your fault. But someday you'll be with Tyler again. You'll get your happy ending. No one else deserves this as much as you do!"

I cried day in and day out from being dizzy. No one believed the pain I was in because of my tube. The only thing that guaranteed that I wasn't completely insane was the websites that I found with other people that had the same pain I was suffering through.

"YES! I'm not crazy," I thought. "Damn it! I'm not crazy!"

Mom still yelled at me for considering the surgery that would be done on *my* body. *I* would be the one to die, not her. She would have everyone else that she loved. She wouldn't have to deal with me anymore. But sometimes in life, you don't get everything you wish for.

Chapter 20

A New Beginning and another Ending

Mom and I argued one night over the MRI that I had. She said that it was probably my ears. I knew that it wasn't and I wouldn't let her tell me that it was. I *knew* that it wasn't, but of course she didn't want to hear it. She thought she was right and, of course, I was wrong. I was the one who was dealing with this and yet I didn't know a thing about my own body. I was so over come by anger and betrayal by everyone.

"They won,' I told myself. "Why can't they just leave me the hell alone? I never asked for this kind of pain, but I was cursed with it anyway. They should be happy that I'm going to die. At least then they'd be set free from my consist annoyance."

I was so sick and so tired of the pain that I was going through, that I simply couldn't handle it anymore.

I was suffering with a broken heart that I never asked for. "Tyler was my true love," I told myself, "but not anymore. If he doesn't want to even be friends with me, fine. There's nothing I can do about that. But you have to tell him about your illness and let go of him forever, kid. You'll be okay in the end. I promise."

I emailed Tyler, tired of waiting for him coming back. I told him how sick I was and how I couldn't wait for him. I told him how much I did like him, but I was sick. I told Tyler that it was something that the doctors couldn't figure out. Maybe when I was better, maybe, just maybe, Tyler and I could be friends. I apologized for everything.

I regretted sending that email and I wanted to take it all back.

I received an email back from Tyler a week later.

"I've been so damn busy," he wrote. How many times have I heard that? "I consider you a friend. Maybe if we got to know each other a little better, things could change."

No, I thought. They can't change and they're never going to.

"I hope things get better for you. I want to hear more stories," he wrote.

I texted Tyler back right away and begged that he would forget everything that I wrote before. I told him that I might go to the improv that Friday.

I was over come by so much heartbreak. Kelly and Essence weren't talking to each other and I wanted to do anything that I could to put them back together, but they both told me no. They always asked about each other and I hated being the one in the middle.

Ben and Conan had moved out in September, but Mom needed to loan Ben $5,000 for him to get a condo with his girlfriend.

He'll be back, I thought, hating it more and more. I hated Ben and Conan so much already. I actually considered them family at one point in my life. But they were always mean to people and getting away with everything.

Ben would have gotten away with murdering you, I thought to myself.

As more and more time passed it was getting harder to go on in life with the heartbreak that I was feeling. Tyler wasn't coming, I knew that deep down, but I couldn't let myself come to terms with that. Everyone in my life was telling me to go a certain way. I yelled and cried at every open moment I had.

On September 1st, 2008, Essence and I were going to go to the mall. Tyler said he could meet me that day, but I didn't show up. I asked if he could talk that night instead. He replied with what time. I asked if 10:30 was alright.

10 PM came around, and I was trying to hurry up with getting ready for bed. I was done a little after 10. I hugged Mom goodnight and went to my room to wait. I didn't want to seem desperate so I waited another 5 minutes. At 10:35 I called Tyler. The phone didn't go through. I tried again. One ring, two rings.

"Hello?" I heard one the other line.

"Hi, Tyler. This is Mary Beth," I said. I felt stupid because he probably saw my name on his phone. "How are you?" I asked.

"Fine, how are you?" Tyler asked.

"I'm doing okay at the moment," I said, being honest.

I read all the notes I had written of the things that happened over time.

"Are you reading this?" he asked.

"Yeah," I admitted and then went on.

Tyler had asked a little about my car accident, so I told him. "My mom thought I was a dog at first. Then she bends down and she asks, 'Mary Beth, are you okay?'"

His response seemed genuine.

"My three legged cat can beat up my mom's German shepherd," I told him.

"Wait," Tyler started in. "Your cat can beat up your dog?"

"Yeah," I said as if it happened to everyone.

"Is your dog a puppy?" Tyler asked. "Maybe when she's bigger she'll get revenge."

The dog was a big puppy.

"Maybe," I said, agreeing. We spoke for a little longer. There were a few pauses in the conversation, but things went well.

"My friend Natalie plays Barbie on the east coast," Tyler started saying.

"Wait," I said. "Natalie plays *Barbie*?" I asked out of disbelief.

"Yes," Tyler said.

"I've never heard anyone having the roll of Barbie before," I admitted. I had heard rumors before, but that's all that I thought they were; rumors. The conversation dragged on for a while.

"So..." Tyler said in that sweet voice of his. I didn't want to be embarrassed so I said goodnight, but I could tell he wanted to talk. I didn't want to hear it if it meant that I would only be embarrassed in anyway possible.

I asked Tyler on Wednesday, September 10th if I could go to the improv. He asked if I was bringing anyone and at the time I was going to go by myself, but I asked Essence.

Friday came. Essence called to say that she couldn't go because her car wasn't working. I begged her to reconsider. I told her that Tyler had put aside two tickets for us to come and see the show. My mom said she could drop us off. Mom and I picked up Essence at her house and then we were dropped off. Mom had to work on a dress that she was doing for a wedding that Susannah was going to. She was stressing out about that a lot!

Essence and I got lost trying to find the Starbucks so Essence could get something to eat as well as a coffee. I got a bottle of water. We went back. Karen was at the desk.

"Hi, Tyler said he had tickets here for me," I told her.

Karen went to the side if the wall. "Mary Beth?" she asked.

"Yeah," I said.

"You can go in if you want."

"Do you want to go in?" I asked, turning to Essence.

"I don't know," Essence said.

"Fine, we'll wait out here."

"You can go in," Karen said again. I got the door for Essence and we sat in the back. The first show was good. Then there was a thirty minute window until Stranger than Fiction came out. Essence and I moved to the front from the side seats that we were at.

Tyler was coming and going. He didn't notice me, though. Essence told me that Tyler did see me.

The lights darkened and we saw a little skit on the television. Then the actors came out. Tyler noticed me and stared with those dreamy eyes of his. Zeke gave Essence and me high fives. The skits that they did were really funny!

There was another act afterwards, but Essence and I had to leave.

Mom was waiting outside.

Essence told me that she wanted to see the improv two more times, which I found to be ridiculous! I told Tyler through a text message and he said the same thing.

My heart began to break again. It was getting worse and worse to deal with. I cried all over the place.

For a stupid guy? I thought, almost laughing through my tears. *But he was the one! You'll never be happy again!*

NO! Another voice inside me shouted. *You don't need him or anyone to survive in this world.* It made since.

But he was the one! The first voice kept crying over and over. *He could have been the one!*

I fought with myself constantly.

October came and New York was the subject now. I wanted to go, but I would soon regret that.

Mom and I were shopping at the mall for something to wear to the wedding. I found a beautiful dress that I wanted to buy and wear to the wedding.

"You can't look prettier than the maid of honor, Mary Beth," Mom argued.

How am I going to look "prettier" than the maid of honor? I asked myself. I'm not even close to looking anywhere near pretty to begin with. Mom and I fought. She was mad at me because I "wandered off" from her in the department store. I wasn't two! I didn't need my mommy to look out for me or hold my hand. When she "found me" I was spoken to in a tone that I had heard very often from her. I was always doing the wrong thing and getting put down for something that I knew was right. It was okay for a 20 year old woman to be alone, to walk by herself at the mall, to have her own opinions. But it wasn't okay for me to do that? How was I different than any other human being?

After arguing for what felt like much longer than a few minutes I has tears come to my eyes. What had I done wrong? Where does it say that a woman isn't aloud to walk alone or to sit and think *by herself*? I was outraged, but I sat in silence and drank the coffee that Mom had bought afterward. I stared at my cup, unable to have any thoughts running to my head. My thoughts were of hatred, betrayal, loneliness, and outrage that I had felt for too long in my life! I finally settled on getting a plaid dress at another clothing store that was a lot cheaper than the dresses at the mall.

Mom and I baby sat my niece that night. I made her laugh by reading a book out loud to her.

My symptoms had started up again on October 6th. The tube in my neck was killing me.

"Your tube can't cause you pain, Mary Beth," everyone would always say. Then explain to me why I am in such pain. Explain the vomiting, the nausea, and the headaches while you're at it!

I was so angry at Tyler, but the tears and rage and heartache I had for him weren't going away. Was I not meant to be happy?

On Saturday, October 13, I had a dream with Tyler in it. He was down on one knee, proposing to me. It was only a dream, I told myself over and over. Just a dream.

On October 14, I was online.

I have suffered through these symptoms long enough, I told myself. Maybe I am crazy and I am just making this all up!

But I wasn't. There were other people out there just like me that were suffering through the pain that I had. 'Yes!' I thought. 'I'm not crazy!' which quickly turned into, "DAMN IT! I'm not crazy!' There was a little hope that if I was crazy that the pain that I was dealing with would just go away and I could regain everything, again, or at least try. But at the same time, I knew that I could never make up this kind of pain! I never *asked* for this. And yet I was the one who was lying about my own body. I prayed to die and waited for my death to come after Tyler left. He's the one thing that has kept me going, I told myself, but then a rush of guilt that I never understood before swept through me.

I cried to my psychologist about Tyler and I raged about him. I told her that every emotion that was ever felt in the history of humankind had filled inside my head and heart every second of everyday because of him. I was so angry, so sad, so scared. And soon I found out that I was so in love.

Kelly had told me that there was someone out there for me, but it made me so angry that she thought that. Who is out there for me? No one. If they are out there, and that's a big *if*, they sure aren't looking for me. No one wants me and that's fine, I'd say. I knew that I was better off alone anyways.

I wanted to go to an improv by myself, so I asked Mom she could drop me off.

"I'M NOT DROPPING YOU OFF BY YOURSELF AT AN IMPROV!" she yelled at me. I was 20 years old and not aloud to be by myself? How did that make since? It wasn't as if I was going to jump into a car with some guy that I didn't know and have sex just because I could. 'Dude, I'm not anywhere near being attractive,' I thought. I ended up crying and staying home with Mom. She won.

I was crying at least nine times a day by October 22nd. Some days were better than others, but it was still a bitch to go through. Since when was I allowing myself to let any man take that much control over my life? Everyone was saying that I was in love, but was love supposed to hurt this much?

On Friday, October 24, Mom and I left for New York on a red eye flight. The plane was late taking off. There wasn't enough gas, but the pilot asked everyone if they just wanted to take off. The pilot said that it shouldn't be a problem. I slept three hours on that flight and woke up. Trying to keep myself distracted by the fact that I was up in the air and hated heights, I listened to my music and read a book. Things seemed to be going okay until we were in New York. There was a nasty storm that we had to fly threw. The airport wasn't ready for our plane to come in. They didn't have enough room. So there we were, stuck in the air with a storm, and running out of gas. The plane started to shake. I was clutching Mom's hand and she was clutching onto mine. I prayed to God that we would make it out okay.

There was finally room at the airport, but the plane was dropping out of the sky. 'Are we going to die?' I thought. I was worried about Mom because of her heart problems and she was worried about me because of my height problems.

We landed okay, despite the dumpy landing, at JFK.

Mom and I got our things and went on the subway heading towards Brooklyn. We arrived at Tom and Cameron's apartment just fine. Mom and I fell asleep in the extra bedroom that they had. A few hours later we woke up and enjoyed the rest of the day.

On Sunday we went to Tarrytown and a woman asked me to take a picture of her and her sun. Mom took my picture next and I faked being scared.

"Oh, she looks scared," the lady said to her son.

"Yeah, you should have seen her yesterday," Mom said. I knew exactly what she was talking about, but I only laughed.

"You were just as scared as I was," I told her through my laughter.

I kept telling myself that Tyler was a jerk and that he was not the one for me. For some reason, part of me was still hanging on to him. He lied to me. That was the only explanation that I had. He lied.

Mom and I saw a passenger from our plane ride on Monday. We were in Central Park and I noticed this guy looking at Mom and at me. He motioned for me to get Mom's attention for him. She noticed the man when I pointed him out to her. She went over to talk to him and left me to sit where I was in silence.

They spoke for a while and I joined them after a few minutes.

Susannah had gotten to Tom's place by Thursday.

It was Hell getting to the wedding on Halloween. Susannah, Mom, and I left the house by 2PM. We had a rented a car and were going to go to Queens to pick up Mom's cousin Henryette and then driver to Amityville for the wedding. It took two hours trying to get to Queens, only a short distance away. There were trick or treaters all over the place and Susannah was lost. I knew that we were going to miss the wedding.

Finally, we arrived in Queens. We found Henryette's house. She was dressed in a nice black Halloween dress. I was wearing my denim dress. I started to get a little upset, because I was told that you didn't dress up for weddings.

The drive to the hotel wasn't long. When we got there, the ceremony of the wedding was almost over. They had said there vows and we missed it. We got there just in time to hear Christine say, "I do." Then the reception was going to happen. Susannah and I sat at a table and ate the dinner that was served. Mom was off with Janet, Christine's mom, at the bar.

Then the dancing took place. First the bride and groom had their dance. Then it was the father and the bride that danced.

Mom and Janet were dancing. Mom came and got me to go dancing with her. I was okay at first, but then I got more and more upset. I knew why, but I never wanted to admit it to myself. I tried my very hardest to keep a smile upon my face and enjoy what was going on. For Mom's sake, I told myself. But I couldn't help it. I pulled back while Mom kept dancing. I pretended to be tired and went back to the table that Susannah was sitting at. She was texting Tom and telling him how Mom was dancing. Tom thought that was funny. I tried to smile and laugh it off. At least pretend that you're okay, I thought, but I found out that it wasn't working.

Tears sprang to my eyes as I sat there. Not wanting anyone else to know that I was crying, I turned my head away from the crowd. It was there that I realized that was what I really wanted: a happy ending with Tyler. I wanted to marry him and live happily ever after.

You missed your chance, I told myself.

The dress that Christine wore was beautiful.

I was very upset that the entire wedding party and ever single guest there other than Mom, Susannah, and I, were all dressed in the traditional way that one would dress while attending a wedding. And here I was wearing some stupid plaid dress that I felt I was forced into buying for the wedding.

I eventually ended up crying in the restroom at the hotel. I cried over everything: over Tyler, the situation, the dress, and being pushed around and having no other choice but to take it!

Wiping my eyes and checking my make up in the mirror, I returned to the room and sat with Susannah for a while longer. She had to make a call, so she left, but she had Mom come over to the table to sit with me. Was I not even allowed to sit by myself? Was I that naïve that I would do something stupid like sticking a spoon up my nose? I was outraged at this! But I didn't say anything the entire night. I just let it boil inside me all night long.

We were there a few hours before I started to say that I wanted to go. Mom told Henryette and then Joe and Janet.

"You tired?" Henryette asked me, looking at me like I was four and couldn't handle anything. I wasn't tired. I just couldn't be somewhere where I knew I would never have the same happy ending as everyone else. Another part was boiling inside me, just adding to the mixture.

We said our goodbyes and left. Getting back to Queens wasn't hard. We said our goodbyes to Henryette and drove back to Brooklyn.

`I was being pressured by Tom to go back to college. He wasn't the only one that gave me that talk. I heard it from Mom, Tracey, Robert, Essence, and Kelly. They couldn't hear how I was screaming in my head to go back to college. There was always a part of me that wanted to go back and not be afraid anymore.

Both Mom and Tom thought that I should take a photo class. I wanted to, but that retched fear that hung over me was always there. I couldn't do it. Not if I was going to have to deal with everything else in my life. It was *my* life that everyone always screwed around with. I'm the one who suffered through it, not them.

My left rib cage began hurting very bad by November. Mom took me to my doctor and I had x-rays taken. After a week, the doctor called back with the results and everything was fine. The nausea, however, was still there constantly. And no one believed me. I was beginning to lose weight from the diet that I was on, but I still found myself to be hideous!

I was still crying from all the pain from the tube and the nausea. It hurt like Hell and no one believed me.

Tyler was constantly on my mind and it bugged the Hell out of me! 'Why did he text me back with an answer like that?' I thought of after telling him about my car accident. Annoyed by this, I texted him asking why he said such a thing. He replied, saying that it wasn't something that could be said over text messaging. I saw his point and told him that I couldn't talk about it over the phone. There were a lot of hand jesters that went with the story. How was he to know when there was a joke?

In person would be better for me, I told him. Tyler said that the 17th would be good for him.

We agreed on the 17th, I told myself. The 17th. I didn't really know what to say. What was he going to ask? How would this turn out? Would I end up crying in front of him from all the shit that I've gone through? I was already feeling very angry at him for leaving me there alone before, but this wasn't fair! How am I supposed to act now?

Part of me was still expecting the worst would be happen. If he's there, fine. If not, you'll still be okay. You'll be fine. You don't have anything to worry about. You can still have your coffee and you'll be okay on your own. If he isn't going to show up for this one, I told myself, you'll be done with him forever. I won't allow you to keep hurting yourself, Mary Beth. I won't.

Monday, November 17thcame. I got up at 6 AM and ate my breakfast. I did my normal thing, knowing what was happening that day. I left at 9 AM, but I wasn't sure what time Tyler wanted to do this. I texted him asking what time he wanted to meet.

I got my coffee and waited. 10 o'clock came. Nothing happened. I decided to leave. I ended up walking around the parking lot for a while. No where to go, nothing to do, I told myself. Do I stay or should I go?

I ended up getting another cup of coffee. Walk around a little more, I said to myself, again. No, another part said. He's not coming.

I ended up at the park. Sitting down, I couldn't help but find that tears had sprung to my eyes. Tears out of rage and frustration, I told myself. Not sadness. You won't let him get away with that. No, don't do it, kid. He's not worth it!

I texted Tyler, again, asking if he still wanted to meet. No reply.

The next person I texted was Essence. She said to call him. I didn't want to, but I forced myself to do so. He didn't answer. I didn't leave a message.

Tired of waiting, but no where to go, I sat and cried. Getting up a while later, I wiped my eyes until they were dry and left the park. I felt my phone buzz. Checking it, I saw that Tyler had sent me a message.

He couldn't come. What a surprise, I thought. He had been filming and had gotten sick do to all of the smoke in the air.

That's understandable, I thought. Maybe it just wasn't supposed to happen, I thought to myself. I texted Tyler back and told him that I hoped he got better. He asked if we could meet another time. This kind of conversation had been boiling down inside me for far too long so another time wouldn't happen, I decided. It wasn't possible.

Angry and pissed off, mostly at myself for allowing this to happen, I didn't return home. Not knowing where I was or where I was going to, I wandered aimlessly. I finally ended up back home four hours later. This wasn't going to happen again, I shouted to myself. He doesn't want to even hang out with you, fine. Who needs love anyway? My heart is broken, but it's not a surprise to you, kid. You have enough going on with all the pain you're in, so you don't need this.

I ended up at my computer, sending Tyler an email of what happened to me. Just a short email, nothing long, I said. He won't come back. You're doing yourself a favor.

Unable to move on with my life, I still loved him. I hated myself for doing that. What the hell is wrong with me?

I was dealing with so much pain already. Obsessing why Tyler wasn't there certainly wasn't helping.

Joe was thrown in jail for being on a roof. Mom paid for his bail money, but things weren't changing in any way with him.

On Thanksgiving Day, after the big meal, everyone was to draw a name from a hat. I ended up getting my own name first.

"You can't do that. It isn't fair to anyone else," Susannah said in her high pitch voice. So I drew another name. I got Joe.

I was busy looking up different improv classes online.

"It will make you feel closer to Tyler," I told myself. I found a free class in Encino at someone's house. I emailed back and worth for a week and asked about it. I decided to go.

The teachers name was Sean and he was nice. Everyone in the class was nice. I felt okay. I was a little embarrassed, but I was fine. I wasn't the only new comer there so that was nice. Everyone went around in a circle and introduced themselves. Sean paid a little more attention to me for whatever reason. I saw that it was a lot like the acting class that I took before, but improv. It seemed alright. The class went well, and I did want to try it again, but for different reasons.

"He'll come back," I kept lying to myself. "Tyler will come back for you."

I first told Mom that I wanted to go back to the improv class. Five days later, I changed my mind. Doing this wasn't going to make Tyler come back. I was stupid for thinking anything close to that would happen. It seemed to me that it was pulling me further apart from him. It's not worth the heartache, I told myself.

When I told Mom I didn't want to go back, I said it in tears. Instead of her being sympathetic and saying, "It's alright. You don't need to do anything you don't want to," I was yelled at instead.

"You can't give up on everything, Mary Beth." She made me feel worse than what I had already felt. "You said that going to school gives you *anxiety*. You can't keep running away from everything." She said this as if I was the one who *chose* to feel this way. I would much rather be confident and not always having to be with you than to have everyone always making fun of me. I already have Susannah saying that I'm going to live with you forever. This statement had all the anger that I felt for everyone in it. I was always on my own. I had no one to confide my trust in and God only knows how much that hurts!

Tyler really hurt me and I was hurting myself more than ever over it.

It felt like I couldn't love anyone else or be with the man that I loved because of statements made by Mom and everyone else around me.

I was busy getting ready for my first recital. I was going to be singing "One More Girl" by the Wreckers. The recital was on December 21st. I wanted Kelly and Essence to be there, but things weren't looking good. I was heartbroken.

I refused to go through with it. I wanted Tyler to be there, and I had asked him, but he said he had to work. I was tearing myself up inside.

Mike and Ashley said they wanted to come.

I was having difficulty breathing at night in early December. My dizziness was still there, as well as the nausea.

I knew that Ben had gotten my name from the bowl, but I would rather end up getting nothing than to receive anything from Ben, I told myself. He never had a heart to begin with and I certainly didn't want anything to do with him. I told myself that the *only* thing that I would ever want from Ben would be for him to keep his promise from the year before and just kill me. I wasn't doing anyone any favors by being alive, so he'd be doing everyone else a big favor by killing me. This way, they don't have to keep pretending that they care, I thought to myself. They can go on with the rest of their lives. I never mattered to them anyways. Wouldn't change much, I told myself.

The feelings that I had for Tyler were getting stronger and stronger. I obsessed over every word he wrote to me.

"He said 'love'! He loves me," I told myself the day before my recital. I told him that I had crazy stories to tell him and he said that after the holiday season is over he would be less busy. Tyler said we could hang out then. I hated myself more and more for being so obsessed over some stupid guy. I already told myself that love didn't exist.

Pam, Essence, and Kelly all said that love did exist, but I knew better. I was suffering in too much pain from being so obsessed with Tyler that I left any chance I had with love behind.

The day of the recital finally arrived. I received nothing form anybody. Essence couldn't come because she had a Christmas party that she had to be at. Kelly wasn't saying anything and no one else was coming. I was so heartbroken that I couldn't help crying my hardest. I didn't want to go through with it.

"You're going!" Mom yelled at me. "You're going to do this!"

I was more and more upset. I cried for over two hours.

"Tyler's not coming," I cried, only saying it to myself. I ended up in my bed just crying there.

After I was yelled at for sometime, I just went to the bathroom and wiped the tears away from my face while I stared at myself in the mirror.

"You're doing this," I told myself as I wiped the tears away. "You're not doing this for them; you're doing it for you! You can do this!" I had to say this over and over until I convinced myself that it would be okay.

Mom and I left soon after. We got to the music store where the recital was being held kind of early. We went inside and then came out and waited.

Pam drove up, so Mom and I got out and went inside.

The other students showed up all at once. After everyone was there, the students all had to practice their vocals and tune their guitars.

When everyone came back in, I saw that Kelly was there.

The guitar students went first. Then there was a break.

I ran to the restroom after drinking so much water.

The singers were next and I was the fourth person to go up. When the first student was up, I started practicing my warm ups.

"I can do better than that," I thought to myself.

The second girl did her routine while I was still practicing my scales.

"I can do better than that!"

The third girl went up and did her song.

"I can do better than that!"

"And now, Mary Beth Holliday," Pam announced.

Crap! I thought.

I went up on stage and turned around. I saw no on in the audience. I can do this, I thought.

"Hi. Hello," I started to say. "My name is Mary Beth Holliday and I will be singing, "One More Girl" by the Wreckers."

The music stated and the only person I could see in my mind was Tyler. I heard myself mess up on a few notes, but no one seemed to notice. There was only silence in the audience as I sang. You could hear a pin drop, I thought. As the song ended, I waited until there was the last strum on the guitar of the CD.

"Thank you," I said. Out of the silence that there was, the audience cheered and one person shouted out, "WOO!" I thought it was Kelly. She was just that kind of person.

As I made it back to my seat, Amanda's mom smiled at me. The girl in front of me, Mia, turned around and told me what a great job I did.

Everyone else did their songs.

Finally it was the finale. Amanda and I stood in the back and everyone sang Christmas songs. We were dismissed to our families. I ran to the bathroom. I came back to find Kelly and Cody talking.

I gave Pam her Christmas present and then Mom, Kelly, and I left.

We dropped Kelly off at the mall where she was meeting some of her friends.

I felt satisfied that I finally accomplished something like that in my life. I felt a hallow part in my heart, though.

Where was this coming from? I had sang in front of so many people, so why did I feel emptiness inside of myself? So what if Essence and Tyler weren't there? Who cared? I didn't do this for them. I did it for me, but I felt empty without Tyler.

He's just a man, I told myself over and over. *He shouldn't matter. Then why are you feeling this way*, another past jumped in and said. *It was love. It has to be. No one else has ever made you feel this way.*

But you know that love is not supposed to hurt this way, I told myself, again. I cried out in agony and misery! *You've never felt this way for any man before in your life! It has to be love!*

I emailed Tyler the next day and told him about my performance. I told him how someone in the audience was shouting out, WOO!" at the end. I told him how Pam's husband, Chad, told me "three records," after the recital was done.

"Nice!" Tyler wrote back. "I'm going to get your first record!"

"Ha-ha," I wrote back. "Very funny. Thank you."

Tyler was the only person I was thinking of when I was singing.

Christmas day had come at last, a day that I was not looking forward too having. A big part of me did not want a present from Ben. I wound up in my room after the mid morning had passed and everyone was over. I ended up in half tears, because to my predictions, Ben didn't get me a gift. I told Mom.

"No," she said and she pointed to an envelope on my dresser.

"I don't want it," I said. It would probably end up being trash. Mom had gotten angry at me for saying this.

"UH!" she let out a heavy breath. "Well, it's here. You can open it or remain in your mood. It's your choice."

Why would any mother be so cruel to her daughter? I thought.

Eventually, later that day, I opened the envelope to find a $15 gift card to Borders Book Store.

"Wow," I thought sarcastically. "He really put in a lot of thought into getting me this."

Joe had not opened the present that I got him.

"You paid for me to get out of jail," I heard him tell Mom. "I don't deserve anything else." Joe was really putting a damper on Christmas after I had already gotten him his present. Finally, after all the Christmas festivities were done, Joe opened his presents. I didn't get a thank you from him, but I didn't really care either way.

I was terribly sick on December 27th, 28th, and the 29th. I was throwing up every 15 minutes Saturday, December 27th, and then I made it once every half hour. I was running back and forth to the bathroom half of the day. Finally after so many trips back and forth, I asked for a bowl. The vomiting was slowing down at this point to only once an hour. I had to make it to the bathroom at 11 PM that night to throw up, finally making it two hours without vomiting.

Sunday, December 28, I woke up feeling terrible, again, but not as bad as the day before. I barely made it too the coach in the living room. Everything was loud! Joe's music; the washing machine; talking just above a whisper!

I didn't make it too singing Monday, December 29th, because I was still so sick!

I told myself over and over again that I was never going to fall in love ever again. *The lest man that I will ever fall in love with this is Tyler,* I told myself. *And he's not coming back!* I hated feeling this certain and uncertain at the same time! I was so in love with him, but I hated him at the same time.

It must be infatuation, I told myself, just to sleep threw the night. I was still crying myself to sleep each night over him.

On New Years Eve Day, I noticed a friend request in myspace. It was from a guy named Sean, whose profile I liked a lot. He was a musician which I respected.

Time heals all wounds, I told myself.

Chapter 21

Almost Too Late

Tyler was in a dream of mine on Saturday, January 3rd.

I couldn't help but send Tyler a message that day, asking if he'd like to hear all the stories I had for him.

"You'll laugh. You'll cry, because you're laughing so hard," I told him.

"Crying from laughter," he wrote back. "What a thrill!"

As far as I knew we were going to see each other again. It was going to happen soon too! I was nervous and excited, as usual.

But don't give your hopes up, a voice inside me said. It was going to happen, I could feel it.

On January 6th, I cried really hard. Mom kept saying, "You need to make more friends." I already knew how isolated I had become, but there was no way in Hell that that was my fault that this was the way things turned out. I wasn't the one who beat the self confidence out of me. I was just one kid, living in this messed up life that I had to deal with. I had to take on every other person's emotions and if I didn't and ignored it all, I would get yelled at for not caring!

It constantly hurt, getting so discouraged from my own dreams and goals.

"No, Mary Beth," everyone would say. "You need to do something more realistic." Why don't you tell Joe that? I would ask. "Joe's worked really hard at his art," they'd all say. And I haven't? I let everyone get away with *so much* shit in controlling every movement that I went through. I let this happen for so long that my body, mind and spirit were giving up. I was giving in to everything and everyone. And it hurt.

It felt as though no one believed that I could do music or anything that I wanted. Mom told me that she and Kelly thought I did a great job. *Then why didn't you support me in my dreams when I first started? You never just said that I did a great job after singing lessons. Not like with Joe. Oh, but I'm sorry. That's Joe we're talking about. Joe, the genius, the golden boy.* That was what it felt like for far too long. Enough was enough.

I told myself that I let go of Tyler. It was easier than holding onto someone that wasn't coming back. I knew it. It hurt though. "It was only a dream," I told myself, "nothing more than fantasy. I will never love another man again. He was only a dream…"

I told myself that I was better off alone. "You'll be okay in the end," I said. "I promise. Maybe not today, and maybe not tomorrow, but one day you'll be okay." I held onto that. It was all I had left.

Pam had asked if I wanted to record the song "You Left" that I had written a few years back, but I didn't think that fitted me anymore. It was dedicated to a guy that I no longer thought about and a feeling that I no longer had.

Mom had asked if I wanted a boyfriend, but I told her no. My heart wasn't going anywhere. All I wanted was Tyler, but he never wanted me.

By January 8th, I had texted Essence. She told me that love exists for everyone. But I knew that it wasn't meant to be for me. I tried my best to except that, and I was doing a good job at it, but Essence told me that there was someone out there for me. I knew that there wasn't and frankly I was tired of looking for someone that was never going to exist for me.

I was angry at Susannah because she was mocking me due to the fact that she said that I was going to be the last one to leave home. She said that I would never leave home. I cried out of anger and hatred towards her and everyone else! How *dare* they tell me that! How old were they when the Reynolds' family *finally* left home? In their thirties! I had ten more years to go, but I swore to God that I would have my own place in less time!

Love was going further and further away from me in my mind. It never existed and I wasn't going to wait and get hurt by falling in and out of love as quickly as I had done before. "It just doesn't exist," I told myself over and over. Saying this over and over again made the nights easier for me to deal with. I still cried harder than I had ever cried about anything or anyone just because Tyler wasn't there, but it wasn't as bad when I convinced myself that love just wasn't meant to be for me.

I had bought a Pilates DVD Sunday, January 18th from the $15 gift card that Ben bought me for Christmas. I told myself that I was going to get in shape. What else did I have to do? What did I have to lose?

The first week I started, I could only do three of the exercises on the DVD. Mom wasn't making it easier. When I told her that it was hard, I was referring to starting out something new. She told me, "You can't get there in one day." It hurt. I wasn't trying to get anywhere in one week. She said I couldn't. Fine, I thought. I'll show her! I'll show all of them!!!

I did the Pilates week after week, increasing the exercises and the days I did them.

Stimpy, my cat, wasn't doing too good. Her hair had a lot of tangles. Joe had to cut off her tangles with scissors, they were so bad.

I was so heartbroken over everything and everyone in my life that I told myself that I was going to lock myself away from everyone and everything forever. I was hurt. No one else was making it easier for me to deal with the heartbreak that I was feeling. What else did I have to lose if I swore off everyone and everything?

Well, that only lasted a little while. I knew that I couldn't hide away forever. I had to live my life without everyone telling me that I was stupid for evening thinking that there was a light on at the end of the hall for me. I had to deal with my life without anyone else interfering in it. I had enough!

I was so angry at myself for ever believing that love existed for me. That fairytales came true. I was fed lies as a child, I thought. Lies and deception. Love never existed for me and it wasn't going to start now! I hated myself for ever believing in happy endings.

Ashley was in the hospital on January 28th, giving birth to her son. Mike and Ashley had chosen the name Aidin. I didn't agree with the way that Mike and Ashley had their child first before getting married. Mom told me that she didn't like that either, but she never said anything to Mike about it. When it was me doing what she didn't approve of, she told me flat out, but it was different with Mike. Just because he's a Marine? *That isn't fair!* Mike was still living at home when he got Ashley pregnant!

When Aidin was born, he wasn't breathing. The feeding tube was wrapped twice around his neck, so they had to cut Ashley's stomach to get him out. A little while later, Aidin was breathing on his own.

I was still beating myself up very badly over Tyler!

"He's the one who said we should do this again!" I cried. "Where is he now? You're better off without him, kid. Don't worry," I told myself over and over, crying to an extreme that I had never been at before. "Essence and Kelly both told you that you're better off without him," one part of me argued. "But what do they know about it? They didn't have anything to do with him! I did!!! No one else can feel this way except me and it's not fair!"

After making myself believe that there was no such thing as love, life and the heartache starting hurting less. Life was easier to deal with when I wasn't waiting for some dude on a high horse to come and rescue me from the hell that I lived in each day.

I told Mom that I wanted a dancer's body and that I was going to work hard for it. Her response to me was, "Well, it's going to take a long time. Don't expect anything right away. You can't do it in one day." I told myself that no matter what I was going to do it! Screw everyone else! It still hurt a lot that my own mother had no confidence in me.

I hated myself so much that I was still so in love with Tyler. What did he have that I really wanted or needed? What did I have that I could give him? Not much on my account, that was for sure. Just because someone says one thing, doesn't mean that they'll stick to it. I knew this for oh, so many years, but I still believed that there was someone good inside every person. I was very wrong, I told myself over and over again.

I kept telling myself that it would be the last time I would ever contact Tyler. Over and over. Whatever lie I had told myself, came back and bit me in the ass. The crying at night wasn't getting any easier! I was done and it wasn't my fault, I would tell myself. I never asked for this life. To be in this amount of pain. No one could ever last if they spent five minutes living my life!

I started wishing that June 14th, 2008 had never happened. That was the first night that I ever saw Tyler.

Valentine's Day was the hardest day that I had to go through now. Mom and I were going to baby sit Miranda, so Tracey and Brian could go to the movies. I told myself that I was okay, but there are only so many times that one person can lie to themselves over and over again. Mom and I were driving to Bed, Bath & Beyond to get something for Tracey and Brian. I saw a couple holding hands and right then I felt like crying. Why was everyone shoving in my face that they had love and that I never would? How was that even remotely fair? I wasn't going to have true live and I knew that, but why did everyone have to remind me of that today? I felt like crying all day, but I wouldn't let myself.

I waited until I got home to let my emotions out. I cried myself to sleep that night.

I wanted to cry the entire next day, but I wouldn't allow myself to. Parts of me were arguing with each other. "Its true love…..It's not true love…." Make up your mind! I shouted. You're in pain either way! I'm never going to fall in love ever again, anyways, so what's the big deal?

On February 18th, Joe was acting up again. He was yelling about the fact that he didn't have enough money for school. He was going out that night. Before he left he said he was going to make someone pregnant. Mom and I were sitting on the coach. She pretended to not hear what he said. I hated Joe more and more, because he got away with *everything* and no one was doing a damn thing about it! I had to suffer with everyone being so negative towards me, but everyone else could get away with murder.

I had started asking everyone that I knew what I should do for my 21st birthday. I didn't want it to be like my 16th where eleven days beforehand my grandmother had died and that was what my birthday was about. I got messages from Essence and Kelly saying that I should drink and get so drunk that I forget my own name, but I swore to myself that I would never have beer. Tom told me to do the same thing. Finally, my friend Sean told me that he and his friends went hiking until 6 AM the next day for his 21st birthday. I wanted to do that right away! I did my research after that and I finally found the Red Wood Forest. Mom was very excited, because she had always wanted to go.

Life was getting more and more rejecting, though. I felt as if I didn't belong anywhere and that no one wanted me around.

"You hate everyone," I' got shoved in my face. I only acted the same way as everyone acted towards me. I let that everyone hated me, so I felt that it would only be fair to act the same way towards them.

Happy ending weren't real to me. Not anymore, I thought over and over. It was drilled into my head at a young age and that was what I ended up saying over and over. A small part of me wanted to yell and say that happy endings were for everyone, but I was stubborn and refused to get hurt again.

I was waking up at three in the morning every morning to have Tyler in my head. I could never get to sleep! I cried every night with him there in my head and I couldn't sleep a full night. It went on for months. I'd cry at night to get to sleep!

On March 3rd, I found a mermaid doll for Mom's birthday. She loves mermaids, I told myself, and this'll be perfect! I had to hide it in my room where she couldn't see it. I left it unwrapped, but in the bag that it came in.

On March 7th, I had heard the most disturbing news in the world! Little Tom was getting married! I didn't know how to feel about it, or if I should feel nothing at all. I was mixed up feeling hurt and anger towards him, sadness and betrayal, love and loss. Did I still love him? Or was it simply regret and loss?

Love shouldn't hurt you, I reminded myself. *But you felt the same way for Bill Greenlee. What is the difference?* The difference was that I knew Bill longer. He promised me forever, but forever with him would have been hard either way.

Tyler was constantly on my mind! No matter what I said, did, or thought, he was there! It annoyed the hell out of me more than ever!

What right does he have in doing that? I was furious with myself for always thinking of him! *No one controlled you like this before*, I'd say. *What gives anyone the right to do this to you now?*

I wanted to write to Tyler and tell him, "I love you but if you want someone else or other people then just let me know, so I can let you go." A Kelly Clarkson song inspired me to want to say that, but I never could. I wanted to say this more than anything, but I couldn't. Sometimes fantasy is better than nothing.

I kept reminding myself that Tyler was nothing to me. Nothing. He couldn't be anything, especially if he's not there! *It was not love*, I'd tell myself. *Then what are you? A stalker? NO!* I'd shout over and over. *I am not a stalker!* I'd fight with myself constantly, which turned violent. Maybe *I am in love*, I'd say, *but does love feel like this? Is it supposed to hurt this way?*

Essence and I had lunch at the Olive Garden on March 12th. Our waiter, Justin, was really cute! He was flirting with Essence and me! It was fun! It seemed that Justin was always looking at me, which was nice! I left him a $5 tip when we left.

Essence told me to never get in contact with Tyler again. He wasn't good for me. I knew this too well, but my heart was physically hurting from all this. I had to pretend that it was getting easier. That didn't help, so I decided to pretend to pretend that it was going to be okay. *Only time will te*ll, I told myself. *Memories will fade. You'll be okay.*

I wished that the love that I felt for Tyler wasn't there anymore. It kept me up at night, kept me crying, and I would yell out loud and I hated people for that. Who was this man turning me into?

Part of me knew that I was stronger without him, but the other part always questioned, *well, what if?*

I was saying, "Whatever dude! Whatever," so often that Mom would get mad at me and said to stop saying that. I would repeat it 20 times in a row. It annoyed her, but it annoyed me even more! The only reason I kept saying that was to not cry. I cried too much over Tyler and it had to stop! I continued saying that I was better off without him. I knew that.

I had to put on a brave face every day and every night just to keep from crying, even though I was screaming at the top of my lungs on the inside!

I asked myself why I wasn't good enough for him. Was I too loud? Was I too quite? Was I too nice? Was I not nice enough? I used to get made fun of for being too nice! Why would I even consider that I was anywhere close to being good enough for Tyler? I wasn't. I never could be.

On Mom's birthday, I gave her the mermaid, which she loved! She and I went to Pasadena and we went to a used bookstore. We were just tripping around in the store. I was looking for some author, when I look up and see this gorgeous guy! He had thick black glasses on and was wearing a black leather jacket. He looked almost exactly like Tyler. Could I never escape him? I wanted to find this guy. I was determined. I lost track of him. Mom and I decided to leave, but he was there when Mom and I walked out. He was beautiful.

I woke up at 6 AM on Wednesday, March 25th, because I was thinking of Tyler too much! He wasn't going to take over my mind! *Not like this,* I'd say. *Tyler lied to you anyway. He was never coming back, and you knew that. You have every reason to blame yourself for this.*

I always had the urge to contact Tyler. It wasn't going away. *But I shouldn't have asked him,* I'd tell myself. *This is as mush your fault as it is his. Maybe more!*

Mom started saying that I was going to get married and have kids. *With who? What kind if sick, twisted mind would find me attractive? I was pulled away from the only man that I will ever love. I will never love again!*

I was yelled at for being sad. How did that make sense? Mom would get angry at me for being sad. That made no sense to me. A mother should be there for her daughter when she's going through heartache.

I was mad at Tyler *now*, because he never even said goodbye. It just ended and that was it. It was never over for me.

I hated day dreaming about Tyler. Where was he? What was he doing? Who was he with? I didn't need to know! No matter what, he wasn't thinking of me! I hated thinking of him when I woke up; when I went to bed; when I was just sitting in my room! He wouldn't leave my head alone!

I found out in April that Sabrina had a new boyfriend. I hated that she had a *new* boyfriend! She will just be getting in trouble, I thought to myself. Mark my words!

On Wednesday April 15th, Essence went to the Olive Garden. She saw our waiter from March, Justin. He was working the bar when he decided to come over and talk to Essence and her friends.

"Justin asked about you," Essence told me on Friday.

"He did?" I asked excitedly.

Essence asked if she could give Justin my number.

"YES!" I told her.

Essence was seeing this guy Todd who was friends with her brother. Todd kept telling her that he wasn't good for her and that she shouldn't be seeing him. Her relationship with Todd ended the friendship he had with her brother.

In the back of my mind, I was never going to be okay without Tyler. He was the one, I said. He was the one and now he's gone and it's my entire fault! But there was this little voice that was screaming at me, "NO! You're better off without him! Let go! You'll be okay on your own. He doesn't want you? Fine. You're better off alone!"

I kept falling further and further in love with Tyler and for that I hated him! How dare he do that to me! What the hell did I do to him?

By April 29th I told myself to give up. A part of me was saying to give up and die. My body was tired and hurt all the time. Life wasn't meant to be this painful, I knew that much. Forget the part of being heartbroken forever, my body wasn't supposed to give up like this!

In my head, Joe was the saint and I was the ugly duckling. Mom always complimented Joe on everything and I was lucky to have a place to sleep.

Tyler was continuously haunting me.

Mom and I went to Arizona and visited family. We went to the University of Tuscan. It was nice, but Tuscan was way too hot for me!

After the trip I had no desire to ever go back to Arizona again! It was too hot and there was nothing to do except be around family. I couldn't be around family that much.

On Saturday, May 16th, Mom and I were invited to a pampered chief event at her friend's house. Mom told me that her friend invited me. I wanted to go. It might be fun, I told myself, to cheer up. But it will be awkward. You'll be the youngest one there. I had changed my mind, but Mom said, "It will be fun and my friends expect you to be there." I felt guilty and went.

We got lost first. It took us over an hour to get there. Then when we got there, Mom knocked on the door. This one lady almost closed it on me! She looked like those creepy house wives. There were quite a few of those there. I didn't belong. Of course I was the odd one out. I always was, but did it have to hurt like this? I felt like screaming the entire time I was there, but I didn't make a sound.

There was one woman that I found to be interesting. She used to sing to the army guys 50 years before.

I tried to control myself from screaming, crying, and running away. I made it through the event, fake smiling and all. Then Mom and I made it out to the car. I closed my door and broke down crying. I pointed out to Mom that I was the youngest person there and how much I hated that. It wasn't supposed to be this hard! When I told Mom how uncomfortable it made me feel, she said she'd back off. Yeah, like she did last year? I wanted to say, but I was too busy crying. Mom said, "The next time Pam and Chad have a show, I want to invite Julie."

"Fine, just leave me out of it," I felt like saying, but kept my mouth shut.

I told Tyler that I went Arizona. He sent me a message back telling me that he went to college there. He said he loved it there. Tyler told me to keep him posted on when my next recital was.

My goal from there on out was to drop 40 pounds. I felt like a whale, even though the scale said another thing. I was so obsessed with my weight. I was losing weight because I wanted to be with Tyler? I used to make fun of girls like this. When did I become so obsessed with a guy? I hated being this way and it was killing me.

Mom was going to see her friend Peggy one Sunday in May. I was invited to go, but I refused. I didn't want to be the odd one out again. Kalib, Peggy's son, was going to meet his biological father, as was Peggy.

Mom had a nice time there with everyone.

I went to Rite Aide to get some stuff for myself when Mom was in San Diego visiting Peggy. A car passed me and some guy whistled at me. I felt like yelling at him, "You want to come over here and say that!?" or, "You have problems!" but I said nothing and continued on my way.

Dr. Shirman told me that I was in love with Tyler. I hated him at this point. He was all I thought about and it annoyed the hell out of me!

I had to be thankful that I wasn't crying so much on the outside by May. Inside, though, I was screaming! It felt like I was going to tear down an entire building with all my pent up rage and sadness that I had! I felt so broken inside and nothing was ever going to change it!

I cried that Monday night, because I wanted what fictional characters had: true love. I was never going to have it. I cried to Mom. She told me that all of her friends thought I was pretty.

"They all need medication!" I screamed. I wasn't pretty. I wasn't smart. And I certainly was *not* funny! That was the way I grew up. The ugly duckling was a hard job, but it was all that I knew. I was the ugly duckling and no matter what, that was what I was going to stay as forever.

I wanted to be with Tyler, again, by the 29th. What was changing? Nothing. I mostly wanted to be free of him. He wasn't coming for me, I told myself over and over. Why should I go after someone that doesn't want me, again? I began to lose count of all the nights, months, hours, minutes, and seconds that I spent crying over him. This wasn't love, I told myself, again and again. This was torture!

On June 5th, I met Kate Voegele at a Borders bookstore in Hollywood. She performed three of her new sings acoustically. Mom and I were very excited to go. I got an autographed CD.

I decided to pretend that I was okay without a response from Tyler. I had to keep reminding myself that I was done with Tyler, anyways. "He's not coming back!"

On Friday, June 14th, I was in the living room when Joe came home. Joe left the house by 3:30 PM. I was alone to watch TV in peace.

Ben came at around 4:30 PM. I was still in the living room. He went to the kitchen and I heard him doing something, but I wasn't paying much attention.

Mom came home at around 6 PM. She smelled some smoke in the kitchen. I started freaking out, because I thought that maybe I forgot to turn off the stove after using it, but I remembered that I did turn it off. My mind was racing around. Had Joe not turned it off? No, I walked through there earlier. Then my mind went to Ben. Was Ben so mad at Conan not graduating from elementary school that he would kill me?

I thought that Mom would believe me as to what I thought happened. Turns out I was wrong.

"It was the ghost. *OOH*", Mom said.

"It was Ben," I said with tears forming in my eyes. "Ben tried to kill me."

"It was the cat," Mom said again.

"Ben tried to kill me," I said, even though I had no actual proof that it was him. All I had was a theory because of a noise I heard in the kitchen and the fact that he was the last person in the kitchen. Mom got mad at me for being afraid. I was pissed off that she didn't believe me. I almost died, but I was blamed for something that I never knew started.

It took a while for me to come to terms that I couldn't explain what happened exactly on that day. I was already blamed for a lot. Why should this be upsetting? It had a lot to do with the fact that I was so mistreated when Ben and Conan lived at home.

Essence and I had dinner Thursday, June 18th. We were going to go to the Olive Garden. I was excited and nervous to see if Justin was still there or not. I had nothing to lose in the long run. I was already so broken inside that it was amazing to still be standing, let alone breathing. Essence said that she called and asked, but the restaurant said that Justin didn't work there anymore.

"I don't think they'll tell you if someone works there," I told her. "Isn't that a little like stalking, anyways?"

"Yeah," Essence said. "You're right."

We went anyways to find that Justin wasn't there. My heart was a little let down, but I couldn't really tell anymore.

Maybe I was just selfish in love, I thought. Maybe that's who I am. I want everything to go a certain way. But life doesn't go like that, kid. You can't force someone into doing something or loving someone a certain way. Life breaks your heart. Some people have it easy and some people don't.

Chapter 22

Love, Life, a Broken Heart

Mom and I left the house a 10 Am on Friday, June 19th. We headed towards Berkeley. Mom got us a motel room for the night and everything was set. We got up to Berkeley at 4:30 PM that day.

At the motel we stayed at, there was a family in front of us; a mother and father, and their two children. The little girl said something about her Uncle Tom. I thought of the Toms'.

After getting our room we walked around the Marina for a while. We found a little children's yard where the kids would build things. It was fenced off so Mom and I couldn't go inside and check it out. On the side of a wooden board was the name "Mike." Immediately I thought of the Toms and the Mikes from Tom's graduation day in Berkeley.

For dinner that night, Mom and I had pizza and a salad from the Cheese Board just down the way from the motel. We had our dinner outside on a park bench facing the water.

We watched *Ghost Adventures* that night. They showed a rerun.

Saturday came at last. It was my birthday! Mom and I were going to the Red Woods to hike around all day. It was a free weekend up there, so Mom only had to pay for the bus trip.

We were really lost for two hours trying to find the bus pick up area. Finally, after over an hour of trying to find it, Mom and I saw a group of guys that were just sitting around. She decided to park the car and we went over and asked for directions. The guys were nice. They didn't seem much older that I was. This one guy that caught my attention reminded me of a cross between my high school crush, Josh, and Tyler. The guys were nice and gave us good directions. We thanked them and then went on our way.

Finally getting to the bus area, Mom bought our passes and we waited for the ride to come. The bus came and 40 minutes later we were at the park. The ride was up hill, so I didn't do too well. My eyes were closed through most of it. Mom and I started hiking around at 12:30. We went up and down all there different paths. We saw birds and took picture of the trees. There was one trail that I didn't think I would be that much of a fan on, so we started going back a little bit. There were people coming down the little road that it was on.

"You know, it's very nice up here," a guy said while he was coming down.

"She's afraid of heights," Mom said. *Why not just put a cardboard sign over my head that says, "Freakish girl. Watch out"* I thought.

"It's not that high," the guy said.

"Let's do it," I told Mom. So we went up and it was wonderful!

We walked around the national park and in the state park for three and a half hours. It was great!

The ride back down the hill went okay. Closing my eyes through most of it kept me from crying out in fear.

For dinner that night, we had crepes at a small restaurant in Berkeley. We ate ice cream and cookies for desert. It was a great day. One of the best birthdays I ever had.

The next morning, Mom and I were leaving Berkeley and going home. First we were going to have breakfast with Mom's cousin Lee and her husband Gordon just out of town a little way. Gordon and I were talking and joking around the entire time. It was fun. Gordon said that I should count the restrooms that Mom and I stop at on the way back. I asked if the one there counted.

"Well, you have to start somewhere," Gordon said.

We said our goodbyes and Mom and I left. On the ride home, I saw a lot of cows and I thought of Tyler, of course.

For the one present that I got that wasn't the hiking experience, I received the movie "Corpses" from Mom. I watched it and laughed all the way through it.

I realized that I was in charge of my life. *No more fear!* I thought. Well, that only lasted a little while.

I realized the reason I was so anti-social was because I was never in groups in school. I was always off with different adults doing therapy. I never had the opportunity to be with kids my own age when I was younger and that was where my fear to be social came from. If they liked me, I always thought it was out of pity. The kids and some adults seemed like they were always in some way poking fun at me. It hurt and that was why I lashed out at people when I was a kid.

The anniversary of the first day that I met Tyler was coming up. I wasn't sure how I felt. Was I happy that I wasn't with him? Was I sad? Angry? Depressed? Betrayed? Disgusted? Confused? Was I in love? Was it lust? Was I stronger? Weaker? The list went on and on. I was massively hurt, that much I knew. Every emotion I had ever felt in my life, I was feeling now. People would make me feel worse just because I didn't believe in true love. It was just fantasy and I needed to grow up, but they held me down by saying: True love exists for you, Mary Beth. I'm going to wear this to your wedding. On and on and on! I knew better. True love, or love itself, wasn't meant for me. I had to except that and deal with it. But it was harder when everyone around me said that somewhere love was waiting for me. I'd rather deal with the truth than to believe in some kind of fantasy and get even more hurt.

But how can you break a broken heart? I'd ask myself. *The truth is: you can't. You're heart is broken, kid, and there's no getting out of it. And since when is it okay to tell me that love exists for me. When I grew up, believing that I would get a happy ending, everyone else made it clear that it would never happen for me.*

Mom told me that I didn't try hard enough at making friends, but she didn't know how I *hard* really tried. But no one had to take in every negative thing that was always thrown at me. They didn't cry themselves to sleep, praying not to wake up in the morning. I always felt so isolated, but I was never allowed to be alone. I was yelled at for being lonely and in the end it was my entire fault. That was what it felt like. I never asked for the life that I lived to get harder. God and my angels were the only ones that I knew were there for me, but at times it felt lonelier than ever.

My eye doctors were very pleased with how well my eyes were doing.

July 7th finally came. I cried all morning and all afternoon. *Why didn't he come back?* I thought. *I mean, I know that I can be annoying and I know that I am stupid. And I have always been that ugly girl since childhood, but why did he have to pretend that he wanted to see me? He didn't need to act like he really wanted to see me. Was I just a joke to him? That's it, I was only a joke. I was only a stupid experiment and someone for him to laugh at.*

The crying grew more and more intense from there on out. The rage took over my body. The fear sunk into my skin. The self hatred grew stronger and stronger that day. I told myself I had to let go. *He's not coming back. And frankly, he's not missing out on anything.*

My second recital was coming up. July 12th was going to be the day. I cursed myself for inviting Tyler, again. *He's not coming, kid. When are you going to get that?* I still had hope.

No one wants to see me. Robert's not coming. Tyler's not coming. Essence is off doing her thing. No one wants to see me. I thought. *NO!* I screamed at myself. I also had Mom yelling at me too. *You're not doing this for them! This is for you! No one else matters! Get that in your head. This is for you! NOT THEM!*

I didn't cry too long this time. Mom and I went to the same music store as the last time. I wore a little black dress and my black sandals.

Getting there, we went to the back and went inside to wait. Pam, Chad and Cody were already there, along with some of the other students. I checked the schedule and saw that I was the fourth person up, again, on the singing. The students had to warm up, of course, so the parents left the room.

Kelly had gotten there when the family members came back in.

The guitar students were up first. They all did their thing. I thought the little girl Andréa did the best job with the guitar. Amanda did a good job as well.

The break came and I ran to the restroom. Kelly and I hung out a little beforehand. We waited. Afterwards, I went back to the recital room and Tracey showed up. I introduced Tracey to Kelly. At last, the singing was going to start, so everyone had to take their seats.

I practiced my exercises in my seat while the first three students went up and sang. *I can do better than that!* I thought after each performer had there turn.

"And now I would like to bring up Mary Beth Holliday," Pam said with a smile.

I went up, not really knowing how to start introducing myself, again.

"I love you," I heard someone shout from the audience. I figured it was Kelly.

"How's it going?" I asked and paused for a second. No one said anything. "You're good? Good. So, hi. I'm Mary Beth Holliday and I will be singing 'Only Fooling Myself' by Kate Voegele."

"Remember your diction," Pam told me before she started the CD. And then I was off. I did my hand jesters like I practiced at Pam's. The only person I saw was Tyler. Part of me broke because he wasn't there, but I had to remind myself that I already knew that was going to happen. It hurt, though. It still hurt. There was no getting over that.

"Thank you," I said as the song ended. The audience went crazy!

I had reminded myself, once again, that love didn't exist. *It wasn't written in your cards. GET OVER IT!*

Little Tom's wedding was coming up. Tom and Cameron had come out from New York for the wedding that was in Big Bear. I was pretty upset, but I did my best to hide my emotions.

Mom and I went to Manhattan Beach to see Tom and Cameron and to meet Cameron's brother. Everything was fine there. Tom and Cameron were coming out for a barbeque at home the day after the wedding. I was going to make the jalapeño burgers that I liked so much from a cooking magazine.

Saturday, July 18th, Mom and I were going to make the coffee cake that I had in one of my other cooking magazines. Everything was going okay, but I suddenly felt overwhelmed by sadness and heartbreak. Tyler and Tom were both on my mind. I wanted to marry Tyler and spend the rest of my life with him, but I was forced to do otherwise. I started crying as Mom and I were making the coffee cake.

"What's wrong?" Mom asked out of panic and concern.

Like you care? I thought.

"I have a broken heart," I cried to her.

"Oh," she said and that was all. She didn't say, "It's going to be okay," or anything comforting of the sort. No. I just felt worse and worse. I had to make the tears stop. The rest of the day passed.

Sunday finally came. Mom and I were getting ready for the barbeque. Tom's friends were coming over, which was going to be a weird kind of experiment for me. I had hidden in my room before, but I was determined to sit with everyone else now!

Mom and I made the burgers, but doubled the recipe because there were going to be more people. I only made eight of the burgers, but I knew that I was going to have one and I hoped that Tom would have one as well.

Mom was away at the store when Tom and Cameron walked in the house.

"Hello?" Tom said as he and Cameron walked in.

"Tom," I said and went over to give him and Cameron a hug. I was wearing an apron, so they knew that I was cooking. I told them that Mom was away at the store. She came back a little later. Everyone went out to the backyard.

Someone knocked at the front door. It was Ara and his girlfriend, Karen. I gave Ara a hug and told him that Tom was out back. He and Karen went in the back.

After everything was good, I went out back and sat down with everyone else.

More of Tom's friends were there. Robert came. I met Tom's friend Joe. Everything was going well. I was social at last!

Tom was going to get a drink.

"Hey Mary Beth, do you want a drink?" Tom asked me.

"Oh, I can get it," I said, getting up. I had to know what my choices were.

"You know, you're 21 now. You can have a beer," Tom told me.

"No, I'm good with a soda," I told him

Ara jumped in. "You're 21? I remember when you were a kid. You can't be 21! That makes me feel old!"

"Why does everyone still think that I'm 17?" I asked. I chose my drink and went back to my seat.

I looked Ara in the face and said, "Hey, Ara. I came back over here just to make you feel old." Ara laughed.

Ara was telling all of these different stories.

"Karen's friend has the fear of cotton," he said. Everyone laughed. "This one guy dressed up in a giant cotton custom and walked in the room. Karen's friend screamed, so the guy just walked out backwards."

I was laughing all through the story!

"Hey, Mary Beth, good job with the burgers," Tom told me and gave me thumbs up as he ate one.

Desert was served. I was the first one to get a piece of the coffee cake.

"Hey, Mary Beth," Tom said again. This time I was on the other side of the yard. "Good job with the cake," he said with another thumbs up.

After the party was ending, Tom's friend Chaz and Robert were leaving. Chaz told me that he really liked the coffee cake.

"I had three pieces of the coffee cake," Chaz told me.

"I'm glad you liked it," I said.

Tom and Cameron were going to drive back to Manhattan Beach where they were going to get a flight out the next day.

"You look good Mary Beth, "Cameron told me.

"I've been doing Pilates," I told her. We all said our goodbyes, and then they left.

The refrigerator broke the last week of July. Mom was mad and took it out on me, again. She yelled at me because Ben was supposed to come over and make sure that the refrigerator guys knew what to do. It was then that I wanted to move out, because I was sick and tired of getting yelled at for things that weren't my fault and that I had no control over.

Ben didn't come that day and neither did the refrigerator guys.

Tom always told me that college was a good place for me. He always encouraged me to go back to college and I really wanted to, up to a point. So much talk about college and that I belonged there. That was just too much for me to handle. Tom told me that if I was interested in writing that I should talk to Ben because he wrote a short story online. I was *so angry* at Tom. He knew that I hated Ben and yet he insisted on me talking to someone who would have killed me. Maybe it was my fault, but I cried myself to sleep too many nights when Ben lived at home and I wasn't going to talk to someone that I loathed that much!! I hated typing back to Tom about how much I hated Ben and how I was never going to talk to him again! I hated typing his name; he had that much of an impact on me! My eyes twitched with rage from only looking at it!

On August 5th, my heart pounded in fear. Joe had come home and started throwing everything out of his room. Nothing was to out of the ordinary there. He threw all of his art in the trash and was yelling and screaming at Mom. I quivered in fear. Joe yelled at Mom, "Get the fuck out of my room!"

"This is my house," Mom said in a surprisingly calm voice. I was so terrified of what Joe might do that I hid behind half of a wall.

I was sitting on the couch, trying to stay calm as Joe rushed to the kitchen and I heard him use the scissors. I heard them drop to the floor, but I was too horrified to go pick them up in the kitchen, only a few feet away. I decided that I was going to take the empty bowls which were once filled with cereal to the kitchen. There, I would have an excuse to pick up the scissors.

Joe screamed he hated Mom and that he wanted out of the house. He left in only his underwear, but soon came back and changed into clothes.

He took a bag with more clothes in it this time as he left the house, screaming. My heart pounded from fear the entire time.

Mom told me that he was drunk. She said he had been drinking vodka.

Only a few years ago, Joe said he would never drink. He said that he would never do that. Why did he change his mind? What is wrong with him? I thought.

Mom had gotten a call later that night after we went to bed. Joe had called her from a bush somewhere. He cried that he was sorry.

I hoped that a situation like that would never happen again.

I was dealing with too much from all the emotions that I had for Tyler. I was angry at him one minute and the next I was in love and I couldn't live without him. *What is wrong with me?* I'd ask myself, but I could never get an answer that suited my curiosity. I was crying so much and so hard over Tyler. It was hurting me more than ever! Mom would tell me that Tyler is simply "too old for me." What about Mike and Ashley? She'd never tell them that? Why was Mike "allowed" to be with Ashley who was only two years older than I was, but I wasn't allowed to be with the man of my dreams? Mike and Ashley fought all the time anyways. They had a baby, so that makes everything okay? No! That doesn't change anything. I'm sure I could find a guy that I liked the same way, but I knew that I would approach things differently. My dreams for marriage were over, what else did I have to lose? I never saw the difference.

I always thought that I was only fooling myself with Tyler. He was perfect and I was a freak of nature!

I spoke with Kelly. She had a new boyfriend. I cried so hard over the fact that Kelly had someone and I never would. I told Mom and I was yelled at. Her response was always, "You need to get friends." What I needed the most was confidence in order to *try* to get friends, but she already took that away from me. Everyone took that away from me, so there was no looking back on that now.

I had begged Essence to talk to Justin and see what he said. She told me that he was still broken up about ending his relationship with his ex-girlfriend. Moving on was the hardest thing, I knew that from too much experience, but you're better off in the end, or so the story goes.

I wanted to see an improv by myself. I told Mom and she yelled at me.

"I'M NOT DROPPING YOU OFF ALONE!" she yelled. I cried.

"Okay," she said, after calming down. "I can take you."

"No," I responded. "I don't want to go anywhere ever again!"

I stayed at home and watched my misery happen for another night. I hated it, but tried my best not to show it.

I had let go of every guy that I held onto for so long: Tom, Jeremy, Bill, and Jose, but nothing hurt as much as Tyler. Not for me, at least. My friends kept telling me, "You're better off without him. He's not good enough for you." On and on and on. But no one ever felt the pain that I felt. I had erased Tyler's number from my phone more times than I could count, but I kept coming back. It hurt and it drove me insane! Since when did I need a man in my life this much? This was taking over my life and I hated the feeling. Was I doomed to always think of Tyler and to always want him?

I fought with myself and cried harder and harder everywhere I went. At the dinner table, in my bed, at my psychologist's office, in the shower, at the park and in my dreams. It was a never ending battle. I began to hate the world more and more each day.

On Sunday, August 23rd a crisis had come. The phone rang and I checked to see that it was a payphone, so I didn't answer it. Mom came in and asked who it was.

"It was just a payphone call," I told her.

"That could have been important, Mary Beth. You should have answered it," Mom said. "Maybe they left a message," she said while checking the phone. The phone rang again a minute later and Mom answered it.

"Hello," I heard her say in a scared tone.

Joe was on the other line calling from a police station in Sylmar. I felt guilty right away for not answering the phone, but how was I to know who was calling?

The assumption that was made by Mom was that Joe's girlfriend Juliet broke up with him. The next few minutes were a blur for me.

"Joe was put on medication. Joe sounds down. Joe gets out Tuesday. He was going to be in the hospital for 72 hours." I knew that 72 hours wouldn't fix anything with Joe. He was stressed, but then again what else was new? Joe's unorganized. Again, what else was new?

I had a feeling that Joe's car was impounded before I had heard anything, and in the end I was right.

I was right that Joe and Juliet never made any sense. Someone so messed up as Joe with someone nice like Juliet just didn't add up in my book. Still everyone thought that they were meant to be.

I was crying over Joe for the rest of the day. I was scared that I had lost a brother. I was scared that I had lost Joe, of all people. It didn't make any sense that I was crying five times a day for a person that wasn't very nice to me to begin with. But I was scared that I was losing a brother. I wouldn't have him anymore, despite that he and I fought most of the time or that I was afraid of him most of the time. It didn't matter. I was afraid.

Joe thought that no one cared about him, but everyone was worried what might happen to him. Mom went to the hospital that Sunday. I stayed at home, crying.

Monday came around. Joe was still at the hospital, but I kept my singing lesson that night. I thought I'd get through it okay.

Amanda was still there. She asked how I was.

"Not too good," I told her through a fake laugh, trying to keep my tears down. She left and Pam asked how I was. I broke down crying and told her what happened to Joe. It was the first time that I ever cried in front of her over Joe or anything concerning him. Pam gave me a tissue before I told her what I heard that happened to Joe.

I apologized for crying and did my lesson.

Tuesday night came around. Mom and Tracey went to the hospital to see Joe. They never saw him, because Joe thought that Mom was mad at him. Tracey and Mom stayed outside and spoke for a while. Tracey ended up writing a letter to Joe and gave it to the nurse to pass it on to Joe.

Joe's only concern was Juliet. He thought they broke up and he wanted to see her.

Joe was released on Wednesday, and he ended up walking home.

I was put through hell and back, again. I spent those few days that Joe was in the hospital crying every few hours on how worried I was about Joe, knowing that he wouldn't change, but always hoping that there was some small hope that he would be okay through it all and would seek help or at the very least not drink anymore alcohol.

I saw my eye specialist on September 4th. The doctor was very pleased with my vision! I had been practicing the eye exercises a lot. I told myself that I wasn't allowed to see anymore double vision and that my right eye needed to come in and work harder than ever to make that happen.

The doctor said that I would always see double in my life, just not all day long. I needed to work hard, and I knew that.

Tom came out or a wedding for one of his friends in September. He was very busy with his school work, but he made time to spend with me and Mom. On Sunday, September 6th, Mom, Tom, Susannah and I went to the Getty Museum to see the new art there.

The art work at the museum was great, but I was feeling too sick so I couldn't sit still for too long.

Tom gave me the big lecture of how I should go back to college. I assured him that I was going to start taking a dance class that month.

"Oh, that's good," Tom said. "You're going to have to take it more than just one time. I'll be really disappointed in you if you just drop it after one time."

"I'm going to take it more than once, Tom. Don't worry," I assured him. I was trying to think of going more than just once. Things were hard for me to do just one time, let alone to keep doing it over and over again. But I made a promise to Tom and I was making a promise to myself that I would go for a month or two just to try it out. My first day was September 10th. I was sweating a lot, but I was highly active and I loved it. I wasn't the only new person there and the teacher was nice so it felt comfortable.

Essence and I had lunch on Thursday, September 17th, after my dance class. She was away at the restroom and our waiter came over.

"Is someone else here," he asked me, looking at Essence's jacket on her seat.

"Yes," I told him.

"Can I start you off with a drink," the waiter, Brett, asked.

"Iced tea," I told him.

Brett left. Essence came back. Brett came back with my drink and Essence ordered a Shirley Temple. I got a salad, of course.

I felt adventurous and a little flirty, so I left my number, but he never called. I wasn't too disappointed.

The week of September 21st, I was feeling so terrible! The dizziness was there, full blast! I was feeling nauseated at well.

Kelly and I had a late lunch that Thursday. She and I went into a clothing store afterwards.

"I know what I'm wearing to your wedding," she told me. I knew that I was never going to get married. My mind was already set on that. I wasn't going to fall in love ever again anyways.

That week, Mom and I found out that her cousin was diagnosed with a rare liver cancer. There wasn't much the doctors could do for her. But I prayed a lot that she would get better. Every night she was in my prayers before I went to sleep. Her brother Joe was dealing with this terrible illness that was taking his sister away and I'm sure he had to act brave for both of their sakes. It was a hard thing to do, I knew too well from experience of my own, pretending that everything was okay when you were really crying and screaming on the inside! I felt so horrible about what Henryette was going through.

Susannah had her Kiwi friends out from New Zealand. They were nice enough. They were both actors, so they were looking for work out here.

We were all going to go to a go-cart-derby down town. Mom and I were going to meet Susannah and her friends down at the subway. Ben, Vicky, and Conan were coming too. I hated them, so right away I changed my mind, but I forced myself to go. You never know, I told myself to try and feel better of the situation.

I wore my red punk-rock skirt and a black tank top.

We all got there and waited for the derby to start. There were these two guys with black sunglasses on that were coming our way through the crowd. They had nothing on except black thongs. They squeezed there way past me. The first guy that came my way had a banana peel coming out of his thong. He was shaking his ass at me while he came past. Mom and Vicky were laughing at that. The second guy brushed past my left hand.

Mom was upset at me because she said that my underwear was showing. I thought that no one was looking at me, but to her that whole word was looking at me. Looking at what, I thought. There's nothing to see. What do they see when they look at me? A big scar? A freak of nature? A hideous beast???

Tom won first place in a contest that he and another student entered for the New York Times later that month.

I was determined to never get in contact with Tyler ever again! He wasn't doing any good for my health.

I was working on "Forever and Almost Always" by Kate Voegele on my guitar and it seemed to be getting better and better throughout time. I was getting better at not taking up an entire half hour, trying to get through the song. I made it to 15 minutes and then 10 and finally 5 minutes for the song. I was very pleased with myself as the song went.

I hated myself more and more for falling for Tyler so hard and so fast. He wasn't the only man in the world! And I knew that. There were plenty of other guys out there. Even though I told myself that I was never going to love again, I was determined to move on. It hurt way too much holding on to nothing. But somehow it hurt worse letting go. I would wake up at 2 AM and Tyler would be on my mind. It was too much. I would toss and turn for hours, always unable to fall asleep until the sun was coming up, and then I would only get two more hours to sleep.

Tom was always pressuring college on me. I wanted to go back, but I didn't want to have a try and fail like the first three times that I went.

Mom was determined to go out to New York before the year ended. There were miracles out there, so that was what I prayed for. Henryette had to be okay!

I was dealing with too much myself. My headaches had all come back. I was dizzy mostly in the mornings and it lasted until early afternoon, most days. Some days the dizziness was there 100% of the time and it was driving me insane! Why should anyone care now? They all ignored me for so long and said that I was crazy and stupid and that I was making up the pain. Why would I do that to myself? Why would I even consider making up the pain that I was in? I was in tears from the pain and everyone thought I was making it up!

On Saturday, October 3rd, I had gotten my hair cut. I was going to get pictures done in my little black dress.

While at the hairdressers, I had the feeling that I was going to end up like alone in the end. I did not want to do that. I had been through too much. I was screaming at myself for even thinking that. It seemed that I was never going to have true love or love at all and I was trying to except that. I felt so guilty for thinking bad thoughts, so I tried to ignore them.

Mom and I went to the photo place and this Asian lady tried to make me smile so much. I didn't feel like smiling, but I forced myself to do so through some of the pictures. I purchased two pictures out of the ten that were taken. I was still battling this awful feeling inside me. The Asian lady gave me a free photo booklet to keep the photographs in. I thanked her and left.

Mom and I were going to go see Pam and Chad play that night. I was very upset, so I cried and screamed to Mom. She and I were in a heated argument at the kitchen table when we got home. I was so mad and I took it out on Mom, which in the end made me feel so much worse. She always asked Joe what was wrong, but never bothered asking me. That hurt a lot! I had to keep everything bottled up inside until it exploded out into tears that caused me to hyperventilate. I didn't want to go anywhere ever again. So I fought with myself.

I finally told myself, "Too hell with it," and I decided to go to the show to see Pam and Chad that night with Mom. My favorite song that they did was called, "Worth the Wait", that Pam had written. It was a sad love song. I didn't believe in love anymore. It certainly wasn't looking for me, so I wasn't going to waste my time searching for it. It was still a nice song, though.

I wanted my first kiss so badly that I begged Mom to find a guy for me to kiss. She only seemed to forget. Joe was causing so much mayhem at home and in his life that Mom forgot about me. I was left alone to deal with a feeling of loneliness and frustration. My tears seemed as if they were only friends now. I was feeling worse and worse about myself and the fact that I lost the only man that I would ever love.

On Friday, October 9th, I went to see my regular doctor at UCLA. I explained all of my symptoms to my doctor. Ruman. She didn't have an answer as to why I had all this pain to deal with. She gave me the referral to see a neurologist at UCLA. I explained that my tube in my neck was bothering me again and how the pressure was hurting me so much.

Mom made an appointment for me to see the Neurologist on Friday, October 15th.

Great, I thought. *Someone new that doesn't have a clue what they're doing with me.* I was going to give it a shot and see what happened. Maybe there was someone who had a solution to the pain that I was going through.

I was practicing more and more to "Forever and Almost Always" on my guitar and I was getting better. I still had a long way to go before I was as good as I thought I could be. I was going t do it for the next recital, I had decided.

My mind wandered all day long. I had everything and yet I still had nothing at all. I wanted love. I wanted to wake up next to the man that I loved and then, I thought, everything would be okay. I only woke to disappointment and tears. There were times that I feared for my life because of everything at home.

I had a strong hatred of everyone that always said how "cute" or "adorable" I looked. *You can't ignore me for 21 years and then all of a sudden say, "Oh, Mary Beth. You look so pretty." No! It doesn't work like that. You and I both know that I am not pretty or adorable or anything to that nature!* It was annoying as Hell to hear this. I hated it and I hated myself more and more.

I felt even more lost and alone by October 23rd. Maybe it was my fault, but I didn't ask for a life like this. I was just one kid trying to get through life like this as best I could. Even through the hard times, I always thought that there was a light on at the end of the tunnel. I never liked blaming the world for what they all did to me. I tried to only focus on what I could do, but I had others tell me that I put myself down. I wanted to scream louder and louder 24/7! No one would hear me, though. I wanted a life that had nothing to do with the fact that I was run over at such a young age. I wanted to fall madly in love and have that person love me back even more. I wanted to feel confident again. I never knew what that felt like. I wanted my dreams to come true and not be put down by so many people out there. But mostly, I wanted Tyler to come back for me.

I had calmed down a little on October 24th. I wasn't crying so hard.

Every morning, Tyler was there on my mind. It hurt, but I had to get up and start each day as if something good were going to happen.

My neurologist didn't seem to know what to do, so I saw Dr. Lazereff in November. I always seemed to have three options with him. 1) do nothing; 2) Have a surgery to move the tube further in my neck. This was dangerous, f course. What surgery wasn't? Or, 3) the doctor would have the shunt taken out completely. Mom seemed really relieved with the third option. I was drawling a blank. How dare anyone think that I had so many options! I was the one suffering through all this pain, emotional and physical, and *now* they believed me? I was ignored for months. Centuries, it felt like! You can't just decide that *now* I can have the surgery that I wanted from the very start!

I had dreamt that Tyler sent me four emails saying that he wanted to hang out with me. That was all that I had now, just dreams.

I was angry about Tyler and took it out on Mom the next day. I felt so horrible about doing that. *But, why?* I thought. *She's yelled at me hundreds of times for things that were never my fault. And I had to take it. Why should I feel guilt over this?* But I did.

The pain was still coming and it drove me insane! I was in tears because of it, but I made myself wait.

You're not going to have the surgery, yet. I said. *Not until after New York.*

I had finally found an angel necklace for Henryette at the mall. It did cost a lot, but it was nice. She would have her angel looking out for her through all of her chemo and radiation. Everyone else was worried about her, but I had my faith that everything was going to be okay. All I could do was hope. All anyone could do was hope.

My singing had really improved. Pam thought I was doing such a great job! I had decided that I wanted to record a song that I had written called, "Two Lovers." I had decided against recording that song after only a short while.

On Friday, November 13th, I was so angry! Mike and Ashley were getting married. I was hurt and confused. How could Mom be "okay" with this? She wasn't okay with me and Tyler, but she was okay with Mike and Ashley? *This isn't fair!* I screamed at myself. *What? Just because they have a baby? Women have been getting pregnant from the beginning of time.* I felt angrier and angrier as time went by. *Why are they allowed to do that, and Mom is still making me feel terrible about Tyler. Is it because Tyler and I didn't sleep together? Or was it because I didn't kiss him? Was it because I would have gone the slowest with him?*

I wanted the world to pay. I wanted Tyler to pay for everything that he did to me. For every emotion that I felt for him, I wanted my revenge. Love wasn't supposed to feel this way. I wasn't supposed to be this angry at the one man that I thought I loved. And yet at the same time want nothing else to do but hold him forever. It was nothing more than a fairytale that kept me going on in life. Having Tyler come back and we lived happily ever after. It was nothing but a fairy tale.

Sabrina had gotten a hicky from her "boyfriend" in Arizona. This made me feel a lot worse. My world was already ending, why did you have to do that to me? Why share such a thing that I will never have?

I was so angry. Not only at Sabrina, not only at Mom, not only at Mike and Ashley and the rest of the family, but I was angry at Essence. She said that she was going to go back to the Olive Garden and give Justin my phone number. It wouldn't have changed anything, but there was hope that things could have been better. Maybe I wouldn't have cried so much anymore. I was crying over a man that didn't feel the same way for me.

Joe was making the family deal with too much! He would have his "episodes" as Mom called them. I would be sitting in my room or on the couch minding my own business. Then I would hear, "Fuck *this*....Fuck *that*...." And I would be very scared, as usual. I would quiver in fear if Joe so much as walked in a room. You could never tell what kind of mood he would be in. He had a rifle in is room that I had only found out about from Mom going on and on with the anxiety that she was feeling over him. This outraged me, of course. He had a parking ticket that never got paid, and he wasn't taking any responsibility for it.

Joe would go wild in rage and get away with it.

Mike and Ashley had set their wedding date for December 4th, 2009. I was so angry and heartbroken, again. I would never have my wedding day. I would never walk down the aisle to the wedding song that played and see anyone there waiting for me.

How is it fair that Mike and Ashley are "okay" together, or "perfect" together? But I'm not evening close to being "allowed" to live the life that I want with Tyler? I thought about this over and over.

When Joe was having one of his blow ups on Tuesday, November 17th, I was so scared that I emailed Tom and told him what happened. I was terrified to leave my room that afternoon to just go out and get coffee. I was terrified to just wash the dishes that afternoon. Joe was at the computer in the living room when I was at the kitchen sink after getting back from Starbucks with my coffee. Everything was quite and seemed calm, but this freaked me out even further. What was coming? What was going to happen?

I was harder and harder on myself for my looks. "I'm too fat...I'm too ugly.... I'm not smart enough...." All of this and then some had been dumped on me for years when I was jus a young kid. Most of it was Conan or Ben's influence on him, but even Mom was harsh on me at times.

I hated how other people would always put words inside my head and make me feel even worse about myself or the situation. I had been through so much already. Why can't you just leave me alone with my own thoughts, I'd think, but I would never say. Not until it all blew up on everything and everyone. Everyone in my family always made fun of me or would be mean to me and I would just have to take it. "It's all just light heartedness", Mom would say. "She didn't mean it." Or the worst would be when Ben would get away with such bull shit and never look back. Nothing bad ever happened to him. And that was what sickened me the most.

I was made fun of by my own mother for the choices that I made in life. I told myself from a very young age that I would never drink alcohol and I had even told Mom that at such a young age. I told her that I would never smoke or do drugs. I would be laughed at and mocked for making my own decisions. Just because I didn't want to be like Chuck or Joe or Ben or Mike or Susannah. Just because I didn't want to get drunk with a homeless guy in Central Park for the company like Tom. How much more did everyone want to beat out of me? I had no confidence and I was heading down hill fast!

On Friday, December 4th, Mike and Ashley got married. It was the only time that Mom was "okay" with me wearing my little black dress. I was the only person there to get dressed up.

It was a small room and the "bride" didn't walk down the aisle or wear white.

Ashley wore a grey dress and Mike had on a suit. The best man was Ben; a terrible choice, I thought. The maid of honor was Ashley's aunt. It was a small group and I felt horrible the entire time because of Tyler. I felt worse and worse, but I swore to myself that I wouldn't let it show. I couldn't allow myself to cry in front of these people.

We all had Chinese food after the wedding. It was a great meal after a wedding, but everyone was lost getting to the restaurant.

That night, I asked Mom if she could drop me off at LA Connections. I wanted to talk to Tyler or at the very least, see him and wave hello. Mom agreed to drop me off by myself, for once. My heart was pounding as I existed the car and walked up to the door. Karen wasn't behind the counter this time. It was some dude whom I had never seen before. I paid for my ticket and decided to wait in the lobby. Maybe Tyler will be here and I'll get to see him again, I thought. I sat down and waited, thinking of everything that I had to say to him. Would I yell? Would I scream? Would I walk or run away? What would happen? Would I cry? Would I hug him?

A lot of other people had shown up, but they were all in there little groups on the side of me. I was excluded, what a shock.

Finally the doors opened. The first act was over. I went in right away and found an empty seat in the middle of the second section. Everyone else came in and sat to me right. No one sat in my section, but I thought, *Good. More room for me*, just to make myself feel better with the situation. I switched my seat three times. A guy was looking at me the second time, so I switched and another guy looked at me. I just ignored them all. I had too much on my mind. *Was this love?* I thought. *Or is this just obsession?* I would find out soon enough. The lights darkened. The little video clip of the actors playing football with a baby came on. Then the actors all came out.

Natalie's not here, I thought right away. But Karen, Tyler, Lindsay, Lisa, Zeke, and Chad were all there.

Zeke noticed me right away. He had that familiar looking grin on his face as his eyes caught mine.

"You're here alone tonight," Zeke said looking up at me. How did he notice me? Or better yet, how did he remember me? Who can remember someone from so long ago that they've never even spoken to?

The improv started. Tyler asked the audience for a suggestion on being addicted to something. He and Chad were paired up together for the scene. There were three groups and the group that started had to say the same sentence as the last.

As Tyler came out, he asked for an addiction to something. Someone in the audience shouted out something, but in the middle of them I shouted out, "Twizzlers!"

Tyler looked up at me with squinted eyes.

"What?" he asked again.

"Twizzlers," I said again.

"I love Twizzlers," I herd Chad say. Tyler turned back to Chad and said that they would have an addition to Twizzlers. That scene was funny.

In another scene, Karen and Lindsay needed an accent. No one in the audience was giving one, so I shouted out "French". They asked me what I said and I told them again. Karen was in the scene with Tyler and Zeke. Tyler was a bear, which was selected by the audience, and Zeke had turret's syndrome.

I had a good time that night, despite Tyler. I had feelings for him, but they weren't as abundant as they were before. I didn't understand why, though. Tyler had changed his hair, but that didn't matter to me. I still cried over Tyler, but something was different now that I couldn't explain it.

I had gotten really sick on Tuesday, December 8th. Mom and Joe were making fun of me by saying that I had the swine flu. My temperature was a 101.4, and then it kept on increasing. I was stuck inside, something that I hated. I was coughing very, very hard all the time. I couldn't eat anything and everything in my body hurt.

I didn't get out of bed that Wednesday until 4:30 PM, and that was just to feed the cats. I got myself a glass of water while I was up, but then I went back to bed. I thought I was dying, and I was laughing at myself for it.

Mom got me a lot of soup to eat and she made me garlic bread to go with the soup. I wanted to get better for that Saturday because my cat, Stimpy, had an appointment at the vets. I wasn't okay, though.

I had an appointment to see my neurologist, Dr. Kim at UCLA. That got canceled.

I had to cancel an acting class that I scheduled with an actress over in Santa Monica because I was sick.

My temperature was up to 102 by the end of Friday.

My appointment to see the neurologist was rescheduled for January, but I had already been having second thoughts about that.

On Sunday, Mom told me that if I wasn't better by the end of the week that she was going to take me to the doctors. I was sure that I was going to die. I kept feeling worse and worse, so it wouldn't be a shock to me if that really did happen. But I was not convinced that I was going to die of pneumonia or the swine flu. No, heartbreak was more like it.

Everyone kept telling me, "Don't get me sick!" I wasn't going to get anyone sick on purpose. "If I do, I apologize", I told them.

I was over the flu a week later.

I had signed up for eharmony online. It was embarrassing, but I figured I had nothing to lose. Just time.

I waited weeks, months to get a match that might like me back, but nothing came.

"No one's out there for you, kid," I told myself. "GET OVER IT!" I just felt so broken inside and that there was nothing that anyone could do for me to cure the heartbreak that I felt. Not heartbreak that was this bad. Nothing ever felt this bad. I had never felt so alone before in my entire life. I didn't cry, though. I wanted to. Oh, God, I wanted to, but I didn't I wouldn't let myself. I couldn't let myself shed one tear.

I felt so angry, hurt, frustrated, confused, betrayed, pissed off, lonely, est. I knew that telling Mom anything at all that concerned my "love life" was suicidal for me to do. But for once I thought she'd be happy that I was venturing out on my own and trying to find love again. She said I should do this, so why the hell not? I thought to myself.

Mom started freaking out, of course. I pointed out Mike and Ashley for the millionth time.

"They're in love," she told me. That isn't love, I thought to myself. I was in love with Tyler and you said that he was too old for me. Mike and Ashley have the same age difference. I was always in violent tears when I told her this. If I can't be with Tyler because of everything that you say, then why should Mike and Ashley get that *privilege* that I don't have? Love isn't even a privilege. It's a curse!

Christmas went fine. I got five presents. Tom and Cameron got me a pair of skinny pants and a red t-shirt.

I picked Mike's name, so I bought him a book on history.

Mom got me a shirt, a book, a soundtrack, and the final season of Flight of the Conchords on DVD.

Sabrina was out for Christmas. She and I got into an argument. She said that saying a ghosts' name would bring it to you. It was the stupidest thing that I had ever heard. I made my point by saying Chuck's name out loud. Nothing happened.

"Stupidest thing ever," I thought. Susannah yelled at me that Sabrina was allowed to have an opinion. And I wasn't? How did that make sense?

I had been taking diet pills and had run out, so I ended up buying more. It didn't make any sense to me. I used to make fun of women who were like this. And now I had become my own worst enemy? I was already down hearted and broken, but I knew that if I did this, at least I had something to hold onto. Whether or not it was healthy to do this, I did not care anymore. My life seemed to be breaking apart faster and faster, and there was nothing that I could do about it. I was so lost without love in my life.

Chapter 23

An Unfair Story

New Years Day had come at last. I was shocked that I was still alive.
Surely you should have died from a broken heart, I told myself. *But you're still here. How does that make sense? It hurts thinking that I was going to die from a broken heart last year. Death hasn't come.*

Not yet, another side of me has said. *Just because your alive now, doesn't mean you won't die soon.*

Tyler's, "We should do this again," had haunted me everyday. Every second it's been there. Taunting me. Teasing me.

He didn't mean it, I told myself. *If he meant it, he would have been there. If someone isn't there the first time, they're not coming.* It hurt me saying this, but past experiences taught me just that.

And just because a few million bastards broke my heart throughout life, that doesn't give anyone the right to have the power to control my life. Or it shouldn't.

By Sunday night, Susannah was at home with one of her friends Nurell. She said to her friend that Mom and I were like a package deal. I hated her for saying that. Or more, I hated myself for not telling her to shut up and what a horrible person she was for saying that. I waited until after they left and then cried to Mom. She claimed that she didn't hear that. I had let Susannah borrow one of my CDs and I was treated like garbage? Well, what else was new? But I thought that she would at least act nice to me. It wasn't like it was a hard thing for her to do. But she and Ben acted like toddlers. And they all treated me *worse* than shit, except Mike. I told Mom that I wanted my CD back and that Susannah could *not* burn a copy for herself. I was sick of being treated this way and I knew that it was never going to end. No matter what I did, it wouldn't stop.

Love had broken my heart even further through using the website eharmony. And life broke my heart a million times a day for over 15 years.

Mom and I went to the movies on January 3rd. It wasn't until half way through it that I felt a very sharp pain right where my shunt is. I became very dizzy at this point as well. I told Mom and she seemed very angry at me. What reason does she have to be angry, I thought. This is *my* shunt, not hers.

"I'm taking you to the hospital," she told me.

"No you're not," I said. If I was going to die, I wanted to die at home.

Two days later, I felt horrible for yelling at Mom. "Just because I'm mad at Susannah, doesn't mean I should take it out on Mom," I told myself.

I was seeing Dr. Kim that Thursday, so I skipped my dance class. I thought that maybe, just maybe, he would have an answer as to why I was in so much pain.

Joe had given me sponges that turned into little animals and he gave Mom a sea shell. It was so out of character for him to do. It was a nice thing to do, though.

My heart and my head were arguing over Tyler, again. *I'm going to love him forever,* I told myself, *but I have to let him go.*

I explained all the pain I had been having to Dr. Kim. He gave me sample medicine for the pain. I took it Friday night before I went to sleep. I woke up at 1 AM and ran to the bathroom, but nothing came up. So I went back to bed.

Not being able to fall asleep again, I tossed and I turned in bed from the horrible headache that I as having. I got up at 3:40 AM and ran to the bathroom a second time. I was throwing up a tremendous amount the first time. I tried to get back to sleep, but I couldn't because I had the worst headache anyone could ever have.

Mom went to the pool on Saturdays, so I heard her leave at 6 as I lied there in agony. I ran to the bathroom again at 7 and threw up the same amount as the first time. And then again at 8:30. Mom made it back by 8:45 and I let her know what was going on. 30 minutes later, I was in the bathroom for the 4th time. I was in such severe pain that it was hurting to breathe. 9:40 am., I threw up in the bathroom for the fifth time. I made it until 11 AM without violently throwing up in the toilet.

It was hurting so much that Mom was saying that the headaches I was dealing with *could* be from my shunt. She didn't believe me before when I was dealing with my dizziness for over 6 months in 2008, why should she believe me now? She always seemed to change her mind about something every minute of the day when it concerned my health. I would never in a million years make up the kind of pain that I was in. I wasn't even sure how anyone could create the amount of pain for themselves. But in a way, I simply started to stop caring about the whole thing. *After all, everyone dies.*

I dealt with waking up with the same headache for days, but it really felt like centuries at this point. I tossed and I turned in bed early in the mornings. Days felt like years while I was in agonizing pain.

I had bought *Post Grad* on DVD. Mom and I were watching it one Saturday night, but I ended up crying because I wanted Tyler. It wasn't fair that Mike could have Ashley and that Joe could have Juliet, but I couldn't have Tyler. It sickened me that I was still so obsessed with him. I was angry at Mom for making me feel so stupid about Tyler and *my decision* over the whole matter. It wasn't fair!

"Are you ever going to forgive me?" Mom asked as I cried out in agony. I wanted to. More than anything, I wanted to. It wasn't as if this were the first broken heart that I dealt with. Tyler wasn't even my first love. It hurt like hell, regardless.

I told Mom that I would kill myself. *It would do everyone a huge favor if I wasn't here,* I thought. Mom told me that she would take me to the mental hospital if I were to do that. *Then you should lock Joe up for everything he's done or could do.*

"Break up Joe and Juliet," I told her. If I wasn't allowed to be happy, why should they?

"No," Mom said calmly, but firmly.

"Break up Mike and Ashley," I told her. This should not be happening to just me!

"No," Mom said again in the same tone.

"THEN BRING TYLER BACK!" I yelled at her. I was crying in such violence that it was scaring me to feel this way.

"I'm going to bed," Mom said after a split second, and she left me there on the couch to cry to myself. I wept so hard, but I got up after a few moments and went to my bed to cry.

The next morning had come and I was still angry and hurt and heartbroken, but there was no way in hell that I could share it with Mom, so I faked being okay and I apologized for the whole thing. She said nothing.

I woke up at 1:50 AM on Wednesday, January 13th, just a few days later. I was in such pain that, again, I went to the bathroom, but I didn't throw up the first time. An hour and a half later, I ran to the bathroom and threw up. Mom over heard me with the bathroom door closed.

I ended up sleeping, sitting up that night. I didn't seem to be in as much pain sitting up and sleeping, but it does takes talent to sleep sitting up.

Later that morning, Mom called and asked if I wanted her to call Dr. Lazereff and get his opinion on the matter.

"Yes," I told her. What other choice did I have?

Mom called back a little later and said that I confused the doctor over the phone, which was a first for me.

I slept sitting up the following night, but it was harder than I thought to sleep sitting up. I didn't wake up with a headache in the morning for two days after that. I was dealing with headaches that came off and on throughout the day, though, so there wasn't a sure sign that I was okay again.

Joe was in one of his bad moods by Thursday night just because he lost his charger to his phone.

I was dealing with too much, but I was still determined to win Tyler's heart back!

I went to my neurosurgeon on January 19th.

"If you ever experience that amount of pain again, immediately call me and I'll schedule surgery for you right away." I told myself that I was ready to die. Without love, nothing else seemed to matter to me. Life was pointless and the sooner I wasn't here, the better off the whole situation would be.

Mom's hurtful words were echoing in my head. 'Date...." Love didn't exist. My life never had meaning. I wasn't even allowed to have my own life without someone else interfering in *my own* decisions.

Aidin's first birthday was coming up. Mike and Ashley were going to have it on the 30th. Everyone was going to be there, including Ben and Vicky. Mom wanted me to go, so that was my excuse for going. Susannah was also going to be there. All the people that I hated were there. I hated being there. I stood out like a sore thumb, again, at a place that I didn't want to be. I was so upset and in such a rage that I couldn't even remember why I felt this way. Everyone else had love; all of my worst enemies; and I wasn't going to fall in love *ever* again.

I told Mom that I was going to head home.

"Okay," she said. "I'll take you."

Why couldn't she see that I wanted to be left alone? It wasn't like it was the first time that I would be left alone anyways. I told her that I wanted to walk home by myself, but she insisted that she drive me. It was a long way. *Good*, I thought. *At least I won't have you nagging at me like you always do or yell at me when I already feel terrible.*

I waited anyways, but I couldn't handle it anymore. I just decided to go.

"Thanks for coming," Ashley told me with a smile on her face as I was trying to make my exit. I was stupid and decided to wait for Mom at the car. *She has you locked around her finger,* I told myself. *Just go!*

All of these different emotions were racing in my head: rage, hatred, anger to sadness, grief and loss.

Mom finally came out to the car and I told her that I was going to walk home.

"Just get in the car," she told me. "It's a long walk, and you don't know the way."

"No," I told her.

"Get in the car," she said again.

"No," I said.

"Get in the car," and she opened the car door. Like I was just going to give in and have her yell at me on the ride home? I knew her games too well at this point.

"No," I said, slamming the door. I continued walking east towards home. I knew where I was. I wasn't lost as Mom told me that I was. She always looked down on me and it was hurting me too much now.

I made it home an hour later, and as I suspected, Mom called everyone in the family. I hated her for doing that. I already hated everyone else. Why did she have to drag everyone in on my misery? Everyone was always happy that I was so miserable anyways, so why did it matter to them?

After I got home, I found Mom in the kitchen. I apologized, but she spoke to me in a certain tone. I already knew that I was nothing that she wanted, no matter how much she tried to fake wanting me.

Mom spoke to Tom on the phone, but went in the backyard to talk about me. I hated that, so I cried at the table. I got more and more upset and decided to go to my room and cry. Eventually I had to feel better, right? Wrong.

Mom came in a little later.

"Go ahead and enjoy being miserable," she told me. This hurt more than ever. What kind of mother says that to a daughter whose heart is already broken? I was just trying my best, and crying was the only thing that, for God knows what reason, was still keeping me breathing. Mom left the room, making me cry even harder now.

I calmed down, for the second time, and Mom and I went to get a movie.

I Hope they serve Beer in Hell. We didn't watch it.

The next day, Mom and I were supposed to go to a clothing museum, but she made me feel horrible. She changed her mind about going.

Mom looked at me and said, "I can't put up with you doing this anymore. I was really looking forward to going out this weekend, but you just had to get up set. And ruin everything."

She thought she knew what it felt like? *I* couldn't put up with myself doing all this shit. I was put through hell and back by everyone, but I felt worse when I put them through a *small portion* of that that same hell.

"I should have crossed the street when Joe told me to," I cried. "It's my fault. I'm the one to blame for getting run over." She wanted me to show emotion. Fine.

"It's not you're fault," Mom said in her soothing voice. "It was an accident."

That wouldn't have occured if I had just crossed the street when your beloved Joe had told me to....or better yet, you should have just let me die. Then at least you wouldn't have to put up with me.

I was heartbroken forever. That was for sure.

Joe and I yelled at each other because his music was too loud and I had a headache. I was talking to Mom. Mom just told me to go to my room. She would have defended Joe if someone was bothering him. I was already the black sheep of the family, so why should this surprise me now? It wasn't fair, though. Joe was the one in the Psyche-ward, not me.

On February 5th, I worked on my guitar, as usual. I strummed a few chords, when a song came to my head. It was an apology from me to Tyler over Tyler breaking my heart. I showed it to Pam. She and I started working on it together. She wanted me to record it. I wanted to send it to Tyler and completely let go of him. I was so stupid, thinking that he could possibly love me. Who could love me? What kind of sane mind would fall for someone like me? Who would ever want to?

I wasn't over Tyler.

On Saturday, February 13th, the Vampire Diaries stars were going to be at a mall. Mom and I were going. It was always embarrassing going out with my mother. It was a great experience, though.

By the end of that day, when everything seemed light and fluffy and that nothing could go wrong, it did. I found out that Susannah was moving back home. I hated her so much and I didn't want Mom to have to give up her room again for anyone. Especially the selfish Reynolds' family. I was so outraged over that! But I knew that there was nothing I could do about it. To me, two years without Susannah was nothing. She said that I was always going to live with Mom, but sure enough she moved back. Just like everyone in her family did.

I had met someone on eharmony the week of Valentines Day. Things were going well for Kevan and me for a week, but he ended things with me. First I was really upset, wondering what I did wrong, so I apologized. Then I realized that it wasn't love anyway. I was never going to fall in love again, so why should this matter to me? Kevan was just someone to pass the time with anyway.

I soon gave up on all of that love bull shit. There wasn't anyone out there for me, and I had to except that and move on with whatever dignity I had left.

Joe moped around in one of his moods on the 21st. He and Juliet broke up. Good, I thought, anyone in the world would be better than Joe. *Anyone.*

Joe always seemed to use up Mom's energy. I got yelled at when I was upset, but Joe's the prince, when he's upset. Joe never knew the definition of what hell really, truly was.

I hated when I threw "tantrums" as Mom called them. She didn't know what hell felt like. No one did.

I can't count how many times I've cried over life not being fair. Life has always been cruel to me from a very young start. You'd think after a while that I'd get used to it. But I never have.

Joe was in a fight with one of his friends, Flip. Out of all of Joe's art friends, Flip was probably the most attractive in my opinion. Joe was upset at Flip over something and he and Flip were going to have an art duel. Joe said that he going to beat up Flip or kill him in the desert. Flip changed his mind and didn't want to do the duel with Joe, for whatever reason he had. Joe still wanted to do damage to Flip. I just wanted to tell the police and have him thrown in jail for good, but I didn't.

Essence and I got lunch the last week of February. I told her that love didn't exist for me. I was getting used to saying it and believing that statement. I had almost convinced myself that there was no such thing as love. At least there wasn't anything like that for me. Essence said, "True love exists for you. It exists for everyone. There's someone out there for you…" No there wasn't and at least I could accept the truth now. Love didn't exist for me, and it only took over 5,475,000,000 years, it seemed like, to finally understand that no one was coming for me. I had to except that and move on. It was better said than done, though.

I hadn't tried to get in touch with Tyler for 61 days by March 2nd. It seemed as if it was the hardest thing that I had to do. I had had my heart broken for over 15 years, and this broken heart was the hardest one? That made no since to me. Why is this experience the hardest thing? Why now? Why ever? I thought I would die by now, but here I was, still breathing. Crying in rage, but still breathing.

Pam and I were working hard at the song I had written and dedicated to Tyler. Why should he have the last word in a broken heart that he caused me?

By March 4th, I saw my eye specialist at UCLA. He was so impressed with my vision.

On March 6th, Mom and I went to the Paley Center to see the *Vampire Diaries*, again. It was wonderful. It was raining that day, as we stood out in it waiting for the doors to open. I wore a skirt and a coat, so I was freezing, but I was fine. The line kept going behind, but Mom and I finally got inside to see the actors and writers of the show.

Joe's friend Jeff had come by on the 12th. He looked good. I hadn't seen him in what felt like years. I thought he would be locked away with his girlfriend who was 20 years older than him. I thought he was adorable, though, but I refused to go out with any of Joe's friends, and it even creeped me out that I found any of them attractive.

By March 13th I had only been screaming out Tom and Tyler's names when no one else was around, so things seemed to be getting better.

Tom was coming out for Mom's birthday and he wanted to do something BIG for her birthday. I told him that Mom didn't want anything for her birthday. Nothing big or fancy, but no one listened. I respected her wishes, though, and I was going to go against everyone else. No one was listening to me, but what else was knew?

Mom's friend Peggy's mother had died in early March. It was sad, but I wasn't too broken up about it. Mom said that she and I were going to go up to Oregon in the summer and that we would bring Peggy's dead brother with us. At first I was okay with the idea. We would be going to Eureka afterwards.

I wanted to go my own way in the summer, but that seemed to be slipping away from me. It wasn't fair! But I kept a calm face and had a polite response. Who knows, maybe I would like it?

Tom came home and he, Mom, and I went over to Mike and Ashley's apartment on Friday, March 19th for breakfast. It went fine. I got to see Aidin again, so I was happy.

I inspired Tom to make a sandwich that afternoon. I was hungry and made myself a sandwich. Tom was in the kitchen and saw my "masterpiece." So he ended up making himself a sandwich as well.

I had been dealing with major headaches and massive dizzy spells that afternoon. I wanted to cry, I was in such pain! But I told myself not to tell Mom because she would only have a certain tone with me and make me feel worse, so I stuck it out. Nothing could be that bad. Then again, maybe it could.

After a very long email from Mom, she said that she didn't want anyone to do anything for her birthday. "It's not a milestone," she wrote. I respected that, but everyone else refused to go along with it. Susannah came to me and said that everyone was ignoring what Mom said and that they were all still going to have the gondola ride. It was already paid for and everything. Susannah asked if I was still going, but I told her no. I wasn't going to do anything that Mom didn't want to do for *her* birthday.

However, sure enough, everyone was ignoring what she said, so I decided to go on the stupid gondola ride. Who knows? I might even enjoy it. I thought the "kidnapping" idea was really stupid considering Mom's heart condition.

Joe decided that he wasn't going to the gondola ride either. He had other plans the night before. He was doing a BBQ with some of his friends. It seemed like it was going to be a good time for him.

The dinner went fine. Then Mom and I went to the restroom. We were gone for a few minutes, but when we were walking back, the gondola people were already there. So much for a surprise.

I had to give Ben create. For once, he did something nice for Mom.

I had a weird feeling that Joe was going to get in trouble or that something bad was going to happen at his party. Sure enough, I was right.

When Mom, Tom, and I got home, Mom received a call from Joe. His party got out of hand. The police were there and his friend Jeff was arrested for hitting Joe over the head with a beer bottle. I just started laughing! I knew something was going to happen. I was kind of disappointed that Jeff was the one who was arrested. Joe was the one who was in the fight, and Jeff got arrested for hitting Joe over the head. Jeff was trying to stop Joe, but he did the stupid thing and hit Joe with a beer bottle.

I didn't tell anyone that I thought something was going to happen. I would have been told that I was stupid or that I didn't have a clue what was going on.

That night, Tom said he was in therapy. It was the first time I had ever heard that he was in therapy. Joe was the one who needed therapy the most out of all of us. Mom never made him get it. She made me, but not Joe. It wasn't fair.

The next day, Joe got home, depressed. What else was new? Joe got a letter in the mail. He was accepted into Cal Arts University. *It's not fair!* Even when Joe puts his own friends in jail, he gets rewarded for being a terrible person! Joe even said that he was done with art. He said that it was a waste of time for him and that he wanted to be a paramedic. *The only reason he wants to go is because he'll have campus housing*, I thought, and I was right. *His "art" is crap and is only good to those people who need as much medication as he does, but they refuse the treatment.*

I was having a small amount of luck on a website plentyoffish.com. I found this one guy that I thought was cute and he seemed cool enough to talk to. He didn't want to talk to me because I didn't have a picture on the website. *Fuck you!* I thought. I was done with love, anyways. There wasn't anyone out there for me and I had to accept that and move on. I loved in my life, but I lost more. I found it unbelievable that after everything, I was still breathing on my own. That was all that I had.

By March 27th, Joe had locked himself away in his room going on three days. He is so pathetic, I thought. It was his fault that his friend is in jail and might be serving 25 years because of a fight that Joe started. Joe always starts something and then it's someone else's fault. PATHETIC!

I was learning more and more about the party. Juliet's ex-husband was there. I didn't know that Juliet was married before she met Joe. Why would she want Joe in the first place? Why would anyone?

Joe got angry and hit a girl in the face. That was what Jeff tried to stop Joe from doing. That was why the police were called. Joe should have been arrested, I thought. Not Jeff. I could be in the same room with Jeff for more than 5 seconds. I could never do that with any of Joe's other friends.

Susannah was moving back in that night. I hated her in a lot of ways. She was so mean to me. Everyone always thought that I was making it all up. That part hurt a lot. I was always trying to make nice with whatever I had. It hurt to be so nice, and then to be made fun of so much or treated so unfairly.

My massage therapist, Frani, saw in my eyes that I was too nice and I got hurt too much because of it. She was right.

I met one of Essence's friend's. She was nice; a little insane, so she fit in with me and Essence. She was an actress, so that was cool.

I was thinking about Tyler too much and it was driving me mad! I wanted him back, but I wanted him to pay for all the heartache that he caused me. He deserved it, but at the same time, why waste my time on him? He wasn't worth it. He's not worth it, I told myself over and over, just to get through the night.

Joe had left home on foot one night in March. He was causing Mom major anxiety! She forced me to get therapy, but not Joe. No. He was the King and if he wasn't happy then everyone else had to suffer. If he hurt, the whole world had to hurt. It was getting so out of control, but I wouldn't let myself cry. I wanted to, though. Oh, God, I wanted to, but I couldn't let myself. Mom was so upset that I had to be there for her, but I had to keep my guard up at the same time. I was going to get hurt over this, and I knew it.

It wasn't fair that Joe got away with so much. Just because he was the one who *saw* me get run over, that didn't him any right to act the way that he did to everyone. I wasn't meant to be the black sheep in the family or in life. Not for this long. Not this much. Not this way. And, yet, there was nothing I could do about it. I was treated so unfairly, but everyone else just didn't seem to care anymore. I did try to forgive Joe. God only knew how much I tried and how much it *hurt* me to be so defeated by so many others, when I was just trying to live *my own* life.

Susannah was back that night and I already felt like screaming. I knew that nothing good was going to come of this. She was going to talk bad about Mom and everyone else, I just knew it.

On March 31st, Mom and I had a red eye to New York. I couldn't sleep on the plane, because I was terrified. It wasn't as bouncy this time, but it still wasn't comfortable.

We landed in New York and everything was fine. It took a while to get our things all together, but we did, and then we got the air train to Brooklyn.

We met Tom outside the station, early in the morning. Then we went up to his place. Cameron was still asleep. Mom and I rested on the couch in the living room for a few hours.

We got up in the afternoon and got ready to go to 42nd Street. I wanted to get my picture taken with the Naked Cowboy. I saw him! Mom and I came around and I waited my turn. I paid him $5 as I went up there, and I felt confident enough to give him a hug. He squeezed me back. Robert Burke played with my hair and squeezed me even more. It was like Heaven for me! It felt so good to be there with him.

When Mom and I were going to leave, I looked up at Robert and I thanked him. He looked back at me with those lovey-dovey eyes I had seen so many times by so many other men.

Mom got a call later that night from Trixie, the girl who got her arm pulled by Joe at the party. More and more information was coming out. I believed that Joe deserved to go to jail. He wasn't a good person in my eyes.

"They were all drunk", Mom would say. And that makes it okay that Joe sprained or broke a girl's arm?

Joe does NOT deserve to go to Cal Arts! I thought. I started to voice my opinion a loud, but no one ever listened to me anyways.

Mom and I saw Henryette the next day. She looked good, considering everything. We had pizza over at her place. It was very hard for me to get over the fear of heights to get over to Queens. There were so many stairs to get to the subway that was up high. Mom and I had a really good time with Henryette, though. I was more outspoken this time and it was noticed. I hated how people would comment on it, though. *Why must you make me feel so incompetent?* I would think to myself over and over.

I noticed that Henryette was wearing the angel necklace that I bought her.

I had a nightmare on April 4th. Tyler was in my dreams and he told me that he had a girlfriend. It was confusing, because I was getting over him, but I still loved him very much. I knew that he wasn't waiting for me anyways, and I just needed to accept that. *Just move on,* I told myself over and over. *He isn't waiting. He's not coming back.*

I had made my decision that I wasn't going to go to Oregon with Mom for Peggy's Mom memorial. I began planning my trip to the east coast instead. *Will it happen? Only time will tell,* I thought. I decided that I needed to venture out on my own. Make my own mistakes and decisions. Live my own life.

At 7:05 that evening, Mom and Cameron were poking fun at me. "You hate a lot," Cameron said. "You need to love more." I did love; too much, though. *I got hurt more than you'll ever know,* I thought.

I wanted to scream at Mom and Cameron, but I held my tongue and didn't say anything as they continued to mock me. I saw the mocking smile on Mom's face. When they were done having fun, I sat there in silence on the couch, barely holding myself together.

"It hurt when you and Cameron were making fun of me," I told Mom.

"Oh, I'm sorry," she said. *No. You're not,* I thought. *But I will show all of you one day.*

On April 6th, the day Mom and I were leaving, she wanted to see Henryette. My foot was hurting, so I told her that I wouldn't go. I had been complaining about my foot pain for four days already. *It should not be a surprise that it still hurt,* I thought. It wasn't as if I needed permission to stay.

Mom seemed to be getting upset with me over the fact that my foot hurt. I had let her know more than once.

Mom decided that it would have taken too long to get to Queens, so she had decided against it.

She and I just went around town for a few hours, getting whatever souvenirs that we could find.

We walked Tom to the subway so he could get to class. I gave him a hug goodbye. The last words he said to me that day were, "I love you."

Mom and I hugged Cameron goodbye and left to get to the airport. The plane ride was very annoying. 20 kids were on our flight.

Returning home was anxiety driven, of course.

Tyler was in my dreams on April 9, 2010. It was annoying as hell! I could only see his back, which was turned to me.

Mom hadn't heard form the girl Trixie when we were finally home. She hurt her arm and Joe was responsible for some of it. "She was drunk," Mom said. And so was Joe. He was an angry drunk too. Much like Chuck. Joe had been in situations like this for years and he always seemed to get away with it. It wasn't fair!

I was in tears when I saw my psychologist. So many bad past memories were erupting in my mind from past events. Why was the world so cruel to me? What had I done to it? I exploded on my doctor, and then burst out of the room.

When I had come back, after realizing that I had no where to go, I found that she was on the phone with my mother.

This isn't going to be good, I thought.

"Oh, she's back," my doctor said as she saw me reappear in her doorway. She and I spoke for a while longer. I was still in tears over everything that Joe had done to me.

"He's an artist," she said. "So, Joe's going to art school."

"STOP TALKING ABOUT HIM!" I shouted! This wasn't about him. I didn't see her to help Joe feel better. I was the one who was forced to come here. Joe had nothing to do with this.

Outraged, I threw my book across the room. Completely unaware of my actions, I saw what had happened. The book fell against the wall and hit the floor.

"Stop it," the doctor said.

You stop it, I thought. I was so angry, I couldn't stay any longer. I got up from my seat, grabbed my book and left. I don't need to take this!

I found my way down the stairs in tears. Continuing to wait for Mom, I already knew that nothing good was going to come out of this. *Nice,* I thought to myself. *You did it again. Congratulations!* I fought with myself for those few minutes, not knowing what to say to Mom when she got there. *Just tell her,* came to my head. *No! She won't understand!* But I knew I had to say something.

My mom got there, just outside the building. I was in tears as she approached me. She thinks she can fix this? What about her adoring son? Joe was everything to her, or so it felt.

Driving back home, I began crying.

"What's wrong?" Mom asked. I couldn't tell her. I wouldn't allow myself to. *She'll only hurt you,* a voice in me said. I just cried and said that everyone else will be sorry.

Mom stopped the car on the side of the street and yelled at me. I quivered in fear. What was she going to do? Beat me????

You're not going to get out of this. Just tell her, I thought. So, I told her what Joe did to me when we were just kids. How terrified I was of him and the reasons why. How I felt his penis behind me.

Mom grew silent while I cried to her. She wanted the truth. Fine. Here it is.

"I'll talk to him," she told me, calmly.

"NO!" I screamed. He'll only deny doing anything. If she didn't want to believe me, there was nothing I could do, but don't you dare call me a liar!!!!!!

We got home a little later and I went to my room to scream and cry to myself. No one cared anyways, so where was I wrong? I did nothing wrong. I finally told the truth, something other people were too afraid to do.

Mom and I didn't completely make up over the fight for about two days. I was pissed and no one was going to tell me how to feel. This wasn't something that you could just say, "Oh, sorry." I knew which ones were lies and which weren't.

My foot was still in so much pain that I had to go to urgent care one afternoon. Luckily I was one of the only patients there on a Saturday afternoon.

Mom and I took a hike the next morning. I told her that there was something that I needed to say to her. I was already terrified of my mom, what else could she say or do to me?

"Now everyone will know what a horrible life you've lived!" Mom said when I told her what was wrong. She promised that she wouldn't yell when I told her what was wrong. She lied.

She walked away when I begged for forgiveness.

"Are you coming?" she said scornfully to me from high above on a hill.

We made it back to a ditch in the road and I fell. My own mother would not help me up.

"I'm not in the mood to do this. I can't drive down here to get you," she said while she stood above me. Why was she being so mean to me? What did I do?

With no other way out of this mess, I got a hand up from her and she sped up to get to the car. We made it home in silence. I felt horrible. Not just because I fell, but I hated making Mom feel this way. I couldn't handle living like this, though.

April 29th, I bought Mom her mother's day gift. It was a difficult day to get through. I had a hard time with Joe and my foot hurt, but I knew I had to get through the day.

Later that night, Susannah and I were in a fight over *my* dead father. I told her that I didn't have a father anymore. It made me feel better saying that. He wasn't coming back. People don't come back from the grave and ask for forgiveness. Chuck wasn't her father. Her father was still alive. If I wanted to say that I didn't have a father, who did that hurt, I thought. It doesn't hurt anyone. No one gets hurt.

Susannah had to argue with me in her high pitch voice, of course.

It was my choice to say that I didn't have a father. He wasn't there. He certainly wasn't coming back.

I was so sick of everyone telling me that I couldn't be an actress. What did they know? But I was too exhausted to fight back anymore.

I found a few acting places online that were in the valley, close to home.

It made me sick that everyone thought that I was just making up the fact that they always said something negative about my dreams.

"Why do you think I gave up my hopes not that long ago?" I'd ask.

"I don't remember saying that," Mom told me. Well, of course not. Why would you? Why stop that dancing or singing that's going on in your head? It wasn't fair!

I fought this stupid battle for far too long by myself. When I finally got tired of doing this one handed and gave in, that was when everyone has to say, "Oh, I've always been there for you." You have? Was I not there? Was I asleep?

Fighting this battle wasn't fair and it wasn't easy. My feet were both killing me. I made it to my doctor and I was told to stay off my feet for another week. It wasn't easy not going anywhere, but I stayed inside as I was instructed.

I was trying my best at ignoring everyone else interfering with my dreams.

"They're yours," I told myself. "Don't let anyone ever take them away from you, again!"

I wanted a boyfriend more than anything. I was tired of being alone. But he wasn't coming for me. That was loud and clear. Tyler wasn't coming back and I had to accept that. Whatever this feeling was, it was not a comforting one for me to have.

Mother's day came around. I was the only one in the family to get Mom something other than flowers or a card.

I had prayed for my death to come for years, but I stood here, waiting. Waiting for something that could happen, but I knew that nothing was coming. I learned that a long time ago.

I found hope. I had emailed an acting school. This was new and exciting, but also very scary!

I made the appointment for an interview to get in. Scared out of my mind, I didn't know what to expect. Was I ready? Was I going to fail, again?

No, I told myself. *Even if you don't get in, this will be a learning experience. You win either way.*

Saturday, May 15th, came around. Brian was leaving for Virginia. I did get to say goodbye to him. *You'll see him again.*

Butterflies started swarming in my stomach! What the Hell had I gotten myself into now? But that voice inside me told me to keep going. I couldn't get my money back anyway.

Just a learning experience, I told myself again and again. *If you get in: great. But if you don't, it'll be okay. You'll be okay.*

Monday came around at last. I had to make my ride with Access Service. At 10 AM, I called and got my ride for the next day. An hour later: *What the hell were you thinking? This can only ended in disaster!*

Shut up! Shut up! Shut Up! I argued with myself. *You're doing this. It will work out okay. You'll be fine.*

My heart was still arguing with itself over Tyler, of course.

Tuesday, May 18th was finally here. Butterflies were still swarming in my stomach before my ride picked me up. They were early.

My scheduled meeting was at 12:30 PM that afternoon. I was dropped off at 11 AM, so I went to get coffee down the street.

I sat there in Starbucks and waited. I got a call from the acting school at 12. The owner, David, had called and left a message. I called back.

"Hello, this is David," David answered.

"Hi, David," I said. "This is Mary Beth."

"Hi, Mary Beth, I called to let you know that my class ended early."

"Oh, well I'm right down the street," I told him.

"Just give me 10 more minutes."

I waited outside, counting the seconds that were going by. Finally, I decided to go in.

"Hi. David?" I asked with my hand out. "I'm Mary Beth," I said to David as he sat behind a desk.

I did a scene with David on camera. He gave me a script to go over beforehand.

"You're a good character actress," David told me. I was shocked and excited!" So on a scale of 1-10, how nervous were you?" David asked. I thought about it. "A 12 or a 15?"

"No," I told him. "Maybe a 6."

"Has anyone ever called you 'quirky' before?"

"No," I said. "I've been called a lot of things, but 'quirky' is not one of them."

"You're charming," David told me. I had never been called "charming" before either. David told me that I had some good parts to the script.

"So, Mary Beth, why do you want to be an actress?"

"I knew you were going to ask that…. When I was very young; a 6 year old little girl, I was in a tragic accident," I said, looking down at my legs. I looked back up to see almost the look of terror on David's face. "It's just easier for me to be anyone else."

David told me more of the school, as I sat there and listened. He showed me pictures of the other teachers who worked there and gave me information on them.

I sat back down and David continued giving me information on the school.

"Look this over and tell me if you have any questions."

David gave me a form to go over.

"My only question is: I may have to have a very intense surgery. How would that work out?"

"How long would you be out?"

"10 days," I told him.

"Well, you would just need to call to make sure that we know."

I had a seat at the table where I put my things. David had me go over the other paper work and fill it out.

I was finished 20 minutes later. I shook David's hand and thanked him.

Mom answered her phone when I called her outside.

"I GOT IN!" I said in excitement. I told her all about it, how nervous I was and everything.

I texted Kelly and Essence and told them.

My ride wasn't coming for another 30 minutes, so I stuck around for a little while.

I had gotten into one of the hardest acting schools in Los Angeles. I waited my whole life for something like this to happen to me! I always thought that there was something out there for me. I had to ignore everyone when they said, "You need to think of something more realistic...You can't be an actress...You can't be a singer...You can't do this...You can't do that."

I finally made it on my own without their help. But in a lot of ways they did help. Without their negativity, I would have no need to want to be someone else and put that into acting. But it was only the start.

David sent me notes on what to expect in the acting class. I had begun to go over them the next day. It was going to be very painful, trying to get out all the emotions that I hid away for so many years.

Tyler was still there on my mind. It hurt, but if it weren't for him, I wouldn't be here, I thought over and over. I still cried when I listened to sad love songs, because I only thought of Tyler. He wasn't coming back, I reminded myself over and over. He's not coming back. I felt so broken without him, but what else was new?

I thought about him more and more every day, and it only seemed to remind me of the heartache that I felt when he wasn't there the first time or the third time. *It wasn't his fault*, I reminded myself. *You need to let go. This isn't healthy!*

But I love him, I still argued with myself. *He's not coming back, and you're going to have to get used to that. If you spend forever alone, who cares? You don't need anyone.* A constant battle was always going on in my head. I could at least sleep through the whole night, now.

I had begun reading "On Acting" by Sanford Meisner. The book was very intense in acting.

My first class was finally here! Mom and I got there 30 minutes early. I felt like a freak when I was the first one there. The teacher hadn't even shown up yet!

Walking back and forth for a while, I saw a car park. I noticed Mark; the teacher who David said was the teacher for that day, get out of his car.

"Hi, I'm Mary Beth," I said with my hand out. He shook it and greeted me with a warm welcome. Then he unlocked the door and showed me where to sign in.

The first person to get there was this tall guy.

"Hi, I'm Jason," He said, shaking my hand.

"I'm Mary Beth," I said.

Jason seemed nice.

Three other people got here that were all women. Most of them were young.

Mark asked me if I brought a DVD, and I told him that I did. We were all paired up to do dialogs. Jason and I did our scene together at the end. I was nervous the first time through, but I started to get the hang of it the second time. Mark always said, "Look at Jason, Mary Beth…. Don't look down….Look at Jason….Use your diaphragm, Mary Beth."

There was a break. I had my sweatshirt on the first time through. During the break, I took it off and went over my lines again and again.

Mark had me hold the script up so I wasn't looking down all the time, which made it easier to be in character and look at Jason. I did a lot better the second time through. It was a try and fail the first time, but I stuck it out.

When I tried to explain to Mark that the reason why I used my chest voice instead of my diaphragm was because of what happened when I was a kid, I choked up. I wouldn't allow myself to cry through. Not here and not now.

When I finally got around to watching the DVD of my first class, I was so embarrassed that I didn't do a great job. It was only your first class, kid, I told myself. Don't beat yourself up over it.

I told Pam and Cody about it and they were excited for me.

Mark was pleased when I finally let myself get pissed off at Jason's character. I thought I had some good parts through it.

Mom hadn't heard from Joe since Sunday. She was worried; I wasn't.

By 7:31 PM on Tuesday, Mom got a call from a payphone. I hadn't answered the phone all day; because it was an unknown caller and I had no desire to talk to those people.

It was Joe calling from a mental hospital.

Great, I thought. What else is new? I was so sick of caring about Joe now. He screwed up all the time and always seemed to get away with it. Every time, Mom would say, "This is the last time I'm bailing him out of jail", but I knew that it wasn't. I always hoped that it was, but it wasn't.

I knew that Mom would probably get angry at me for not answering the phone. I just seemed to grow more and more tired of caring. And, yeah, maybe that was mean, but when were people actually nice to me?

I had started praying for Joe the night before, and instead, he ends up in the mental hospital!

I already knew that Mom was going to go soft on Joe and harder on me. It wasn't a fair game! Nothing has changed, and nothing will change, I thought.

He'll most likely still go to Cal Arts, I thought. *Never getting punished or having anything taken away from him, no matter what.*

Joe had made it two months without going to jail, so there was something.

Still, the fact that Joe was still putting Mom through so much stress wasn't right. I tried my best not to explode from all the rage that I felt. Joe got away with everything and it wasn't fair! Joe should be locked away in the mental hospital forever, I thought again and again through the first few days.

I finally saw my pediatric neurologist. But, of course, he could not find anything wrong.

"Everything seems okay," he said. I hated how every doctor always said that everything was "okay" with me. Everything was *not* okay with me! Why am I still in pain, I thought. Why did it stop and then come back again? The worst part of all of this was the fact that everyone thought that I was making it up. What kind of sane person makes up this kind of pain?

I was given medication for the pain caused by my tube in my neck. Against my will.

"Oh this should help, Mary Beth. Give it a try." That's all I was. "Just a try."

I hated how everyone always just assumed that this was a normal amount of pain. I was throwing up in July of '08, but that was a "normal" thing to do? It was "normal" to feel this way? To be in so much pain that I was crying and praying to just die so I wouldn't have to be in pain anymore.

Joe was supposed to come back home on the 28th. This terrified me! How was he going to act? How was I going to act? When I voiced this out loud to my own mother, her response was, "Whatever," and the way that she said it was as if she didn't give a care in the world about anyone else but her precious son.

I was hurt enough as it was! I always seemed to be competing for just a little attention from Mom. The kind of attention that she always gave Joe, the good kind. It was getting harder and harder for me every second to just breathe and pretend that I was okay and that everything was fine.

Joe had a warrant out for his arrest and of course Mom was coming to his rescue.

I was beginning to tell myself over and over: "It's okay to die young. You'll be okay. God will understand and so will your angels. The world will be alright without you."

Friday had come at last, a day that I had been dreading. Joe was going to come between me and my peacefulness, again. Everything was going to be about him. But he didn't make it home! Thank God, I thought.

I was going through so many different emotions over what had happened during the past week. I went through anger, fear, misery, sadness, and frustration. I was all over the place! And it was all because of Joe.

I felt like I was on the verge of crying, but I couldn't allow myself to. Not now. Mom needed me. I needed to be strong. But it was pissing me off that Mom was going to help Joe get an apartment and she would most likely be paying for it. Joe was just a loser in my mind.

"Oh, he's bipolar."

Nice to finally know, I thought. But that doesn't give him any right to treat anyone the way he does. I thought it was good for Juliet to break up with him. At least now she'll be without the stress.

I got the medication that the doctor prescribed for me. I was still really pissed off that no one believed me when I first told them that I was in pain. Why believe me now? Why? Because I was actually throwing up in the bathroom at 3 AM in January? And no one had any idea if the medicine was going to work or not. I was actually looking for a solution for this pain, but all I was given were guesses.

Joe began to get "better" the next day.

"He's on medication," Mom said. And that will help how?

She went to visit him every night in the hospital.

I thought that you were done with him? You said that last year. You said that it was the last time you would bail Joe out...but I guess it was all a lie.

I began searching for a place of my own. Just some place that was cheap and that was away from this hectic family. Anywhere but here, I thought.

I was dealing with so much hatred. Ashley made it sound like I was stupid, because I chose not to answer the phone. It would only ring three times and then stop. I hated her for making me feel so incompetent.

"Oh, I can't get pregnant," she once said. And, yet, she had a child. I loved Aidin, but I began to despise her!

My acting class was letting out a lot of emotion that I thought I had forgotten. I hoped that I could forget it, but it all came back.

"How does Jason feel, Mary Beth?" Mark asked me over and over while we sat there.

I told Mark a little about my "medical mystery", but I kept it like and fluffy before class had started. Mark told me after class had ended that I needed to get a monologue to do for the next class.

This should be easy, I thought.

The next day, Monday, I was looking for monologues online. After I found a few, I was really excited and I wanted to show my mom.

"Mom, can I get your opinion on something?" I asked as I went to the kitchen.

"Okay," she said in a rushed voice. "But I have to leave right now, so make it quick."

I smiled to this, not knowing what to say next.

"Seriously, I have to leave. What do you want?" she asked out of exasperation. I stood there dumfounded. Had it come to this? Was I not important at all anymore? Angry and hurt, I told her to forget about it, and I went to my room.

"I'll just write my own monologue," I said. I could hear her following me to my room.

She got upset at me! I only wanted help on finding a monologue and getting her opinion, but she was in a rush to go to the hospital to see Joe. I didn't matter anymore to her.

"I have to leave in a few minutes," she said through the tears in her eyes. She was mad at me for everything Joe had done. She always had to take her anger out on me. Why? Because I was the weakest? Because I had nothing? Or maybe because she could never be angry at anyone else?

Joe was coming home the next day, and I knew what that meant: he was going to be treated like the king. It wasn't fair.

Ashley was so worried about Aidin that she was going to have him have an MRI. The kid is only falling down, I thought. Every kid falls down! But Ashley was neurotic about the whole thing.

"There has to be something wrong with him if he's always falling down," I heard her say.

The only thing that's wrong with him is that he had you as a mother, I thought.

"Let her get this out of her system," Mom said.

Whatever, I thought. You're all stupid!

I had decided on doing a monologue from "10 Things I Hate About You." I practiced and practiced all week, but I couldn't cry. I cried all the time, so what was stopping me now?

I stared at a picture of Tyler that I got online. I practiced the monologue in the bathroom and tears were pouring down my cheeks the first time. I tried again and again, but nothing came. I thought I would be okay for Sunday in class.

I thought it would be easy to cry in class, considering the fact that I was always treated like dirt when I was at home.

Susannah's birthday went fine. I had gotten her a necklace. She, Mom, Joe and I went out to eat that night at a restaurant.

I had asked Mom what she would do if I was terribly sick. She said she wouldn't do anything. What a shock, I thought.

For the guys and everyone else in the family, she would be concerned and actually do something. But I wasn't important to her anymore.

Mom and I had to say goodbye to Tracey that day. I didn't cry, though.

You'll see her again, I thought. *Maybe you won't be alive, but you'll still see her again.*

I knew how to cry on camera, though.`

"Just think of all the shit you've been through," I said to myself.

The day of class had finally come. I was the first one there, of course. I signed in and sat down.

"Did you write something?" Mark asked. I had, but it was only two hours beforehand.

"You've had all week, Mary Beth. Why did you wait until the last minute?" Mark asked as he was getting out scripts for everyone else.

"I did!" I said. "I just couldn't get the right thing out on paper," I told him. "I do have something else, though."

Everyone else got there. They all did their dialogues. I was last to do my monologue. I messed up the first time. I couldn't cry and I forgot a line.

"What do you hate, Mary Beth?" Mark asked me.

"What do I hate?" I asked.

"Yeah," he said. "I hate those parking meters."

I looked up at the ceiling. It had come down to this.

"The answers not up there," Mark said.

"I hate the fact that I got run over by a car," I started. "I hated the fact that the women who did it got away with it. I hated my brother because he gets away with everything. I hate my other brother, who I don't even consider family anymore, for getting away with everything. I hated how my mom favors my brother for every bad thing that he does. I just---I hate everything!"

"Who were you thinking of, Mary Beth?" Mark asked when I did my monologue again.

"Tyler," I said.

"What would you say to him if he was here right now?"

I stared at Jason, who was sitting in front of me.

"Fuck you!" I said at last. "What did I do to you? What? Was it because I got run over? Was it because I asked you out? Was it because I told you that I was sick? What did I do wrong?" I was finally in tears as I poured my heart and soul out. What had I done wrong with Tyler? Was I too nice? Was I not nice enough? Was I not good enough? Was I too young? Had I been through too much in my "young life?" Had I not been through enough in my "young life?" What had I done wrong?

Then the break hit. Jason patted me on my knee as I sat there in tears, before we both left the front of the room.

"You did a good job," he said.

I returned to my seat. Osra came up to me with her sunglasses on and told me I did a good job.

When the break was over, everyone else did their scene, again. I did mine last.

"Sing," Mark told me. I tried to song, but I was too embarrassed!

After class was over, Mark told me that I needed to get another monologue to do for the next class.

"Okay. Bye, Mark." And I went outside. My phone was already in my hand and I was calling Mom to pick me up. As I opened the door, I saw Jason talking to someone. He came up to me after.

"You did a really good job," he said.

"Thanks," I told him. I was flattered.

"Hello," I heard Mom say.

"Hi," I said back. I looked at Jason to see that he looked a little rejected. I knew how that felt. Jason had told me that I did a better job than the week before.

Jason walked to his car. I waved to him as he drove away and he waved back at me. I stood at the corner, waiting for my ride, when there was a tap on my shoulder.

"You did a great job," Sue said.

"Oh, thank you," I said back. Sue was leaving, so I said goodbye to her. I continued waiting.

Mark came out, on his phone. "Good job today, Mary Beth," he said.

"Thanks Mark."

I waited a little longer for Mom to come.

It had been 699 days, and I was still waiting for Tyler. How pathetic could one person get?

Mike came by that evening and said that Ashley might be pregnant.

I hated her for being so rude to me.

The crazy part about the afternoon was the fact that I was actually crying in class. Real tears were coming down my cheeks and I remembered all the pain that I went through because of Tyler, Joe and Ben, and my illness.

I cried myself to sleep that night. Acting made me get out all my emotions and I ended up crying myself to sleep.

The next day I went to the library in search of a book for my monologue. I found the same book I had in college and decided to do the same monologue. I was older now and had a lot of different experiences happen to me that I could get to the point that I needed to be for the monologue.

It annoyed the hell out of me that Tyler was still there on my mind every day. It annoyed the hell out me and I hated thinking about him. I hated myself for thinking that he was still coming back.

"He promised," one part of myself argued.

Yeah. A lot of people had made promises to me that they never kept. What was the difference now? I should be used to this, but my heart was still so broken just from one stupid guy, I told myself over and over to get through the day.

The medicine that the doctor had given me wasn't helping, so I emailed him and told him that. I wasn't going to keep taking something that made me feel worse. I didn't want to take it in the first place. I was forced into thinking that the idea of this medicine would help, even though I knew otherwise.

I was feeling really lightheaded that day.

Two days later, Wednesday, I was feeling even worse!

I had made the decision to email my regular doctor and explain everything to her, or as much as I could. I was beginning to have shortness of breath!

I felt so lost and confused with life.

I managed to call my doctor's office and get an appointment. Unfortunately, I wasn't able to see her until the following week.

I was told that I needed to just let go of Tyler, something that I had been trying to do for the past year.

Just let go of him. He's not doing you any good. You need to let go! I had told myself over and over again.

I had changed in the past few months. I was meaner to some and more confident to others. Life just seemed unbearable and I couldn't do a damn thing about it. There are only so many times a person can be knocked down in so many ways in their life. That was proven to me now more than ever. I had lost the man I loved, my dreams had been crushed in the past, I had been lied to too many times, and nothing was going to stop! I needed to start fighting back to have my own life, apparently. But it was anything but okay with everyone else, or so it seemed.

Friday morning, I woke up to find that my heart was hurting me more than ever before.

"It's probably anxiety," Mom said.

Gee, I wonder why that is? I thought.

I was working on redoing my monologue for the 5th time, making corrections. Joe had his music blaring and I couldn't concentrate. I was so angry that I yelled and asked if he could turn it down.

"Just close your door," he said back to me. I had to be quite when he wasn't feeling good, why couldn't he do the same?

"No," I said. "Turn it down."

"I'll close your door," he said. I was so mad, but I blocked him from doing that. Then the anger that was inside of me came blasting out, again. I rushed over to him when he pretended to be funny and put the hallway closet door as if it were closed to block out the sound from the computer. I slammed the door on him, knowing very well that he could kill me himself after getting released from the mental hospital only weeks before.

"I HATE YOU!" I yelled, but I went to my door and slammed it shut. I could still hear Joe's music. *What a shock!*

I left and went to get coffee. Peace and quite was there when I was away from home and sometimes it was my only friend when I was at home. I didn't like the person that I was becoming, though. Who was she? A monster?

Mom was home when I arrived back.

"You can't always do this every time you get mad," she told me. And Joe can? Its okay for him to do stupid shit that is much worse than this, but it's not okay for me to do anything? I can't even say the word "hate" anymore? I'm sorry, but how is that fair?

I had woken up in pain the next morning. My heart was hurting, my head was hurting, and I just felt worn down. I stayed in bed for a while that morning.

I finally told Mom that I wanted to move out and get my own apartment. She thought was a good idea for me.

What is that supposed to mean? I thought. Why was I suddenly against this?

It had disgusted me how angry and heartbroken I had become. I hadn't asked to live life this way.

In acting, we had a substitute. I was actually looking forward to having Mark be there. I liked how he challenged me in ways that I actually hated. I had such a difficult time getting in touch with the sadness that I had for Chuck when he died. I had written a goodbye letter to my dead father, but it wasn't worth crying over it. It wasn't like that now. He had been gone and part of me wondered if he knew about my car accident. If he did, where was he? If he knew, why didn't he care? I cried for him too many nights when he died and why? Something I never got an answer to.

Our substitute, Brett, was nice. He was a lot mellower than Mark is. Brett still had me do my monologue. I couldn't get there emotionally in the scene.

After class, I stood outside waiting. Jason and Osra were going down the street. I had decided that I wanted coffee. As I walked down the street, I saw Jason and Osra in front of me.

Please don't go to Starbucks, I thought. I saw them turn at the corner. *Damn it!* I had a small crush on Jason, but I couldn't handle getting rejection, again.

I walked in after a few moments of getting there. Jason saw me.

"Hey," he said with a smile.

"Hey, Jason," I said back. Where was Osra?

"You had a hard monologue today."

"Yeah, it was hard getting there emotionally," I told him as he got his drink. Osra came out and got her drink.

I continued to order my drink. I saw that Osra and Jason were sitting outside. I had to walk past them.

"Are you leaving?" Jason asked.

"Yeah," I turned and told him.

"Aw," Jason said. *He wants me to stay! Oh my God!* I thought. "Okay, see you next week."

"Bye Jason." I walked to the parking lot to wait for Mom to get me. Jason liked me being in the class!

I finally made it to my doctor on Monday. First I had to change, and then the nurse came back into the room and put wires all over my chest. Afterwards, she left the room and I sat there in my hospital gown.

My doctor came in and asked what was wrong. I told her about my chest pain, dizziness, headaches and everything else that was going on with me. She mentioned the brain surgery that my neurosurgeon was talking about. If those head aches came back, I already knew to just call him. But that wasn't what was happening here. After writing everything down, the only solution was to be put on anxiety medication. I hated admitting it to myself, but it could help.

You never know. I mean, what other options do you have?

"If you don't like the effects that it has, you can stop taking it," she told me. "Just give me your psychologist's phone number so I can ask her what she thinks about this."

I started to feel so overwhelmed being there and having to admit it to myself that it was probably anxiety. But there was nothing that I could do about the stress and I knew that. I was the only person who could admit that out loud.

"Are you okay?"

"Yeah," I lied, looking down.

"Are you sure?"

I nodded my head back and forth. I wasn't okay. Then I spilled everything to the doctor. About everything that had been bothering me since 2008. I had made it this far with being in pain and no one believed me to begin with, so why did they care now? Were they just that good of actors, pretending that they cared?

The first thought that came to me, out of all of this, was Tyler. Why was I so in love with him? Love wasn't supposed to hurt you like this, and I knew that. Still, there was nothing that I could do about it. There was nothing that could ever be done. There would always be things that would just be unsaid between us. Things that I've dreamt of that I couldn't say out loud to him. Tyler broke me down and built me up like no other person had ever done before.

I had problems breathing the next day.

"The world will cause you more anxiety than this family does," Mom said to me as we were sitting at the table talking. I doubt it, I thought. Nothing could be worse than this. I had to leave the room where Mom was to just keep breathing.

I had to write a sad love poem that day and I dedicated it to Tyler, of course. The man broke my heart and I wasn't even able to say goodbye to him.

Relationships were ending everywhere I turned, except Joe and Juliet.

Maybe she just feels sorry for him?

Part of me knew that I wasn't going to have a happy birthday. Yes, I did have class, and yes, I was going to see a tribute band, but I knew that Joe would ruin it. Mom only thought of him now. I was lucky if I got scraps.

Mom couldn't go see whatever "art" show that Joe had that was four hours away.

Wow! There's something. Joe doesn't get too much attention today. He still got all the rest of her attention, so I still had to keep my guard up. I couldn't wait to move out so I would be done with both of them. It wasn't fair, the life I lived, and I had to at least know that there might be something out there for me that didn't have either one of them in it.

My birthday was finally here! I went out for breakfast with my mother and my sister. I had class that day also.

"Hi Mark," I said as I walked in.

"Hi Mary Beth," Mark told me. "How are you?"

"I'm good," something Mark had never heard me say.

"Good," he said.

Everyone else showed up after a few minutes. They all wished me a happy birthday.

I still did the same monologue from the week before. I couldn't stop smiling, though. I was getting more and more angry at Chuck for everything that he did. The class went well, despite the fact that I laughed at myself all the way through it.

"Next week, I want you to bring in a comedy, Mary Beth," Mark said.

I went out to find Mom's car and we went to the park to see Desperado.

After the concert, we went back home. I was given two CDs for my birthday. The house was quite for the rest of the night.

My eyes had gotten worse, and my fibromyalgia was intense over the next few days.

I was put on medication for my mood swings, but it only made me want to commit suicide that much more. I complained to the doctor over an email. She said to give it a few more days, so I decided, "Why the hell not?"

But the medication made me more and more anxious, so I stopped.

My heart seemed to break more and more over Tyler every second of everyday. It drove me insane for the first few months that he was there, but this time it was more torturous than ever!

Chapter 24

Conclusion

Can life have a conclusion? After all the madness and all the heartbreaks, is there still a chance of a happy ending?

I've lived my life. Maybe not the life I wanted to live 100% of the time, but I've learned a lot. I've had more happen to me in my young life than most people can experience in a whole lifetime. It hasn't all been "a fairytale come true", as some people have called it. I've been to Heaven, but I've walked through Hell.

You can't erase your past. I learned that *a long time* ago. It has taken me a lot of work to be who I am today, and to achieve everything that I have. I have hated people, and I'm not afraid to admit that. But I have loved others with all of my heart. I've waited and hoped and prayed to be loved back. Not for who I was or for the girl everyone knew I was once upon a time, but for whom I have become in my life, for everything thing that I have done.

After losing my childhood and all my dreams, I've risen up to become something more. I have had to ignore and laugh off every negative thing that everyone has said to me and it hasn't been easy. I have had to work harder than most people I know.

I've been mocked by so many people, both family and strangers. I was lied to, pushed and bullied by a lot of people with whom I've loved.

I found true love in my young life, but that was taken away from me.

But out of everything, I've learned to live again. Sometimes that's all you can ask for.

About the author

Mary Beth Holliday studies acting at the David Kagen School of Film Acting in Southern California. She lives in Granada Hill, California, but she hopes to one day see the whole world one day. When she's not in school, Mary Beth enjoys her singing lessons, dance lessons, and working out. She enjoys reading and writing poetry, as well as spending time with her animals.